David Mercer

Plays : Two

Flint, The Bankrupt, An Afternoon at the Festival, Duck Song, The Arcata Promise, Find Me, Huggy Bear

By 1970 David Mercer had become established as one of Britain's leading television playwrights on the strength of more than a dozen original works broadcast since his debut with *Where the Difference Begins* in 1961.

This volume, containing his work from the early seventies, shows a creative and questing intelligence seeking new modes of expression and new dramatic forms. The plays also present a certain darkening of mood and closing down of individual and collective options as the characteristic Mercerian oppositions of private/public and psychological/political are set against a new and somewhat changed backdrop. However, the range and flexibility of Mercer's dramatic imagination in the later play, *Huggy Bear*, indicates a certain rebalancing of his vision, marking a prelude to the major achievements of the late seventies.

This is a companion volume to *Mercer Plays: One*, which contains his major plays from the sixties. *Days of Vision*, an account of working with David Mercer by Don Taylor, is also published by Methuen Drama.

D1586424

David Mercer was born in Wakefield, Yorkshire, in 1928. He began his career as a television playwright with *The Generations* (a trilogy which opened with *Where the Difference Begins*, 1961) and *A Suitable Case for Treatment* (1962). In 1965, with *The Governor's Lady*, he began an association with the Royal Shakespeare Company during which they premièred, among others, *Belcher's Luck*, (1966), *After Haggerty* (1970), *Duck Song* (1974), *Cousin Vladimir* (1978), *The Monster of Karlovy Vary* (1979), and *No Limits to Love* (1980). Throughout his life, he continued to work with television, writing, among many television plays, *On the Eve of Publication*, *The Cellar and the Almond Tree* and *Emma's Time*. His screenplay, *Providence*, was filmed by Alain Resnais. David Mercer died in 1980.

DAVID MERCER

PLAYS : TWO

Flint
The Bankrupt
An Afternoon at the Festival
Duck Song
The Arcata Promise
Find Me
Huggy Bear

with an introduction by Stuart Laing

Methuen Drama

METHUEN WORLD CLASSICS

This collection first published in Great Britain in 1994
by Methuen Drama
Methuen Publishing Ltd
215 Vauxhall Bridge Road
London SW1V 1EJ

www.methuen.co.uk

Flint first published by Methuen and Co Ltd in 1970
Copyright © 1970 by David Mercer
The Bankrupt, An Afternoon at the Festival and *Find Me* first published by
Eyre Methuen Ltd in 1974 in *The Bankrupt and Other Plays*
Copyright © 1974 by David Mercer
Duck Song first published by Eyre Methuen Ltd in 1974
Copyright © 1974 by David Mercer
The Arcata Promise and *Huggy Bear* first published by Eyre Methuen Ltd in
1977 in *Huggy Bear and Other Plays*
Copyright © 1977 by David Mercer

This selection copyright © 1994 The Estate of David Mercer
Introduction copyright © 1994 Methuen Drama

A CIP catalogue record for this book is available at the British Library

Methuen Publishing Ltd reg. number 3543167

ISBN 0 413 65200 9   1005197270

Front cover: *In the Harbour* by Josef Herman, Boundary Gallery, London

Transferred to digital printing 2002

Contents

screened (December) in the Omnibus series.

1976 *Huggy Bear* broadcast on Yorkshire TV (April).

1977 *A Superstition* (August) and *Shooting the Chandelier* (October) are shown on Yorkshire TV. *Providence*, a film directed by Alan Resnais and scripted by Mercer is released.

1978. *The Ragazza* shown on Yorkshire TV (April). *Cousin Vladimir* opens at the Aldwych in the Autumn.

1979. *Then and Now* opens at the Hampstead Theatre in May.

1980. David Mercer dies in Israel in August. *No Limits to Love* opens at the Warehouse Theatre in October. *Rod of Iron* shown on Yorkshire TV.

1988. *A Dinner of Herbs* shown on BBC 1 as part of Mercer retrospective season.

Introduction

By 1970 David Mercer had become established as one of Britain's leading television playwrights on the strength of more than a dozen original works broadcast since his debut with *Where the Difference Begins* in 1961. At the age of 42, and with the beginnings of a successful career also in live theatre, he was at the height of his powers with every possibility of another decade of further successful development within both media.

Certainly his work of the early Seventies (contained in this volume) indicates a creative and questing intelligence seeking new modes of expression and new dramatic forms. Equally, however, it presents a certain darkening of mood and closing down of individual and collective options as the characteristic Mercerian oppositions of private/public and psychological/political are set against a new and somewhat changed backdrop. Three different kinds of pressure seem to exert themselves through the plays of 1970–4. First there is increasing uncertainty about the viability of socialist or Marxist politics – in either their theoretical forms or in any aspects of the actually existing socialism of Eastern Europe (about which Mercer had always been deeply ambivalent). Secondly, in British society itself the generalised liberal optimism of the Sixties had given way to an increasing sense of manifest decline and collapse (rising unemployment, galloping inflation, increasing industrial strife, the post-1968 institutionalisation of the troubles in Ulster). Finally there is Mercer's personal sense of his own ageing and mortality; in 1973 he reflected that, 'when

ix

you're into your early middle age that sense of the possibility of dying at any moment ceases to be a question of all the accidents that could overtake you . . . and is supplanted by an increasing sense of the death contained within you, as an inevitable biological process.' Taken together these three contextual elements help to shape the vision of a series of works in which the location of a position of value or ideals from which to generate an affirmative criticism of the existing social arrangements becomes increasingly difficult.

In this respect the stage play *Flint* stands as something of a transitional work. *Flint* was premièred in London only six weeks before the June 1970 General Election, which was to replace the Sixties Labour Government of Harold Wilson with the doomed Conservative regime of Edward Heath, and the play explores the collision between the exuberant excesses and personal explorations of the Sixties and the inherited power of established institutions – apparently obsolescent, but soon to reassert their power in a society rapidly polarising.

The continual energy of Ossian Flint himself drives the dramatic structure of the play with its mixture of farce, monologue and moments of violent destruction. Flint (the seventy-year-old swinging vicar who believes in 'crossing lines not drawing them' and espouses the romanticised Communism of Lenin and Guevara) himself centres a form of desire and dynamism which is in revolt against both a range of social conventions and institutions and the more intractable facts of age and death. In the former case the Church (specifically an empty and compromised Anglicanism), the law and marriage (embodied by his wife's self-induced paralysis) focus the deadening effects of a society in which access to fulfilment is blocked off. It is however Flint's consciousness of his old age and approaching death which gives the play an underlying desperation which takes it beyond a fairly obvious kind of social criticism. Flint's activities constitute a form of absolute refusal to accept restraint. He is 'a demented old man raving in an empty church about matters which are the province of the Devil rather than God' – riding a motor-bike, visiting bowling-alleys, making love in the vestry. However, even while envying the young lovers of the Sixties who 'couple freely and guiltlessly', he asks 'do I only *imagine* they have not yet handled their despair?'. The repeated fires with which he is involved and his final explosive accident show a desire (in the words of the alternatives offered in Conrad's novel *Under Western Eyes*) to 'burn rather than rot' which, while endorsing the value given to energy, spontaneity and anarchy in 'the Sixties', also shows their logical terminus.

Flint shows more consistent hesitancy of tone than any earlier Mercer play. It is in part self-regarding and joky about the Sixties' radical perspective on psychology, love and repression (as when Esme calls Flint 'a polymorphous perverse'). It caricatures many of the representatives of the establishment, yet finally offers no secure place on which to stand. 'My world' says Flint 'has always been precarious'; the play opens the increasingly uncertain terrain on which Mercer's works of the early Seventies are set.

Ossian Flint can nevertheless be placed, with Morgan in *A Suitable Case for Treatment*, for example, among Mercer's catalogue of anarchic and ultimately optimistic heroes. More typical of Mercer's bleaker mood in the plays of the early Seventies is a series of studies in personal failure. In the BBC television play *The Bankrupt* (November 1972) Ellis Cripper, another of Mercer's middle-aged male figures under pressure, has, at nearly fifty, become a discredited bankrupt through operating at 'the dishonourable end of the system . . . capitalism'.

The focus of the play is, however, not predominantly on the attribution of systemic or personal guilt nor even on the processes of psychological breakdown. The main dramatic issue is rather how to define or re-find meaning and direction when all the props of a life have disappeared; the 'bankruptcy' is as much mental and moral as financial. Cripper's 'limited amnesia' is then a means of avoiding a focus on 'what went wrong' and replacing it with the question of how to live from now on. His interview with the doctor crystallises this – 'Why not focus on twenty to thirty more years of fruitful existence?': 'That's it, I can't'.

Cripper's search for meaning is conducted through a number of comic encounters – both real and imagined. His dialogue with the worm is part of a light parody of *Hamlet* which runs through the play, while his dreams summon up a series of historical figures to propose a series of more abstract and general answers. Behind both lie his family and Angela who attempt to re-make him in their various preferred images. The construction of Cripper's father Gowran must lead to a qualification of Mercer's view that in his earlier play *Haggerty* (1970) he had finally come to terms with his own roots. Here Ellis Cripper returns to live in his father's cottage since it is all that is left of his assets, and identity. Gowran Cripper is a deliberately stereotyped Northern working-class figure whose values and identity are equally as unacceptable to Ellis as those of his middle-class sister and lawyer husband.

Through the construction of the pentagram Cripper attempts to re-find significance through an abstract formalism; instead the remaining real social relationships of his life invade and engulf him. The play's medium, television, provides the fluidity of form to allow a swift intercutting between dream and reality as part of a circular movement around a sequence variously grasped as dream and as deliberately willed reality. There is a similar free use of the potential of the television in the Yorkshire Television production *An Afternoon at the Festival* (May 1973) which again centres around a version of middle-aged Mercerian man. The main character, Leo Brent ('around fifty') is more akin to earlier Mercer figures in being simultaneously a tolerably successful artist (in this case a film-maker), an extreme egoist and a failure in his personal relationships. There are also even more conscious echoes of the figure of Robert Kelvin from the 'On the Eve' trilogy (published in *Mercer Plays: One*). Leo McKern (an actor with a very distinctive physical and vocal presence) played both leading characters and the film which Leo Brent has just finished making (and which is to be shown at the festival) is based on Robert Kelvin's last novel. Less explicit, but more extensive, connections with the earlier trilogy lie in the relationship between Leo and the young student Anna (which replays some of the issues explored between Robert Kelvin and Emma) and the concern with the European dimension which provides a wider context for the particularities of English culture.

The play is structured in a rhythmic patterned way, moving between scenes from the film and its making, in the house and garden with Howard (Leo's brother) and Dana (his ex-wife) and of Leo and Anna in a bedroom elsewhere in the city. The pattern contrasts and mixes different levels of reality – from the opening shooting of Dana by Jack (revealed as only part of the film) to the close of Anna playing the cello (reminiscent of the close of *Let's Murder Vivaldi*) and Leo's suggestion that the whole play constitutes only the subject matter of his next film. In many ways the play constitutes an elegant and concise gathering together of a range of concerns from Mercer's earlier work, now organised into a reflective meditation on failure.

The following year, 1974, proved to be as significant a transitional year for Mercer's drama as it did for British political life. His three works of 1974 combine important and often daring dramatic innovation with an insistent probing into a complex vision of personal and social negation. With *Duck Song* Mercer returned to the live theatre after a gap of nearly four years. The play was first produced at the Aldwych in February 1974, the period of the three-day week, the miners' strike and the dying days of the failed Heath Government and it catches the mood of this moment of crisis and dissolution. The first act provides a fairly conventional analogy between the state of a family and the state of the nation, imaged through the naturalistic mode of a comfortable room in a middle-class London house. The characters represent a society in decline – the older generation themselves non-productive and attempting to stop time (throwing walnuts at the clock), pre-occupied by the world of Bloomsbury or the events of the Second World War, while the younger are unemployed or attempting to find some novel solutions (psychiatry, feminism). As the first act progresses, however, and new influences enter from the outside, the dialogue and situation become more fragmented and bizarre. The blinding flash at the close of the act is a culmination of this and simultaneously a dissolution of the theatrical naturalistic metaphor within which the play has been operating.

With the disappearance of the furniture and the foregrounding of the American Indian symbols (buffalo's head and clothes), both characters and audience are puzzled. By collapsing the initial metaphoric correspondences Mercer switches the mode from naturalistic to absurd, but leaves the characters trying to re-construct the original parameters. There is an enaction of each character reaching for essentials but finding the impossibility of achieving solutions through actions with naturalistic consequences (thus acts of violence – shooting, strangling, the firing of arrows – have no effect). The possible 'swan song' of the first act – a formal and explicable marking of the end of a culture – is replaced by the less comfortable 'duck song' – the final breaking in of the noise of an uncontrollable public world swamping a barren set. *Duck Song* is, of all Mercer's plays, the one which most clearly conveys the sense of 'a world to which one cannot relate, which one cannot control, which one can't understand, which one can't manipulate'.

While *Duck Song* deals with collective loss of meaning the Yorkshire Television production *The Arcata Promise* (September 1974) deals with individual collapse. Here Mercer set himself the difficult task of writing a play about a protagonist's self-indulgence of self-pity that is not itself then experienced as an exercise in authorial self-indulgence. It focusses intensely on a characteristic Mercer theme – the mutual attraction between an older male artist (here an actor) and a young inexperienced girl – and pushes this through fully here towards the destructive conclusion of such attraction.

The Arcata promise itself – 'I shall love you. Look after you. You should always do exactly what you want . . . I don't want to hurt you or oppress you, or deny you in any way' – is exposed as idealised fantasy and even contradictory since precisely in Gunge supporting Laura in doing what she wants he helps her to grow away from him and his static conception of how she should be. Laura reminds him that she is not 'just a servicing arrangement to your needs' and that the age difference matters because while he will 'go on being exactly the same . . .' she is changing.

The presence of Laura, and the surprising last scene with its violent conclusion, provide strong points of conflict with at times almost Jimmy Porter-like levels of invective from Gunge towards her; however the central dramatic interest is in the split presentation of Gunge himself. There are in fact three alter ego representations, each using a different dramatic device. The Voice (in effect an adaptation of the television voice-over) is the equivalent of the theatrical soliloquy, while the intercutting of Gunge as Richard II provides a validation and a reference point for the self-pity of one who has fallen from a position of success. Tony the valet also provides essentially an extension of Gunge (a bad angel to the Voice's good angel) rather than constituting a separate protagonist. This multiple personality enables Mercer to link also the problematic relationship between reality and illusion in the world of the actor and the mental instability which is rarely far away from any Mercer hero. For Gunge 'life outside the theatre . . . had always been insubstantial'. The final shooting of Laura is then a transposition of theatrical behaviour into the real world with tragic consequences. Again this play remains as Mercer's most bleak account of individual self-delusion and failure.

Mercer's third work of 1974 had rather different origins. During the early Seventies he was continuing to extend the formal boundaries of the television play in a period when the distinction between television drama and film was beginning to erode. *Find Me* (December 1974) was in fact commissioned by the BBC Omnibus series as, according to director Don Taylor, 'a fully developed film script rather than as a television play'.

The difference between the two forms is apparent in the number of listed separate scenes (sixty-one as against, for example, twenty-one in *The Bankrupt*) and the emphasis on the visual rather than verbal – only one of the first eight scenes contains dialogue. This technique allows fluid movement between different historical moments, from the Second World War to the present of the early Seventies. The film returns in a quite studied and deliberate way to Mercer's preoccupation of the late Sixties with the comparison between the conditions of the politically aware writer in Eastern Europe and those in the West. In Eastern Europe (with again Poland as paradigmatic) the combination of direct experience of Nazi occupation and the sharp ideological conflict between art and politics within Eastern bloc culture produces conditions for an individual stress and confusion which is much more authoritative and explicable than similar states of mind in Western writers. The figure of Marek combines the characteristic drinking and womanising of the typical Mercer hero with a more profound historical consciousness of struggle and defeat. At the same time, it is to the West, particularly the liberal intellectuals, that Marek looks to provide some kind of validation and recognition of himself and his work – to 'find' him. As in so many of Mercer's plays the nature of the hero's political and artistic confusions is revealed through relationships with women in a way which while implicitly criticising the lack of care for others sees this as connected to general social pressures rather than to the specifics of gender stereotypes. However in *Find Me*, unlike a number of the other plays in this volume, the hero is seen and placed from outside by the figure of Olivia.

Mercer's three works of 1974 variously then present a British society in terminal collapse, a vision of individual failure and a further attempt to come to terms with the problematic legacies of Eastern European communism. To turn from these compelling accounts of difficulty and failure to the exuberant irresponsibility of *Huggy Bear* (a Yorkshire Television production of April 1976) is then to find with some surprise that the anarchistic optimisms of some of Mercer's earlier plays were still available to him. Hooper, the infantile and philosophical dentist with 'a failure to integrate', is Mercer's most zestful and likeable character since Morgan in *A Suitable Case for Treatment*. In the face of what is still seen as a decaying and reactionary British society, Mercer (and Hooper) glory in the primal energies of the greedy baby hungry for life, experience and satisfaction. The play's central preoccupation is with the mouth and what it can do. Hooper feeds on egg, tapioca, ice-cream, fish and chips with ketchup, lemon meringue pie, chocolate, milk and blancmange – food whose texture, connotations and consistency (especially when liberally distributed on Hooper's clothes) exemplify the play's celebration of the physcial excesses attendant on oral enjoyment. The dominant mood for playful release also allows speech within the play to become a source of enjoyment; words are played with, snatches of song are interspersed and the final scene includes a character reading aloud from *Finnegan's Wake* – the ultimate example of playfulness with language.

The final scene contains a curious kind of answer to, or at least commentary on, the pessimism of *Duck Song*; set in a typical drawing-room the scene gradually dissolves into chaos and conflict as vodka is drunk in place of sherry, impersonations are made and unmasked and Hooper finally leaves, shrieking, through the french windows. This marks however not an abandonment of the possibilities of all meaning, but a return to the basic human energies of play, physical enjoyment and sensuality. After the controlled, but also, at times desperate, plays of the early Seventies, *Huggy Bear* reminds us of the range and flexibility of Mercer's dramatic imagination and indicates a certain re-balancing of his vision which marked the prelude to the major achievements of the late Seventies.

Mercer on Mercer

. . . that play is really about the obsolescence of institutions, and the contradictions that we create institutions which are intended for our communal benefit, be it material or spiritual, but which become huge kinds of road-blocks in the way of the development and evolution of the society. So that I guess I could have written *Flint* in the context of ICI, but I chose the Church because it is such an abiding institution with such a long history, in such a hypocritical position in our society, which has perhaps ossified even further than the various institutions of political democracy, and because it would simply be more available to people than if I'd narrowed it down to the CP or something.

. . . I get pictures, I hear voices. I might suddenly get the idea of a man on a motorbike driving it fast and furious into a truckload of ammunition, and I think, well, what on earth is thát all about? Then the bits and pieces gradually accumulate to a point where even if I can't consciously fit them together, I know that the pressure on me is so strong that I must begin writing. And then, in that process of writing, I discover what all those pieces mean, and why they should be put together. So, to me, the actual writing is the act of discovering what the play is.

(From 'Birth of a Playwriting Man', *Theatre Quarterly* 3, 9, 1973.)

Gone Away

He doesn't go there any more.
Where cooling towers announce the town
The blackened slums are mostly down
And a new hideousness rakes the air
With a paltry silhouette of roofs and blocks
Which make him yearn for moors and rocks.

His mother died. They burned her corpse
On a windy hill beside a worked-out pit
Where once a young man used to sit
And sketch the reeking works for hewing coal –
Though the crematorium is fairly new
Recalling Auschwitz, it turns his very mind askew.

He went south two decades ago.
His father followed retired and bereaved much later
A working man with no rage against the speculator;
But this is a more gentle landscape, if not unravaged
And these two men live far from their own wrecked earth
Each wondering what the other is worth.

He doesn't go there any more.
Only in his child's mind the towers of the rotting town
And blazing market lamps at night on meat blood brown
Then sooty corn reaches to some tumbling farm above the slag –
His boots rattle through the shale to a sluggish cut
As waking, he kicks the doors of memory shut.

(Poem by David Mercer, 1970, published as Preface to *The
Bankrupt and Other Plays*, Eyre Methuen, 1974)

The Bankrupt

The Bankrupt is a very weird piece, I think. I really don't know
what I feel about it. It still contains bits and pieces of the past,
but it contains also a movement away. There's nothing more
salutary than a developing sense of death, really, and coming to
terms with death, and I think when you get into your forties,
you begin to have a relationship to death which is qualitatively
different from when you're a younger person. Obviously
anybody can die at any moment, but when you're into your
early middle age that sense of the possibility of dying at any
moment ceases to be a question of all the accidents that could
overtake you, or the diseases that you might accidentally have,
and is supplanted by an increasing sense of the death contained
within you, as an inevitable biological process. I would hope to
develop one or two comedies of death, and comedies of
relationship to death. I think death is something I've got to deal
with now.

(From 'Birth of a Playwriting Man', *Theatre Quarterly* 3, 9,
1973.)

Duck Song

. . . there can be no dramatic resolution. I don't think that's
possible any more. I think the play is about what is happening
to us all; the total disorientation of our society, culturally,
economically, morally. The props in our lives are being
removed one by one – recently they have been kicked away all at
once. Even simple things like the milk not coming, the post
never arriving, prices always rising. The tanks at London
airport, the confrontation with the miners. This is a crisis of
values – we are in a moral vacuum. I didn't think about it when
I wrote the play, but I think *Duck Song* is about that, and I think
it's what's happening to us all.

I think it's a play about confusion but I think that if one can say so, that the confusion is sort of lucid. What I mean is, I think one of the things that drama can do is to take confusion and make the point of that confusion comprehensible.

. . . I hate naturalism. I can't bear it. I really think that naturalism is a kind of substitute for the imagination. It confirms people's best suspicions about the nature of reality. I guess I have always written in an individualistic, subjectivist way, since my early, so called social realist plays. I would like to explore the whole question of being human in a world to which one cannot relate, which one cannot control, which one can't understand, which one can't manipulate.

I think it may be an aspect of being middle aged. All I know is that after 20 years . . . 20, 25 years of implacable commitment, I now find myself at an age where I know, not just in my head, that my body is dying. It's giving me illnesses, it's giving me little signs. The entire unit is displaying a sense of collapse, ultimate collapse. Which one knew about, of course. But, now when one goes through it, it's different.

I don't care any more. I think the road to ruin is so clear and that it will be taken, and we're on it . . . I've no faith. Political conviction is not a kind of faith. It's a method of understanding history. But the consequences can be awfully like having faith. That way of understanding history I still accept, but the consequences . . .

(From 'Mercer: Marxism, Madness and a Sense of Tragedy', *Time Out*, February 8–14, 1974)

Flint

FLINT was first presented at the Criterion Theatre, London, on May 5th 1970 by Shield Productions Ltd with the following cast:

OSSIAN FLINT	Michael Hordern
DIXIE O'KEEFE	Julia Foster
ESME FLINT	Moira Redmond
VICTORIA	Vivien Merchant
ERIC SWASH	John Leeson
DR COLLEY	Noel Howlett
MR HODGE	Paul Dawkins
FIREMAN I	Roy Hepworth
FIREMAN 2	Alexander Houlgate
BISHOP	David Bird
MAURICE	Nicholas Clay
INSPECTOR HOUNSLOW	James Grout
RAYMOND	Jonothan Deans
BARNEY	Garry Smith
WAITER & CHOIRBOYS	

Directed by Christopher Morahan
Designed by Peter Rice
Lighting by Francis Read

ACT ONE

Scene One

A church in North Kensington.
Church organ music playing. A file of choir boys passes slowly from left to right followed by the Curate : ERIC SWASH. *He is in his late twenties, a prim and ambitious conformist.*
There is a single pew, which more or less conceals a kneeling girl, DIXIE.
The last choir boy exits. The music stops. SWASH *is about to exit then comes downstage, folding his hands smugly on his stomach.*

SWASH. Faith is the substance of things hoped for, the evidence of things not seen. Hebrews eleven, one. (*Pause.*) Evidence of things not seen. (*Pause.*) The trouble with our Vicar Ossian Flint is that we can see him all too clearly. As one of the church-wardens put it: a demented old man raving in an empty church about matters which are the province of the Devil rather than God. (*Pause.*) There is scandal and shame in the Parish. Item: Miss Biggin, our devoted organist and a sturdy Christian . . . Miss Biggin fled to the island of Jersey in curious circumstances. There, that prim and gentle lady had a miscarriage, took to drink, and publicly assaulted the escort she had acquired through a marriage bureau. Hitherto, Flint and Miss Biggin had been . . . not unfriendly. (*Pause.*) Item: an article in some wretched so-called anarchist magazine. This vilified the Church and State of England, pleaded the cause of one Che Guevara (a deceased communist I believe) and was signed 'Flintissimus'. (*Pause.*) Item: our reverend Vicar was reported by an employee of the Gas Board as having chased the unfortunate man the length of Gorton Gardens with a golf club. The man was empowered to cut off the Vicar's gas and was acting legitimately

ESME. Oh? And what do you do to keep me alive?

FLINT. Well. I ... er ... I provide a bit of tension don't I? Tone up the spiritual muscles, eh? Somebody to vent your spleen on. Judging by your colour I'd say I keep the adrenalin pumping through the system.

ESME. Who needs whom? It's not unlikely a separation would finish *you* off. I'm the one with the money, don't forget. (*Pause.*) Anyway I shall take Victoria with me. I've always had it in for Victoria. (*Pause.*) A small house by the sea, I think. With a garden.

FLINT. Isn't that rather putting temptation in her way?

ESME. How?

FLINT. She might wheel you over a cliff. Or off the end of the pier one dark night. I'm not saying her impulses are unreasonable, but we don't want her put away, do we?

There is a long silence.

ESME. Have you heard the word 'fuddle', Ossian?

FLINT. Fuddle? Fuddle! Odd word.

ESME. Baby talk?

FLINT. Could be.

ESME. Meaning?

FLINT. Could be a contraction of 'frightful muddle'.

Long pause.

ESME. It's what you did with Victoria. For years.

FLINT. Oh.

Pause.

ESME. I get to know everything, sooner or later.

Pause.

FLINT. I wonder how poor Dixie is.

Pause.

ESME. Ossian –

FLINT. Yass?

ESME. Can you account for yourself? I mean, would you say there's anything *mitigating*?

FLINT. Things do seem to have come to a head lately.

ESME. No doubt Lady Susan Moraine has been staving off the worst until now.

FLINT. Good old Sue.

ESME. But can you *account* for yourself?

FLINT. What? The gas? The electricity?

ESME. I believe you are what Doctor Freud called 'polymorphous perverse', Ossian.

Long pause.

FLINT (*sulky*). Been reading the grand old men of psychiatry, have we?

ESME. What I'm trying to say, Ossian, your scope for immoral behaviour doesn't seem to include any *preferences*. There were those boys, and Miss Biggin . . . that awful lesbian woman in Bishop Auckland. What does one get from a *lesbian*? Then . . . Victoria all the time, and heaven knows whom besides. (*Pause.*) What hurts *me*, of course, is your almost wilful rejection of faith. Of God, Ossian. And how many of the clergy, might I ask, base their sermons on texts from that Lenin person? (*Pause.*) One's charitably searched for some kind of pattern over the years, Ossian –

FLINT. Why? What if I'm just omnisexual? What if I just enjoy everything?

ESME. All I wish to know, my dear, is why then you have stayed in the Church?

Pause.

FLINT. Bloody mindedness! (*Pause.*) No. There is a crucial point of strategy involved, Esme. (*Pause.*) The myth of man's fall, redemption and salvation is a mighty one. Is it best subverted from within? Or without? (*Pause.*) I hunger for meaning and poetry, yet fear I am unable to outflank the need for verification. (*Pause.*) Would a frivolous man sit that one out for forty years on the pittance they call a *stipend*? (*Pause.*) *Be* charitable, Esme! Faith is one thing. Fear of total oblivion another. (*Pause.*) The incorrigible believer is immune to me. It is the doubter I must walk with through the intricate labyrinths of agnosticism. (*Pause.*)

One sits ... not upon a fence, Esme ... but a wall topped with broken glass. It lacerates the backside, but it also keeps one hanging by the seat of one's trousers!
Pause.

ESME. We never seem to get anywhere on this subject. I'm tired and I'm off to bed. In the meantime I shall be listening, Ossian. I'm always listening. And if I hear you with that girl I shall beat on the wall with my stick.

FLINT. Bloody wall'll fall down one of these days.

ESME *slowly propels her chair, right. As she leaves:*

ESME. You are a monster, Ossian. The best thing that could happen to you would be a sudden coronary. Good night.

ESME *exits.* FLINT *helps himself to a drink. Raises his glass.*

FLINT. To a cleric so reduced and enfeebled by lust as to welcome the thought of his possible demise at the climax of the sexual act. (*Drinks.*) In my youth, it was known among a certain clique of boys as 'dying on the nest'. (*Pause: drinks.*) But, Dixie! Such a nest! The flesh tints of Rubens. The ribald calligraphy of Rowlandson. The sensuality of Renoir. (*Drinks.*) All combined for the terrible sacrament of my disintegration.

Fade out and fade in to

Scene Three

DIXIE'S *room.*

DIXIE *sits at a small table, writing. Candle light.*

DIXIE. Dear Katie, well it's two weeks now and you can't imagine. Ossy and I spent yesterday afternoon you-know-how. He's bought a polaroid camera that takes indoor photos. He'll come to a sticky end, this one. Said why don't we go off on his motorbike and spend a weekend rubbing brasses. Which I suppose is his funny old way of saying rubbing Dixie. Anyhow we went to the Odeon Kensington and saw a film about a Thing. No sooner home than wash, a plate of spaghetti and into the vestry. This because if we do it here in the vicarage *she* bangs on the wall and it does something to his virility. Down we gets between the Mother's Union banner on one side and the Church Lads' Brigade banner on the other. (*Pause.*) Is this blasphemy, even if it's only Anglican? (*Pause.*) Anyway what with his bungling, the gas and electricity went off today. Still I suppose he *is* a kind of priest.

　　　FLINT *enters and approaches* DIXIE.

FLINT. A kiss? A kiss?

DIXIE. Haven't you had enough for one day?

FLINT. Writing letters?

DIXIE. I've got this friend Katie in Holloway. I wish we had the electric light. What's your wife doing?

FLINT. She waits. She listens. The thumps, bumps and cries of fornication are manna to Esme.

DIXIE. Bible-type manna?

FLINT. Bible-type manna.

DIXIE. Where did you used to have Miss Biggin?

FLINT. In the organ loft. A quick run through 'I know that my Redeemer liveth' just for the sake of appearances, then down onto a pile of hassocks.

DIXIE. Did you like her?

FLINT. Well, she was getting a bit flabby-pooh.

DIXIE. By all accounts she wasn't past having a kid.

FLINT. The Miss Biggins of this world could almost get fertilized by standing in a draught. Miss Biggin was little more than a large, urgent ovary. A sad case of neglect.

DIXIE. I don't know how she could with a vicar. Or you with her either, for that matter. I wouldn't like to be *your* soul on Judgement Day.

FLINT. I'm not the first shepherd to tangle with his sheep!

DIXIE. I just don't know how you *square* it all –

FLINT. How do *you* square it? After all, I should say you're in for a pretty lengthy stretch in limbo.

DIXIE. I think I already qualify for hell, Ossy. But at least I'm

not a priest. It makes me shiver just to think about your goings
on.

FLINT. It's a well-known loophole that God's greatest mercy is
for those who are not of Rome. Sad to think you might be
slogging away in hell when the heathen gets off with probation.
(*Pause: dreamily.*) I can just see an enormous cosmic borstal
full of the spiritually ignorant. (*Pause.*) In my mind's eye. Why
do we say mind's eye? And talking of that, I've got toothache.

DIXIE. Go to the dentist.

FLINT. Not likely.

DIXIE. Well suffer, then.

FLINT. It isn't that I'm frightened.

DIXIE. I thought they were false, anyway.

FLINT. It's the location of the teeth that unnerves me.

DIXIE. Be funny if you had them in your navel, wouldn't it?
      Pause.

FLINT. I'd prefer that.

DIXIE. They look false.
      Pause.

FLINT. What worries me about it, I always feel my teeth are nearer
to me than the rest of me. If you see what I mean.

DIXIE. Your feet are you. Your teeth are a long way from your
feet.

FLINT (*looking down*). My feet are a long way from me. (*Pause.*)
The teeth are close. (*Pause.*) Right in front of me. (*Snacks his
teeth.*) See? That's going on *in front* of me.

DIXIE. *I'm* in front of you. Your teeth are inside you.

FLINT. From your point of view.

DIXIE. Open your mouth.
      FLINT *opens.*
There they are. Inside.
      Pause.

FLINT. I would say that you are simply *more* in front of me than
my teeth are.
      Pause.

DIXIE. Well where are you, for God's sake?

Pause.

FLINT. Behind my teeth. (*Pause.*) And maybe a bit higher up.

DIXIE. Where's the back of your skull, then?

Pause.

FLINT. Behind me.

Pause.

DIXIE. Ossie, all you need is a dentist.

FLINT. And have a bunch of fat white fingers mucking about at the very gates of consciousness? The mouth is rotten with symbolism, Dixie.

DIXIE. Let's have a look.

FLINT *opens again.* DIXIE *looks, recoiling.*

It's just rotten with your brown old teeth. They look like big crumbs of fudge. You know that brown fudge? (*Moving away.*) It's pretty grim in there. Pretty grim just in front of *you*, Ossie.

FLINT. I know. I've got a picture of it in my mind's eye.

DIXIE. I wish you'd go away and let me write my letter.

Pause.

FLINT. Am I ugly, Dixie?

Pause.

DIXIE. Fairly.

FLINT. Was Arthur ugly? Arthur, the anarchist?

DIXIE. He had a lot of blackheads. And seeing as he didn't wash, they'd got very disfiguring.

FLINT. Shall we go to the vestry?

DIXIE. Oh, Ossie!

Pause.

FLINT. I once inadvertently rolled Miss Biggin on to the pedal board of the organ and we made a dreadful noise. (*Pause.*) Diapason.

DIXIE. Arthur wasn't *bad* looking. It was his politics. And he was vegetarian and anti-fluoride in drinking water. (*Pause.*) Fluoride's to do with teeth, you know.

FLINT. Miss Biggin wore curious undergarments. They appeared to be made of ribbed cardboard. (*Sighs*.) You've changed my life, Dixie. I've had the Biggin-syndrome as long as I can remember. There's one in every parish. And even an old man has his fantasies of something better. (*Pause*.) So long as you don't start moralizing.

DIXIE. Moralizing? You take my bloody breath away you do!

FLINT (*abstractedly*). It was so *convenient* when Victoria was still attractive.

DIXIE. Funny your wife being so nasty and Victoria being so nice.

FLINT. I'm not all *that* ugly –

DIXIE (*placating*). You've got nice wispy hair. (*Pause*.) And I quite *like* that bald patch in the middle. It's got freckles.

FLINT. I nearly went to Spain you know.

DIXIE. For a holiday?

FLINT. For the Civil War.

DIXIE. *You*'d have been a hoot!

FLINT. The incumbent Biggin of the period blackmailed me out of it. (*Pause*.) That poor woman suffered. As always, there were rumours. And a nasty gang of little boys used to call after her in the street. 'Flint's bint,' they used to shout. (*Pause*.) One has to make sacrifices. For her sake I didn't volunteer for the International Brigade.

DIXIE. Priests can't fight!

FLINT. Mind you, she was a Superbiggin.

    Pause.

DIXIE. Sexier than me?

FLINT. I would have left the Church, but the huge iniquity of the firm absolutely mesmerized me.

DIXIE. Sexier than me?

FLINT. More . . . more stringy than you. And like most of the Biggins, prone to gentility. But she . . . what do they say nowadays?

DIXIE. Turned you on?

FLINT. That sounds as if it might well describe her effect on me. (*Pause: vaguely*.) Turned me on. Yes.

DIXIE. I have trouble turning you off!

FLINT. I shan't sleep unless we go to the vestry.

DIXIE. Oh, come on then. You're an old goat, Ossy. What are you?

FLINT. An old goat. A doomed cleric. A tower of lust with creaking bones. And the Bishop, who pokes his finger not in the sexual pie but the cake of status and promotion . . . the Bishop will have to act. (*Pause.*) I will say for the Bishop, he looks the other way until the circle of degradation reaches a full three hundred and sixty degrees. (*Pause.*) Then the poor bugger *has* to act.

> FLINT *and* DIXIE *make a stealthy exit.*
>
> *Fade out and fade in to*

Scene Four

The Vestry.
Silence. Darkness. Two banners on poles : Mothers' Union and Church Lads' Brigade. A harmonium. FLINT *enters with a torch, followed by* DIXIE.

DIXIE. Funny sort of smell.

FLINT. Communion port and sweaty cassocks.

DIXIE. I didn't notice it last time.

FLINT. Did I tell you the choirmaster's a butcher? Sings in the shop. There he stands over his wooden block, whirling his cleaver and yelling Worthy Is the Lamb. (*Pause.*) I wouldn't like to cross the choirmaster.

> *Pause.*

DIXIE. D'you feel passionate, Ossy?

> *Pause.*

FLINT. Voracious.

DIXIE. This place puts me off.

FLINT. I assure you. The odour is not of sanctity, but the perspiration of small boys. If you went into the choir stalls you'd smell stale chewing gum. They stick it under their seats after the sermon.

DIXIE. I'd . . . I'd rather go back to the vicarage, I think. (*Pause.*) I've got a premonition.

FLINT. I don't believe in them.

DIXIE. How can you *not* believe in what I've *got*? (*Pause.*) Ossy? (*Pause.*) What are you doing?

FLINT. Getting undressed.

DIXIE. What am I doing in a smelly vestry with a seventy-year-old vicar?

FLINT. The same as last time.

DIXIE. I've been thinking since then.

FLINT. What about a glass of port?

DIXIE. Maybe I ought to get a job and be independent.

FLINT. With a wee one inside?

DIXIE. I can still work. Till quite late on.

FLINT. Where? In a factory? A shop? (*Pause.*) I think you need a drink.

DIXIE. But isn't it consecrated or something?

FLINT. I believe we have a few untransmogrified bottles. (*Pause.*) Mere wine, until somebody does the abracadabra bit on it.

DIXIE. Ossy, you *frighten* me.

FLINT. You should hear my sermon on the mystifying deceits perpetrated in the name of religion. Or politics. For St Paul read Stalin. Or don't. My sermons are not so much Christian guidance, as a bewildering interior monologue. Does it matter? No accident, you know, the amount of blather there is about *sheep* in Christianity. (*Pause.*) I never wanted to come to this ugly corner of Kensington in the first place. (*Pause.*) Dixie, I am racked with lust.

DIXIE. It isn't that I don't like *it* –

FLINT. Well then.

DIXIE. Don't you draw the line *anywhere*?

FLINT. I believe in crossing lines not drawing them.

    Pause.

DIXIE. I've done it in some funny places, but this one! I mean it's part of the *church* –

FLINT. Better than having Esme thundering away next door with her pesky stick.

Pause.

DIXIE. I want to think for a minute.

FLINT. What about a compromise?

DIXIE. *What?*

FLINT. We'll skin off to the underwear. Then I'll have a quiet pipe . . . and you have a quiet think.

DIXIE. I don't see the point.

FLINT. Dixie – where on earth have you disinterred these scruples from? (*Pause.*) Suddenly.

DIXIE. Nothing sudden about it.

FLINT. I just thought if we did what I suggested, it might be – titillating.

DIXIE. As if you needed that!

FLINT. *You* seem to.

DIXIE. No I don't. That's one of my problems. I'm thinking of tomorrow morning. Down at the confessional. Father; I'm having it off with an Anglican parson. Imagine. It's all right for you protestants, thinking everybody's got their own hot line to God. *I've* got to sit there at the grill with me breakfast in me throat and old big ears on the other side! (*Pause.*) It wasn't quite so bad with Arthur and the others. I've only got to look at your collar and I go queasy with fright. (*Pause.*) Don't your lot go in for unfrocking?

> FLINT *has switched off the torch. There is only a faint luminous light, as if from the vestry window.*

FLINT. It's what I'm doing now. Unfrocking.

> DIXIE *is pulling off her dress, in reluctant stages.*

DIXIE. It's not all that warm.

FLINT. Days shortening. Soon be harvest festival. That was nice in the country. St Bartholomew's. Chrysanthemums. Sheaves of wheat. Marrows. These little Norman churches. But I never took to the East Anglian fellaheen. (*Pause.*) We had a tame mouse at Bartholomew's. Used to run up and down the pulpit steps, went mad during the harvest festivals. Grew fat. (*Pause.*) Look kindly upon the gentle mouse. Small cheeks full of grain. There we go. Down to the long johns. Hardly erotic, but functional. Off with the dress, Dixie. (*Pause.*) Here. Two chairs. (*Pause.*) I smoke. You think. Torment yourself into complicity with what you'll do in any case. (*Pause.*) I did not mean that arrogantly. (*Pause.*) Now the pipe. (*He lights his pipe.*) Are you thinking, Dixie?

DIXIE. Yes.

> *Pause.*

FLINT. An old man's love –

DIXIE. Love . . . is it?

> *Pause.*

FLINT. At seventy, one thinks: I could die any day. Healthy or not. (*Pause.*) Some essential part of the mechanism might blow like a fuse. It can happen. (*Pause.*) Nothing really amiss, but . . . aches, pains. I often get a fearful stabbing sensation up the arse. (*Pause.*) I feel death near me. (*Pause.*) Are you thinking?

DIXIE. How can I?

FLINT. When I talk?

DIXIE. Yes.

> *Pause.*

FLINT. I think it is love.

> *Pause.*

DIXIE. Nothing for your wife? Nothing?

> *Pause. We hear approaching voices.* FLINT *leaps up.*

FLINT. Listen. What's that? (*They listen.*) Oh God. Oh Christ. Dixie what day is it?

DIXIE. Wednesday.

FLINT. *Choir night!*

DIXIE. *Now* he remembers!

FLINT. I know. Into the cupboard. Come on. Quickly.

DIXIE. What cupboard?

FLINT. There. Where they keep the sweaty cassocks. And surplices.

The voices are louder – boys laughing and talking. FLINT *is bundling his clothes together. Upstage, a long cupboard, fronted by a curtain on rings. He picks up* DIXIE's *dress.*

Here's your dress. In you go.

DIXIE. But we can't!

FLINT. Where else? Not that way. Church locked.

He pushes her behind the curtain and follows. A moment later he leaps out again.

DIXIE. *Now* what are you doing?

FLINT. Left pipe on chair.

He gets his pipe and goes behind the curtain just in time. The choirmaster, MR HODGE, *and a gaggle of boys come crowding in. The lights go up. The boys gather in the centre, chattering.* HODGE *goes to the harmonium, and places a small pile of music on top. Already there, a stack of hymn books. The harmonium faces away from the cupboard.* HODGE *unbuttons his coat, clears his throat and turns to the boys. He is a large, lugubrious man, full of meat and beer.*

HODGE. Shall we be quiet? Shall we champ our chops firmly together and have a bit of God's good silence? And get ourselves into two rows. And get the sweets out of our greedy mouths? (*Pause.*) Shall we?

The boys quieten down and shuffle into two rows. HODGE *blows his nose noisily.*

Hymn books, Barney.

BARNEY *takes the hymn books from the harmonium and dishes them out.* HODGE *rocks backwards and forwards on his heels, a simple, rather ignorant man playing the schoolmaster one evening a week.*

Well now, as Shakespeare says: If music be the food of love . . . how does it go, Raymond?

RAYMOND. Play on play on play on play on.

HODGE. Right.

He waits for an appreciative titter. The boys, having heard it all before, maintain a glum fidgeting silence. HODGE *wanly sits at the harmonium.*

Right.

HODGE *glares at the Boys.*

Harvest festival coming up. Corn cut. Apples in the loft. The countryside feeds us, and we are grateful. *Grateful,* aren't we? (*A few boys mutter* 'Yes, Mr Hodge.') Without the fruits of the earth, we'd peg out. Go down and see it Covent Garden any day of the week. Right. So turn to plough the fields and scatter. Hymn No. 383. If I remember, it was murdered last year this poor little hymn. Murdered. M-u-r-d-e-r-e-d. By some of those present. (*Pause.*) Some of those present, they did things to plough the fields and scatter I wouldn't do to a dog. (*Pause.*) I quip. (*Pause.*) I only quip.

Long pause.

RAYMOND. Mr Hodge –

HODGE. Son?

RAYMOND. Why do we still have choir practice when nobody comes to church?

HODGE *is thrown by this. How much do they know about the despicable* FLINT?

HODGE. Do you love Britain, Raymond?

RAYMOND. Yes, Mr Hodge.

HODGE. That is why you still come to choir practice.

RAYMOND. Doesn't make sense.

HODGE. Hasn't Mr Swash bashed *anything* into your thick 'eads? Duty? Patriotism? Love of God?

BARNEY. Old Flint was better. At bible class he used to go on about revolutions and that.

HODGE. *Old Flint? Old Flint?* Are you speaking of the Vicar?

BARNEY. Mr Flint.

HODGE. That's better. As I was saying, the earth gives of its fruit – and God, you might say, is who makes the earth toe the line. Push things up. Nourish them. And that's what this hymn's all about, and *that's* what we've got to get into it. Right. Once through quick, then we'll go over it thorough.

HODGE *turns back to the harmonium and starts to play. The boys sing, falteringly:*

BOYS. We plough the fields and scatter
    The good seed on the land,
    But it is fed and watered
    By God's almighty hand.

MR HODGE and the BOYS are facing away from the cupboard. From behind the curtains come wisps of smoke. A smothered yelp from DIXIE. HODGE turns fiercely on the BOYS.

HODGE. Somebody got hiccups? Or trying to be funny? (*Pause.*) Or what?

The BOYS shuffle, and keep silent.

As Lord Nelson said: I know when to turn a blind one, but I have eyes in my *back*, gentlemen.

Abashed silence. HODGE back to the harmonium.

Last lines, first verse and chorus.

Copious smoke from the cupboard.

BOYS. He sends the snow in winter,
    The warmth to swell the grain;
    The breezes and the sunshine
    And soft refreshing rain.

By now the BOYS are aware of the smoke, grinning and nudging each other. HODGE, unaware, bellows:

HODGE. I'll give you the chorus meself and *listen*. This is how I shall want it.

HODGE launches into the chorus. By now the smoke is spreading forwards, the boys beginning to cough and panic. HODGE turns at the commotion and is horrified.

What's all this? What's all this?

RAYMOND. Smoke, Mr Hodge.

HODGE. I know *smoke* when I see it.

BARNEY. Maybe we're on fire, Mr Hodge –

HODGE. Now I don't want any panic. No panic d'you hear? Line up and leave the vestry in a befitting manner. Come on, come on!

At this point, with yelps and shouts, FLINT *and* DIXIE *hurtle out from among the surplices. Each is wearing a cassock, with surplices pulled over their heads. The boys are transfixed,* HODGE *aghast. Wreathed in smoke, the two weird figures belt off right.*

And who was *them*?

Pause.

RAYMOND. Ghosts?

HODGE. Out that door and no pushing and scrambling! Barney, get to the vicarage and tell them ring the fire brigade.

As the last BOYS *exit,* HODGE *leaps to his feet and dashes to the cupboard. A gust of smoke hits him and he is dementedly torn between investigating the cupboard and saving his harmonium. In the end he opts for the harmonium and starts heaving it out of the vestry.*

SWASH *enters, in a flap but nastily authoritative.*

SWASH. Mr Hodge. What are you doing?

HODGE. Trying to save me harmonium.

SWASH. It does you credit but it suggests a lack of proportion, man!

HODGE (*bewildered*). Sir?

SWASH *points at the smoking cupboard.*

SWASH. *That* is nothing! The entire church is ablaze from the altar to the choirstalls. You are not aboard ship, Mr Hodge. You are not required to *go down* with your harmonium.

HODGE. Well, you see, Mr Swash –

SWASH (*frenziedly rushing about*). There used to be a row of red buckets somewhere. With things like water and sand in them –

HODGE *becomes stiff and huffy.*

HODGE. This 'ere harmonium was donated to our church by a close relative of Lord Kitchener. It ain't *any* old instrument, Mr Swash!

There is a clanging of fire engines outside. A FIREMAN *comes haring through the vestry unreeling a hose from a drum.* HODGE *and* SWASH *watch this hypnotically. From the other side another* FIREMAN *also unreeling a hose. Backstage, ladders are going up. There is a great hustle, noise and movement.*

SWASH. Well, since the fire brigade's here, you might as well get on with your fatuous priorities. *I* intend to save the Parish register.

He exits. HODGE *pushes at the harmonium. And, on as much lively stage business as possible, fade out and fade in to*

Scene Five

The Vicarage.

DR COLLEY *stands gazing upstage, where there is a flickering red glow. Sings quietly to himself.*

COLLEY. Jesus bids us shine
>With a clear pure light;
>Like a little candle
>Burning in the night.

 FLINT *slinks in, looking dishevelled and hunted.*

COLLEY. Oss, I think I should give you a sedative.

FLINT. Why?

COLLEY. Have you been out there? There's a black smear on your right cheek.

FLINT. I . . . er . . . I went to see if there was anything I could do.

COLLEY. Looks like it's going to be a total ruin. (*Pause.*) Odd, when you come to think about it. The fire brigade was there in ten minutes. (*Pause.*) They're still at it. (*Pause.*) Where's the delightful young O'Keefe?

FLINT. Having a bath.

Pause.

COLLEY. I'm absolutely with you Ossian. You, know that.

FLINT. With me in what? What am *I* in?

COLLEY. An even worse bloody mess than before, I should say.

(*Pause.*) I . . . (*Quietly*) I saw you and Dixie go into the vestry.

FLINT *sighs.*

(*Looking out.*) Splendid chaps these firemen. They look a bit like gladiators. (*Pause.*) Victoria's enjoying the holocaust from Esme's window.

FLINT. And Esme?

Pause.

COLLEY. Uncannily quiet. (*Pause.*) Want to get anything off your chest?

Pause.

FLINT. I defy any man alive to concoct an explanation of what happened that would satisfy the choirmaster. (*Wanders to look out.*) Sturdy firemen. Going about their lawful business. (*Pause.*) I could swear as Dixie and I fled the vestry Hodge said: Now the old bastard's been and gone and done it.

COLLEY. And had you?

FLINT. It was my pipe. (*Pause.*) Dixie, the doxy and I had been compelled to take refuge among the surplices. (*Pause.*) A few shreds of burning shag . . . you know? (*Looking out.*) One of the firemen's waving a chalice at the crowd! *My* chalice! (*Pause.*) Where does he think he is? Wembley?

VICTORIA *enters.*

VICTORIA. Up it goes, Ossy! A lovely fire. That'll teach them to persecute my darling man. I didn't want to disturb you. The fact is, there are two firemen at the door.

FLINT. What do they want?

VICTORIA. They want to see you.

FLINT. Well let them come in, Victoria –

VICTORIA *exits, but as she leaves:*

What's Esme doing?

VICTORIA *hangs her head.*

Victoria?

VICTORIA. What do they call those things they put under aeroplane wheels to stop them moving?

COLLEY. Chocks.

VICTORIA. That's right. You see, Ossian, I get so tired of her sometimes. And I got the idea . . . I made two little . . . *chocks* . . . out of firewood. And when I feel like a rest, I jam them under the wheels of her chair. (*Pause.*) Esme is *chocked*. And I won't stay here to be criticized.

    VICTORIA *exits.*

COLLEY. Don't we all get tired of Esme! Sometimes.

FLINT. It's cruel.

COLLEY. Victoria isn't cruel. Esme's a domineering hypocrite and a liar. I reckon she's better off chocked every now and then. (*Looking out.*) The roof of the nave has just crashed in. (*Pause.*) And there's Swash. Looks a bit singed. (*Pause.*) *And* dejected! Can it be that he *cares* about the church?

FLINT. I suppose the diminutive of 'doxy' would be 'doxelino'.

COLLEY. What?

FLINT. I was thinking of Dixie's baby.

COLLEY. Are you infatuated, Ossian?

    There is a knock.

FLINT. Come in –

    A FIREMAN *enters.*

FIREMAN. Mr Flint?

FLINT. Yes?

FIREMAN. It's pretty well a write-off, sir.

FLINT. I expect they'll build a new one.

FIREMAN (*shocked*). Sir?

FLINT. I mean, it's a tragedy.

FIREMAN. We found the chalice –

FLINT. I know –

FIREMAN (*turning*). Ron –

    Another FIREMAN *comes in with the chalice and hands it to the first* FIREMAN. *It is black and somewhat twisted, but recognizable.*

FIREMAN. Thought you'd want it, Mr Flint.

    He hands it to FLINT, *who holds it staring at it vaguely.*

FLINT. Thank you very much.

FIREMAN. And there's something else, Mr Flint.

FLINT. Yes?

FIREMAN. Ron –

>RON *goes out and re-enters with two twisted, blackened petrol cans. Sets them down in front of* FLINT. *Exits.*

Petrol cans.

FLINT. Petrol cans.

FIREMAN. Where the altar was. Funny place to keep your petrol.

FLINT. *My* petrol?

FIREMAN. Whoever's petrol.

FLINT. I agree.

FIREMAN. You don't seem very surprised, Mr Flint? (*Pause.*) Ron –

>RON *enters with another can. Puts it down and exits.*

In the ante-room between the vestry and the church proper.

FLINT. How bizarre!

FIREMAN. Do you possess any kind of vehicle yourself, sir?

FLINT. A motorbike. And sidecar.

FIREMAN. Well. I'm not insinuating.

FLINT. I didn't say you were.

FIREMAN. But this'll have to go further, Mr Flint. (*Pause.*) A lot further.

>*He gathers up the cans and exits with them.*

FLINT. How far can anything go, Patrick? Come and talk to Dixie. She likes a chat when she's having a bath.

>COLLEY *and* FLINT *go off. The red glow from the church is dying.* ESME *enters, walking, and pushing her wheel-chair. She looks towards the fire.* VICTORIA *enters. The two women look at each other a moment.*

VICTORIA. Esme dear. The men found the petrol cans.

ESME. They were meant to.

VICTORIA. Isn't it going to be nasty for Ossian?

ESME. I saw him and her doing it, Victoria. Last Tuesday. In the vestry. The entire unwholesome performance. From the cupboard where they keep the cassocks. (*Pause.*) He was *yours*, Victoria.

VICTORIA. And we were *yours*, weren't we?

ESME. I told you I'd get him.

VICTORIA. You did, Esme. Yes you did.

ESME. Shall I tell you the story again, Victoria?

VICTORIA. Yes. Tell it me again.

ESME. I was trembling all the way to Dieppe. In the train, on the boat. Do you remember my lovely going-away clothes? And the sprig of lilac in my buttonhole? (*Pause.*) Thinking of our dear father. Not like other men. (*Pause.*) I sat opposite Ossian in the train. He tried to kiss me and I pushed him off. I watched him out of the corner of my eye. A young clergyman. With a wild look. With roving hands. Perspiring. And that night. In Dieppe. (*Pause.*) He drank too much wine. (*Pause.*) I drank nothing. I didn't know what exactly to expect. (*Pause.*) Frightened. (*Pause.*) And upstairs. I in bed. His clothes off but for his shirt. (*Pause.*) No prayers. (*Pause.*) That monstrous *thing!* Under his shirt.

VICTORIA. Lovely!

Pause.

ESME (*with wooden serenity*). That, dear, is how I lost the use of my legs. (*Pause.*) But knowing you were a born whore, I thought life might be manageable. (*Laughing.*) One parson, coming up! (*Pause.*) I do believe in divine justice. (*Pause.*) Which must often find its instrument here on earth. (*Pause.*) We'll *destroy* him, Victoria. You can see that now the church is burning I am able to walk? My veins throbbed, my legs ached. Then there was a delicious warm thrill, and I *stood*, Victoria.

VICTORIA. Oh, Esme!

ESME (*tartly*). It's a good thing you were an early enthusiast of all those hideous new-fangled ideas, is it not?

VICTORIA. Oh, yes!

ESME. And that you knew at the same time they were *wicked*?

VICTORIA. Oh yes, Esme!

    Pause.

ESME. You are not insane, Victoria. But sex, freedom, atheism and disrespect for authority must be paid for. Not so? (*Pause.*) You might have caught a disease. (*Pause.*) When we and father are reunited in heaven, we hardly wish to take gonorrhoea with us. Now do we?

VICTORIA. No, Esme.

ESME. Mercifully, my dear, we are *both* sane. (*Pause.*) Try to look upon Ossian as having been more a form of prophylaxis than a source of unclean stimulation.

VICTORIA. I will, Esme. Praise the Lord!

ESME. And once and for all, keep that rubbish to yourself.

VICTORIA. I'll try.

ESME. That's better.

    She resumes her wheel-chair.

VICTORIA. Now what, dear?

ESME. There's but one explanation for Flint. He is mad. And what is madness? The evidence of sin. What is sin? The denial of God. What is God? The merciful redeemer of all men. (*Pause.*) Flint must fall, in order that he might be raised again. If they don't get him for arson we shall have to think up something else. (*Beckoning.*) Come along, Victoria. Push me. Push me.

    As VICTORIA *slowly wheels her offstage.*

How many men are privileged to achieve salvation on three gallons of high octane shell?

            Curtain.

Scene Six

The Bishop's Residence.

The BISHOP *has a tape recorder and is walking up and down talking into the microphone.*

BISHOP. In these turbulent years, when we are confronted by

anarchy on all sides . . . denominational antagonisms are giving
way to a search for common ground. (*Pause.*) If there is acrimony
in Rome . . . by the way, Maurice, should I say something here
about birth control? Cardinals dancing on the head of a sperma-
tozoon? (*Pause. The* BISHOP *smiles to himself.*) And, Maurice,
did you order that fellow's book on extra-uterine fertilisation?
Check please, dear boy. (*Pause.*) I retract the cardinals bit. One
must make a fine distinction between what is merry and what is
facetious. (*Pause.*) Maurice, that damned beagle of yours is
yapping beneath my window again. Whilst we're on the subject,
I took my breakfast on the patio this morning. And what did I
see? (*Pause.*) As I spooned a segment of grapefruit mouthwards,
my eye fell upon a dog dropping of awe-inspiring size. A
beagle dropping, Maurice. On the patio. (*Pause.*) Train the
animal, hide it, sell it, or kill it. (*Pause.*) Where were we? Anarchy? Acrimony? (*Pause.*) Rome? (*Pause.*) Nairobi? (*Pause.*)
Wasn't Nairobi horrid! (*Pause.*) The truth is, I've got *Flint*
on my mind. (*Pause.*) The awful Flint problem. (*Pause.*) I
wouldn't go so far as to say there's one in every diocese . . . but
. . . well between you and me I rather admire the aberrated
fellow. His appetites are grotesque, but at least they are matched
by the power of his brain. Which is more than we can say for
some of you. (*Pause.*) D'you remember that surgical little tome
of his on: 'The Colonial Missionary – Vanguard of Imperialism'? (*Pause.*) It was hard-hitting for its time. Nineteen twenty-
six. (*Looking out.*) Damn it, I think that's his motorbike now.
(*Pause.*) I hardly need say these digressions are *not* for trans-
cription. My poor old mind is reeling, Maurice. I've spent three-
quarters of my life preaching tolerance, love and Christian
ethics at home . . . blessing all kinds of slaughter abroad . . .
and now what? Pop music. Permissive society – there's an
enigmatic phrase for you. Black power. Hob-nobbing with
dubious clerics of all kinds. Bland parsons on telly grinning
insanely at renegade Liverpudlian exotics with more money
than talent. On top of all else, Flint burns *another* church.

(*Pause.*) Or did he? (*Pause.*) Oh, and Maurice, will you investigate the prevailing connotations of *underground*? This is top priority. There is not a trend so insignificant that the Church can afford to ignore it. Get young Swindon at St Mary's on to the problem . . .

FLINT *is shown in by the* BISHOP'S HOUSEKEEPER. FLINT *has a paper carrier in one hand.*

Maurice, I don't want to carp, but . . . yesterday's letters . . . there are *two* n's in Connecticut, Maurice. Cheers.

The BISHOP, *warily benign, swoops on the hovering* FLINT.

Ossian! How are you?

FLINT. Well –

BISHOP. I know, I know.

FLINT. Do you?

BISHOP. If one kept dossiers, my dear fellow, yours would run into volumes. (*Looking at the carrier.*) Been shopping?

FLINT. It's the chalice.

BISHOP. Torn from the hungry flames by a stalwart fireman?

FLINT. More or less.

BISHOP. Might one . . . see it?

Glumly, FLINT *takes out the black and battered cup. Hands it to the* BISHOP.

Lady Susan was on the phone this morning. I said you were coming for a chat. (*Examining the cup.*) Looks as if it's been to hell and back. Awful design in the first place. (*Pause.*) Lady Susan said . . . I'm to tell you . . . this time she washes her hands. (*Pause.*) Sorry to be the harbinger of unwelcome news, Ossian.

FLINT *begins the familiar whirling and stammering.*

FLINT. Oh, I expected . . . you know. Delightful woman, your cousin. But I . . . I can *see*, that things . . . the circumstantial evidence. And as you say my . . . my dossier . . . and –

BISHOP. I think she never really got over the Biggin crisis. (*Pause.*) A crisis I might add, so rapidly overtaken by the scandal of the hosing incident. (*Pause.*) I don't reproach, Ossian. I recapitulate. (*Pause*) A glass of sherry? (*With stern emphasis.*) Or a *Scotch*?

FLINT. Er – a Scotch, please.

The BISHOP *supplies the drinks. They sip, eyeing each other.*

BISHOP. You don't seem to be quite yourself today.

FLINT. Would you, in my position?

BISHOP. You have no position. You are an actual . . . and techni-cal . . . pariah. (*Pause.*) Possibly a criminal too, though I for one prefer to distinguish between an unfortunate compulsion and a criminal intention.

FLINT. So *you* think I'm a pyromaniac, as well!

BISHOP. God knows *what* you are, Ossian! How's Esme? And poor Victoria?

FLINT. They –

BISHOP. When you leave the parish, I wish you'd abduct Maur-ice's beagle. I'm so weak with people. I haven't got it in me to get really *stern* with the boy. It barks all the time. Under my window. (*Pause.*) Shouldn't you go abroad somewhere my dear fellow? (*Pause.*) Somewhere extremely far away? (*Pause.*) Swash is already keen to start a fund for the new church. (*Pause.*) *Swash* is one of those people who will go far. Merely by stand-ing in the right place and rising through the attrition of his superiors.

FLINT. Bishop –

BISHOP. Now now, old friend! It's still George, isn't it?

Pause.

FLINT. George. (*Pause.*) Why does everyone *assume* I set fire to the church?

BISHOP. Do they? There hasn't been a breath of it in *my* ears.

FLINT. But you –

BISHOP. It is only I who . . . who have the nagging little thought. (*Pause.*) And I wish to protect you.

Pause.

FLINT. The police are coming to see me this afternoon.

Pause.

BISHOP. I should mention . . . the choirmaster reported a most curious incident. (*Pause.*) Look, I'm the first one to opt for keeping the whole thing under our . . . ha ha, our *mitres*? (*Pause.*) Your startling career in the church has turned me into something of a visionary, Ossian. I see visions. (*Pause.*) For instance I see you with some depraved female in the vestry, poised . . . *pour la volupté.* (*Pause.*) And in your typically absent-minded fashion you picked *choir night.* (*Pause.*) *N'est-ce pas?* (*Pause : sharply.*) Hodge recognized your feet.

FLINT *contemplates his feet.*

FLINT. I wouldn't have said they were so unique. (*Pause.*) Just feet. Inside shoes. Cheap shoes, get them anywhere. Nothing *distinctive*, I'd say. (*Pause.*) Hodge hates me.

BISHOP. It's possibly the way you walk, Ossian. And when running, which the putative you *was* doing at the time. Well! (*Pause.*) My dear man, I fancy you run like an ostrich. Highly identifiable, if not open to proof!

FLINT. It's funny how we say *my* feet, and *your* feet. *My* hat and *your* hat. You might ask me to leave my hat in the hall, but you'd never ask me to leave my feet in the hall.

BISHOP. And we say : *my* church has *burnt down.* Don't we, Ossian? And you probably said it when *your* church was razed at Edgecombe Bassett. Then there was the bell tower of that exquisite little Norman church in East Anglia, wasn't there? (*Pause.*) What was it that time?

Pause.

FLINT. Fireworks.

BISHOP. And by no means sparklers!

FLINT (*sulkily*). Roman candle.

Pause.

BISHOP. Have you been to a psychiatrist?

FLINT. I –

BISHOP. Why not be kind to yourself? And why not give me a series of hooks upon which to hang my evasions? (*Pause.*) Paranoia? Manic depression?

FLINT. I wouldn't dream of –

BISHOP. But I wish you *would* dream, Ossian. I wish you'd bloody well dream up something I can tell the Archbishop! What about infantilism? (*He goes right and calls out.*) Maurice –

FLINT. The human side of it –

BISHOP. Regrettably, I'm an authority on your human side. Were you just any Tom, Dick or parson I'd trounce you with theology. I'd flay you with doctrine. As it is, I shall just ask you to make a statement – which my secretary will take down.

    MAURICE, *a young clergyman, enters.*

FLINT. I had nothing to do with the petrol cans.

BISHOP. God knows – indeed *I* know – the church may be irrelevant, Ossian. Whether people like you should be allowed to turn a dying institution into a chronic farce, is another matter. You are not immoral. You are amoral. You are *a*moral with or without petrol cans. Or fireworks. I'm sure you'd manage even if you had only two dry sticks to rub together. Try to understand. I'm not uninterested in you. I'm positively fascinated and have been for years. But I'm *disinterested*, Ossian, and I wish to make a close study of your own ideas about yourself.

    Gestures towards MAURICE.

Look upon Maurice here as a pair of ears . . . a nimble hand with the Pitman's . . . and between the ears and the hand, a charitable hiatus.

    . *He goes to* FLINT *and pats him on the shoulder.*

Bear up, dear man. Remember Isaiah forty-five, nine: Shall the clay say to him that fashioneth it, what makest thou?

    The BISHOP *exits.* FLINT *and* MAURICE *face each other uncomfortably.*

FLINT. You're Maurice –

MAURICE. Yes.

FLINT. With the beagle –

MAURICE. Oh Lord! Has it been –

FLINT. Yes. Barking.

MAURICE. It's only a puppy. It's not . . . it –

FLINT. Shits everywhere?

MAURICE. Mr Flint. Who am I to criticize your language? (*Pause.*) Would you like to begin? (*He has pencil and notebook ready.*)

FLINT. The fact is I don't know what I'm supposed to be doing. Why did he have to rush off like that? What is there to write down? Why couldn't he just listen to me?

MAURICE. I think the Bishop wishes to spare you any . . . embarrassment, Mr Flint.

FLINT. So he plonks me down in front of a complete stranger.

MAURICE. A nonentity, if one is to believe the Bishop.

FLINT. Oh, I wouldn't take him so seriously. A little eccentric, maybe –

MAURICE. That's what he says you are.

FLINT. Well I'm . . . I'm touched.

   Pause.

MAURICE. Where would you like to begin?

FLINT. Is that a tape recorder over there?

MAURICE. It is. It's what he uses to dictate his letters for me . . . his reflections on life and questions of theology. (*Pause.*) It's pretty entertaining most days. For him it's like talking to himself, and I can tell you he gets quite fruity sometimes.

FLINT. Can't *I* use it then?

MAURICE. The point is, he didn't suggest that. (*Pause.*) No one is more ill at ease than I, Mr Flint.

FLINT. You don't give that impression.

MAURICE. Inside, I am ill at ease. (*Pause.*) The truth is I'm easily shocked. (*Pause.*) Unworldly. (*Pause.*) I'm not the Spencer Tracy type of parson at all.

FLINT. I wouldn't have thought you old enough to –

MAURICE. I watch telly a lot. I like the old films.

   Pause.

FLINT. I like the Shirley Temple ones.

MAURICE. That doesn't surprise me at all.

FLINT. Is that a perception or an insult?

MAURICE. Mr Flint – don't blame me if you're feeling nervous, and on the defensive. You're an old man. I've no wish to seem impertinent. As the Bishop's secretary I have privileged access to all kinds of information. And, like anyone who knows a little about you, I am truly amazed, even humbled. After all, we no longer deal in sin and punishment. We simply insist on life's spiritual meaning. If we seem ludicrous, that is because people cannot respect a religion or a clergy embarked on such a frenetic course of compromise. You make me feel humble because you remind me that there are extremities. (*Pause.*) Would you say . . . I only wish to help, if I may . . . would you say something went terribly amiss in childhood?

    Pause.

FLINT. I'm surprised you aren't a bishop already!

MAURICE. I intend to be one. (*Pause.*) Shall we begin with childhood? Babyhood? (*Pause.*) Much distress in later life can be unravelled, one might say, back to the nipple.

FLINT. Did you have nipple problems?

MAURICE. My mother, I'm glad to say, read some excellent books . . . an enlightened, progressive woman. Fully grasped things like the psychology of the feeding relationship. I think looking back that I can say I'm . . . well –

FLINT. Spockmarked for life?

    Pause.

MAURICE. Do you want to say anything or don't you?

    Pause.

FLINT. I've always *liked* breasts. Don't you?

MAURICE. In their place.

FLINT. No shortage of nice places for them to be *in*.

MAURICE. I gather Miss Biggin was well endowed.

FLINT. Like an atom bomb. Bang the two together and you had a critical mass. An erotic explosion.

    Pause.

MAURICE. It's not my place to interrogate you. Shall I go away?

FLINT. Do I disgust you, Maurice?

MAURICE. Yes.

> *Pause.*

FLINT. Take this down. (*Pause.*) George.

> *Pause.*

MAURICE. Yes?

> *Pause.* FLINT *is wandering up and down, twisting, sidestepping, reflecting.*

FLINT. George.

> *Pause.*

MAURICE. I've got that.

> *Pause.*

FLINT. Revelation of St John, three sixteen: Because thou art lukewarm, and neither cold nor hot, I will spew thee out of my mouth. (*Pause.*) Jeremiah, eight twenty: The harvest is past, the summer is ended, and we are not saved. (*Pause.*) O.K.? (*Pause.*) But: St Matthew, eleven twelve – The kingdom of heaven suffereth violence, and the violent shall take it by force. (*Pause.*) That ought to give him something to think about. (*Pause.*) As to my conduct in this abysmal parish. And others. (*Pause.*) I'd like to say something on the question of the will. Got that, Maurice? Will will will. (*Pause.*) Taking leave of you all. (*Pause.*) The mad mouse of St Bartholomew's was a furry miracle. And it had no will. (*Pause.*) I, that very mouse's vicar – I looked upon it with awe. (*Pause.*) A will-less creature, functioning efficiently in its environment: i.e. St Bartholomew's. (*Pause.*) A mouse, you might say, without petrol can problems. Or police problems. Or bishop problems. Or faith problems. (*Pause.*) An untranscendental mouse. (*Pause.*) The church its oyster. (*Pause.*) Look in the eye of nature, George, and tell me what you see. (*Pause.*) There've been bawdy clerics without number. Queers. Flagellators. Voyeurs. (*Pause.*) Astronomers, experts on saltwater crocodiles. Fetishists. Nympholeptics. Wallingsworth of St Luke's near Heckmondwyke, devoted much time to the life cycle of the malarial parasite. (*Pause.*)

Others collect things, and I knew one with the Stations of the Cross tattooed upon his person.

MAURICE. I am getting all this down. The route to explanation would seem to be . . . circuitous.

Pause.

FLINT. You speak of childhood. (*Pause.*) Thin legs. A spindly torso. A hard round head like an unripe melon. (*Pause.*) Playing on my father's lawns, his paddocks. Once or twice intimately fondled by his maids, who took my little man on their rosy palms and giggled. (*Pause.*) My cousin Oswald once told me the only true love known by young English gentlemen was from those common wenches who peel and scrub, polish and serve. (*Pause.*) Does it still go on?

MAURICE. The question is, does it lead to the later corruption of an adult clergyman?

FLINT. Tears spring to my eyes, Maurice.

MAURICE. Of remorse?

Pause.

FLINT. How many happy grooms have taken their erections to Dieppe, only to be frustrated by brides who had never known a tickle? (*Pause.*) And the mid-twentieth century, charitable only in the matter of retroactive blame . . . I mean, always looking for a start in the early sportings of id, ego and superego . . . and the *nineteen sixties* were a torment. (*Pause.*) I dare not stroll the Kings Road. Last week I drove my motorbike and sidecar into a lamp-post. Gently. No harm. Her skirt, as she took to the zebra crossing, swung no more than half an inch below where my eyes had instantly plotted the position of the *mons veneris*. The swelling little pad. Furrier than the demented mouse of St Bartholomew's. (*Pause.*) I gather the young couple freely and guiltlessly – but do I only *imagine* they have not yet handled their despair? (*Pause.*) An old man looks on, with a swelling heart. And a fairly high proportion seem to have abandoned the brassière. We know that draughts make the nipples rise, and by God the Kings Road can be draughty! There we are, Maurice, back to nipples. (*Pause.*) I see I have not dealt with the issue of fire-raising. Or divinity. (*Pause.*) I fear that in our time, God is only too negotiable. In all hemispheres. (*He picks up the chalice.*) Battered cup! Of mysteries. Wine and blood. Transubstantiation. (*Pause.*) Fired without being tempered! (*Pause.*) Hear this, George. What our choirmaster saw was Friar Dixie, in voluminous cassock. And I myself well-nigh incandescent. Dixie, the dubious colleen. A very Demeter of the Emerald Isle. (*Pause.*) Of petrol I am innocent. I *did* leave a pair or cavalry twill trousers in the surplice cupboard – the flames destroyed evidence of my shame. (*Pause.*) I have profane love gloriously upon me, George. (*Pause.*) You will no doubt think it worth a gutted church to have such incontestable grounds for my liquidation. (*Pause.*) Maurice, adieu! (*He takes the chalice and hands it to* MAURICE.) I add only one further cautionary remark my boy. Injustice, poverty, exploitation . . . well, they've led more than one scrupulous and compassionate cleric from the Sermon on the Mount to the works of Vladimir Ilyich Lenin. Should you contemplate this perilous evolution: beware! Communism is the opiate of the middle classes. *Au revoir. La lutte continue!*

FLINT *exits.* MAURICE *takes up the microphone. Hesitates.*

MAURICE. Bishop, I do not understand Flint. I think I am going to cry, sir.

Fade out and fade in to

ACT TWO

Scene One

The Vicarage.

FLINT *sits gloomily alone: contemplating what future?* DIXIE *enters, touches the old man's bald pate.*

DIXIE. You are down, Ossie?

FLINT. Very low.

DIXIE. You old stick.

FLINT. I await the detective inspector. Policemen terrify me. And later, an inquest to be held by Esme. Have you noticed Esme and Victoria today?

DIXIE. Can't help noticing them. And Esme wouldn't let you carve the leg of lamb. I saw the way she held that knife. But cheering, to see a woman so handy from her cripple's chair. I thought Victoria liked me. But she looks too much at my stomach.

FLINT. We must think of a name for the child. Does anarchy flow in the genes? Will Arthur's political obsessions pursue us even through the womb?

DIXIE. I wish it was yours, Ossian.

FLINT. You feel a tenderness then? (*Pause.*) Your eye drops on the bald patch with its wild fringe, and maybe something in your throat catches? A little lump there? In the trachea?

DIXIE. Don't let them all put you down.

FLINT. What if the detective inspector would put me *away*?

DIXIE. You've had a fair innings, Ossy – And what did that bishop say?

FLINT. He didn't listen. Would my story have burned his ears? This morning, he had it taken down in the vile shorthand. Pitman's, Newspeed, one of those. By a young curate who it turned out was possessed of an unruly beagle dog. (*Pause.*) I ache, here and there.

DIXIE. I'll get the liniment and rub you all over.

FLINT. I admitted the vestry business, but denied the petrol cans. (*Pause.*) Should I survive the police, I think the Church will let me go with a sigh of relief and no hard feelings. (*Pause.*) I see we have power, light and even gas restored to us. (*Pause.*) I think Swash and the Bishop must have done a deal. Swash in triumph, the Bishop in his wisdom.

DIXIE. I'll tuck a few things into the sidecar. And we'll go. Abroad, shall we?

FLINT. I've no money. What parson without private means has ever scraped together a few pounds for the twilight years?

DIXIE. It would be nice to go to Rome and see the Pope.

FLINT. I think I'd like an igloo. On a large ice-float. Polar bears sniffing at the dustbins. Photograph the perennially amusing penguin. Out of harm's way. Blubber lamp for light and warmth. (*Pause.*) It's time for you to relinquish popery, Dixie.

DIXIE. The Liverpool Irish are clingers. They hang on to the faith. I could hail Mary when I couldn't hail me dad. Not that he waited for me to grow up. (*Pause.*) Ossy, I was a scrubber . . . a real scrubber at twelve. I would leave the nuns in their holy business teaching little girls the holy ropes, and away to some boozer. In the yard at the back waiting for the boys to finish their gig. A van waiting for them and their musical instruments. Us girls heaving and panting and nearly swooning. Till they came out, the group. My first was The Smooth. And they used to tip us into the van and have us there and then, still sweating from the sounds. I remember their . . . wet shirts. (*Pause.*) That is youth, Ossian. I never wore a thing under my dress and I never once had delight. (*Pause.*) Till you. (*Pause.*) You're fantastic, I wouldn't have believed. I should think the baba can feel you. And it makes something lovely split inside my head. (*Pause.*) I want you chirpy when the fuzz arrive.

Answer them back sharp, and none of this what you call ideology. (*Pause.*) Ossy, don't grieve.

FLINT. I wonder whether parsons can claim social security? And would it feed three mouths, one a gluttonous infant?

DIXIE. I shall be able to work fairly soon. If you don't mind watching the kid. And you can write your book on . . . what was it? All those pages of notes up there in the study?

FLINT. In Cuba? Under the palms? Where you pull a nut from the tree, slice its hairy top with a machete and drink the cool milk there by the blue and sharky water. (*Pause.*) Only, one asks oneself: where is Fidel *going*? (*Pause.*) I doubt I could manage the sugar cane at my time of life . . . and would they not view an aged cleric . . . *askance*?

DIXIE. As soon as life forces you into dreaming, you really *have* lost!

FLINT. It isn't that I dream. It's that I like the sound of unlikely fancies. (*Pause.*) When I'm left alone to my beastly revels I don't need phrases.

DIXIE. Am I a beastly revel, then?

FLINT. Dixie – no. But how can you . . . I'm baffled that you . . . my old skin and bones repel me. I expect you to cringe, sooner or later. (*Pause.*) Stark naked I am an unlovely sight. And yet I have this brutal energy. (*Pause.*) Knobbly feet. Veins like twisted flex. My bowels constantly bubble. One sly fart from me would asphyxiate a cathedral full of solid citizens. The deformities of my kneecaps practically constitute a work of art. Collar bones like doorknobs. (*Pause.*) It is sad that the pubic hair also turns grey in the fullness of time. I am not so much a body as a relic. (*Pause.*) And without God. (*Pause.*) Miss Biggin and I never once undressed. (*Pause.*) We had to preserve, as she so shyly put it: that certain niceness. (*Pause.*) D'you know, I can't remember what it was that took me into the church. (*Pause.*) I remember a vast, shimmering light – and I fear this was not the handiwork of the supernatural, but one of those rare long and golden summers when the born eccentric transcends himself and turns actually potty. In Cambridge. (*Pause.*) It was not a heavenly light, but the ordinary business of hydrogen combustion from a minor star at, so to speak, the arse-end of a galaxy. (*Pause.*) How many, like my dear dead friend the Reverend Spencer Wilcox, began drunk with Divinity in Cambridge and ended ignominiously with Wolf Cubs in an outlying suburb of Manchester? (*Pause.*) Meantime, the news from Moscow was not good . . . the noble Trotsky holed up on a Turkish island . . . and I have lived too long and understood too much to enjoy anything but the slavery of my senses. (*Pause.*) The naughty parson is not too distant a cousin of the tormented queer in his urinal-haunting. He expects that one day, a policeman will approach, will look upon him. And sneer. And hate.

DIXIE. How d'you think I feel about it then? You should see Holloway. And you don't catch them do-gooders outside naming people like *me* as a Prisoner of the Year. Christ, you don't! There ought to be a society that nominates the Mug of the Century, there'd be a stampede for that one.

    Pause.

FLINT. We're a woeful pair.

DIXIE. I'm not woeful. I'm happy. At least I will be when we get out of this lot. (*Pause.*) *I* don't mind your funny old bod, so don't start making with self-pity. (*Pause.*) Don't you love me you bloody old bastard?

FLINT. I do, but I sniff danger.

DIXIE. From me?

FLINT. Not you.

DIXIE. The cops?

FLINT. Not even the cops.

DIXIE. *What*, then?

    Pause.

FLINT. I don't know.

    Pause.

DIXIE. It's just a feeling.

FLINT. Yes. An apprehension.

DIXIE. Is it Esme? Victoria?

FLINT. Victoria could have married well, as it used to be called in those days. She was lively, honest. Completely un-hypocritical. (*Pause.*) She found her way into that fascinating set of people . . . I mean the Bells, and Virginia Woolf . . . those painters in Cornwall. She had an awfully funny story about once being snubbed by Wyndham Lewis. (*Pause.*) He was a great snubber, I believe –

DIXIE. And now it's all hell-fire and original sin!

FLINT. I suspect, you know . . . I suspect that's a *joke* with Victoria. (*Pause.*) So that sometimes, alone, she can have a little laugh at us all. Because it irritates us so much. (*Pause.*) Quite harmless.

> INSPECTOR HOUNSLOW *enters, pushing* ESME *in her wheelchair.*

ESME. Where's Victoria? Didn't you hear the doorbell? I had to answer it myself. I'm sure you all know how *easy* it is for a crippled person to answer doorbells!

HOUNSLOW. I think it might be useful to have your sister present, Mrs Flint.

DIXIE. I'll find her.

> DIXIE *exits.*

ESME. Ossian, this is Inspector Hounslow. I think you were expecting him. He was kind enough to propel me here in the absence of Victoria. Where *is* the silly woman?

FLINT. How d'you do, Inspector.

HOUNSLOW. How d'you do, sir. (*Pause.*) I hope you *were* expecting me? I told my young sergeant to make the appointment.

ESME. All I wish to know is whether you require *my* presence or not.

HOUNSLOW. I don't know, Mrs Flint. Not yet.

ESME. I thought investigating policemen always went about in pairs.

> *Pause.*

HOUNSLOW. You're well ahead of me, Mrs Flint.

ESME. It is axiomatic, Inspector, that well-born educated old ladies feel an almost *biological* superiority to the employees of our society's institutions. (*Pause.*) One regards you as skilled, intelligent, human – but at some lower and incomprehensible level.

Pause.

HOUNSLOW. You mean you're a snob, Mrs Flint?

ESME. Possibly.

HOUNSLOW. And articulate with it. Or wordy, as we'd say down on our level.

Pause.

ESME. How times have changed!

Pause.

HOUNSLOW. I'll tell you where my young sergeant is. He's wearing a Zappata moustache, a psychedelic shirt, bell-bottomed cherry velvet trousers – and he's at a pot-party in S.W.7. He'll have a ravy afternoon on expenses, leave a chunk of hash in the hostess's wardrobe – and appear neat and innocent as you like at court next Monday morning. (*Pause.*) The co-called clean job's done by the men in blue and a brace of dogs.

FLINT. Inspector –

HOUNSLOW. Mr Flint, we're ignoring you. That's one of the tested techniques as well, sir. Ramble on, scrutinizing hard the meanwhile. I've been taking you in sir. Looking you up and down. (*Pause.*) Haven't I got a pair of penetrating blue eyes?

FLINT. I didn't burn the church down.

HOUNSLOW. I wouldn't have thought you had. What you're going through, Mr Flint, it's more of a ritual than an investigation. (*Pause.*) D'you watch television, Mrs Flint?

ESME. Why?

HOUNSLOW. I like to keep up with what it's doing for our image. There's been progress, I'll admit. No more gawping bobbies in bicycle clips and chin straps. Not by any means. I gather now we're just like you and me, Mrs Flint. Or Mr Flint, here. Or anybody. Some of us tough, some of us kind but stern, some of us half-crazed inside with the thought of all the crime and filth the human race is capable of. Some of us default on the conjugal obligations, due to our erratic working hours. And our occasional brutalities are those of men driven desperate by the irredeemable violence of mankind. (*Pause.*) It's wonderful for public relations is television. Sherlock Holmes would have smiled, wouldn't he?

ESME. Inspector Hounslow, I think you must be a lonely man.

HOUNSLOW. You find me garrulous, I should imagine.

ESME. I do.

HOUNSLOW. No one knows what it's like to be like a policeman any more. Not even the police. Was it Oscar Wilde who talked about life imitating art? The Superintendent is a shocker in that respect. (*Pause.*) No, madam, I'm an old and useless dog in the department. On the verge of retirement. I often look at it this way. If our unit was a monastery, set down on some icy mountain. And the Super an Abbot. *I'd* be the old St Bernard they push off into the snowstorm without its little barrel of brandy. (*Pause.*) That's me in a nutshell.

ESME. If I were you I should retire at once and go into one of those nasty private agencies which concentrate on divorce.

FLINT. The brandy would be for the snowbound traveller, Inspector – not for the St Bernard dog. It would hardly be an injustice directed against *yourself*.

HOUNSLOW. The point is taken, Mr Flint. But basically, sir, I am the one who tends to forget his brandy barrel. And that should reassure you. Because if you were definitely under suspicion, they'd send a better man. What's more, as a swallow doesn't make a summer, three petrol cans don't make a case of arson.

    Turning to ESME

With regard to that, Mrs Flint, and being one who respects the obvious, I can't see you flitting round St Luke's in the dark loaded with gasolene. So you can withdraw from my tedious presence if you wish.

ESME *gives him a withering look and wheels herself offstage.*
HOUNSLOW *takes out his pipe.*

HOUNSLOW. D'you mind if I smoke, Mr Flint?

FLINT (*offers pouch*). Have a fill of mine.

HOUNSLOW *thoughtfully fills his pipe.*

HOUNSLOW. You like a pipe yourself?

FLINT. It's an impregnable motive for carrying tobacco.
Pause.

HOUNSLOW. I can see you're not a talker, Mr Flint. Or should I say I hear?

FLINT. I can babble away when the conditions are right.
Pause.

HOUNSLOW. I'm not a churchgoer myself.

FLINT. This is not an epoch of widespread belief, Inspector. Don't get to feel isolated.

HOUNSLOW. Millions of Catholics in Latin America. Praying. Lighting candles. Crawling up and down church steps on their knees. (*Pause.*) I should think it's hard work for your revolutionary, is Latin America. (*Pause.*) In Western Europe now, I blame affluence for the decline of faith.

FLINT. I didn't burn the church down, you know.
Pause.

HOUNSLOW. Myself, I believe in God all right. But I can't take your modern church. Christmas is a commercial farce, isn't it? And take last Easter. I've got two boys and a girl, came late in life. What's Easter to them? Chocolate rabbits, eggs, chickens. I even saw a chocolate frog in one shop, Kilburn way. (*Pause.*) I do have irreverent thoughts about it all. Imagine if you were there on crucifixion day. Calvary. (*Pause.*) You walk up to the foot of the cross. You cup your hands to your mouth and call up. (*Cups his hands to his mouth*) 'Jesus,' you shout. (*Hands down.*) 'Yes?' he says. (*Hands to mouth.*) 'I've brought your chocolate rabbit' you say. (*Pause.*) That's going to cheer him up, isn't it? *That's* a rare old Christian message, isn't it?

FLINT. There are many paths to grace, Inspector. And irreverence may be one of them. (*Pause.*) *My* childhood was in Somerset. We were rich then, and I thought the farmworkers were yokels. As a boy. One Easter I wrote an Easter poem. I was twelve. It was called: A Yokel's Easter poem. I mimicked the dialect when I recited it, and thought myself very high and mighty. And funny.

HOUNSLOW. What was it, Mr Flint? Might I ask you?

FLINT. When daffodils do be out,
    They gives a little yellow shout.

    Pause.

HOUNSLOW. Who was the girl?

FLINT. You mean –

HOUNSLOW. Who went looking for your sister-in-law.

FLINT. Edna Mary Cecilia O'Keefe.

HOUNSLOW. Late of Holloway Prison.

FLINT. That's correct.

    Pause.

HOUNSLOW. Miss O'Keefe was quite a handful in Holloway. They were expecting her back. (*Pause.*) It's clear you're a complicated man, Mr Flint. And your activities possibly above my head. (*Pause.*) I expect the Church authorities are peeved out of their minds? (*Pause.*) Do you lose much sweat over it all? You never seem to bother with good cover sir, to use an old army expression. There you are out in the open, causing no end of bother. And yet when I look in your eyes, Mr Flint, I perceive serenity. Yes that's the word. (*Pause.*) Well our professions aren't all *that* dissimilar. We chase their bodies – you chase their souls. It all boils down to trying to keep *some* sort of grip on those bloody miserable bastards out there. (*Pause.*) Is there serenity in *my* eyes, Mr Flint?

    Pause.

FLINT. No serenity. No.

HOUNSLOW. Anything at all apart from red veins and mucus?

    Pause.

FLINT. I see that you belong to the police as little as I belong to the Church. On the whole the police have it easier. You tangle with what is visible. We with what is intangible but all too prone to express itself. You with the sanction of the State. (*Pause.*) We with the sanction of a doctrine so totally devoid of rationality that it meets a deep human need. And fears not the implications of the chocolate bunny. (*Pause.*) I say 'we' when of course I mean 'they'.

HOUNSLOW. I brought something to show you.

FLINT. Well I don't wish to impose a kind of anti-sermon on you, Inspector –

HOUNSLOW. I left it outside.

> HOUNSLOW *exits and returns with a brown paper bag. He takes a newspaper from his pocket and spreads it on the floor. He pours out the contents of the bag on to the newspaper – a lot of black powder and bits of charred material.*

FLINT. Now what on earth is that?

HOUNSLOW. You mean what it *was*. I've had it analysed. The lab. report said: a pair of cavalry twill trousers.

FLINT. Oh.

HOUNSLOW. And that's not all, sir.

FLINT. Oh?

HOUNSLOW. Among these charred remains, sir, is also – how shall we say? A pair of carbonized knickers and a multiform bra.

FLINT. Well now. I can't resist quoting you Pliny the Elder, Inspector: It is far from easy to determine whether Nature has proved a kind parent to man or a merciless step-mother.

HOUNSLOW. If this was your step-mother, Mr Flint, she took a thirty-six and there was traces of cheap talc in the left cup. (*Pause.*) And Mr Swash – whilst grubbing about the ruins in his obviously nosey way – found a nickel-plated pipe cleaner. (*Pulling it from his pocket.*) To wit: this one.

FLINT. Mine.

HOUNSLOW. Like the cavalry twill.

FLINT. Yes.

> *Pause.*

HOUNSLOW. I think I'd have split my sides if I'd been the choir-master when you and Miss O'Keefe abandoned that cupboard.
Pause.

FLINT. Are you going to arrest me then?

HOUNSLOW. No. (*He pours the stuff from the newspaper back into the bag.*)

FLINT. Er . . . why not?
Pause.

HOUNSLOW. I'll be frank with you, Mr Flint – this one's a non-starter. I can *smell* a non-starter. Your frolics in the vestry are no concern of mine, though I've no doubt we could have many a smile or two over a glass of port. (*Pause.*) Any little bonfire that started in the surplice cupboard – I'm sure the choirmaster could've put it out with his bare hands. (*Pause.*) I'll be on my way.
Pause.

FLINT. I can't say you placate one's natural anxiety, Inspector. (*Pause.*) I mean – I might even want to know who set fire to the church myself. Mightn't I?

HOUNSLOW. So as to be publicly cleared of any suspicion, sir? Or out of curiosity?

FLINT. I don't like mysteries. Of any sort.

HOUNSLOW. Coming from one who's on theological terms with virgin birth, resurrection, water into wine and cetera – you stun, me sir. You leave the mind somewhat *seized*. (*Pause.*) Can it be that you're an impostor? Don't you accept one jot or tittle of the Church's teaching?

FLINT. Inspector, you've wormed your way into the very centre of my spiritual crime.

HOUNSLOW. And all those little babies that came your way for Christening? All the dying on their way out of life? All the living . . . all those faces turned up to you of a Sunday?

FLINT. What about all those faces turned up to you from behind prison bars?

HOUNSLOW. I *respect* the criminal, if nothing else. And nothing can shake that awful secret respect of mine, Mr Flint. Robbery with violence, assault, rape, murder, it all makes sense to me. But I *do* try to remove those unhappy creatures from the area of temptation, sir. And I would have expected you, likewise, to be a copper of the human soul. (*Pause.*) But I grasp your dilemma. Policemen aren't required to actually believe anything, so long as they enforce the law.

FLINT. Inspector – thank you for grasping.

HOUNSLOW. There's nothing outside the scope of the Almighty, sir. Which enables me to say: God be with you.

> HOUNSLOW *proffers his hand.* FLINT *takes it.* HOUNSLOW *exits, with his brown paper bag.* FLINT *stands a moment, staring vacantly into space. He calls out:*

FLINT. Dixie –

> *Pause.*
>
> *Dixie?*
>
> *There is no answer.* FLINT *exits slowly.*
> *Fade out and fade in to*

Scene Two

The Vicarage.

VICTORIA *slowly wheels* ESME *onstage, places the wheel-chair centre. Stands behind it, her hands on* ESME'S *shoulders.* ESME'S *eyes are closed.*

VICTORIA. I had such a lovely dream last night, Esme. Though it was upsetting at first. (*Pause.*) It all took place in Dieppe and it was about the second coming. (*Pause.*) I've never been to Dieppe. But it makes me think of ships, and cranes, and those green French trains waiting for all the travellers from England.

> *There is a long pause.* VICTORIA *takes a cigarette packet from a pocket in her dress, and lights one. She stands smoking, coughing a little.*

You could walk *before* the church burnt down. (*Pause.*) Couldn't you, Esme? (*Pause.*) You've always had periods of – what do the doctors call it? – spontaneous remission. (*Pause.*) Whenever he took a new woman. (*Pause.*) The painter Sickert painted some lovely pictures in Dieppe. And that was where Jesus came again, in my dream. (*Pause.*) I was in a shabby little hotel. I was waking up. I'd set my alarm to ring exactly at dawn. (*Pause.*) But the sun didn't rise, Esme. (*Pause.*) There was no light of any kind. (*Pause.*) Then it happened. (*Pause.*) Down from the sky. (*Pause.*) A thousand feet tall. A thousand feet at least. (*Pause.*) Jesus descended. (*Pause.*) There was a brilliant aura round him. (*Pause.*) Owing to his enormous size, one could easily perceive each detail. (*Pause.*) He wore a blue velvet cap with a little brim, Esme. And a white cricket shirt. And white cricket trousers. (*Pause.*) He carried a bat too, and had a soft white sweater tied round his throat by the sleeves. (*Pause.*) Sitting there in my little hotel room in that awful French town, I felt a certain pride . . . a pride mingled with awe. (*Pause.*) It is the Son of God, I said to myself. (*Pause.*) And he is batting for England. (*Pause.*) I looked at the heavenly cricketer floating gently from the black sky, and I cried with love and gratitude. But. D'you know, Esme. As those monumental blancoed shoes of His touched the ground – he disappeared in a great flash of light and smoke. (*Pause.*) Like the demon king at the pantomimes only, of course, not the same at all, being Jesus. (*Pause.*) And the sun was in the sky. And I suddenly knew that we were all immortal now. But immortal on this earth. (*Pause.*) Now I know it was only a dream. But it leaves me with the feeling that Dieppe must be an extraordinary place.

FLINT *and* DIXIE *enter, as if sneaking past.*

There you are, my dears.

FLINT *hauls himself and* DIXIE *to a stop. Stares at* ESME.

FLINT. Victoria – Esme doesn't look at all well.

VICTORIA. She *isn't* well, Ossian.

FLINT. Hadn't we better phone Patrick Colley?

VICTORIA. That won't be at all necessary. I was telling Esme all about my dream last night.

DIXIE. We were wondering where you were.

FLINT *goes towards* ESME, *reaching his hand out.*

VICTORIA. Don't touch her!

FLINT (*stops*). I want to know what's wrong with her.

VICTORIA. I expect my silly old maunderings sent her to sleep. We've been out in the sunshine, you know. And the air's rather fresh. (*Pause.*) She didn't like that policeman who came to see you. (*Pause.*) I bought her an ice-cream in Kensington Gardens. Then I brought her home and kept her in the kitchen. Didn't you look in the kitchen.

DIXIE. I did.

VICTORIA (*smiling*). We were in the pantry.

FLINT. Why don't you make us some tea, Victoria?

VICTORIA. Sly one! You're only trying to get rid of me. (*Pause.*) But my sister needs me.

FLINT. Dixie will look after her, whilst you make the tea.

VICTORIA. Esme and I have had a beautiful relationship for many years. Don't think *you* know everything, Ossian! (*Pause.*) She *loathes* you.

FLINT. Well. I do know that.

VICTORIA. She hoped you'd be sent to prison.

DIXIE *steps forward close to* VICTORIA.

DIXIE. Will you bloody well wake her up?

VICTORIA *looks from* FLINT *to* DIXIE, *smiling. Then, almost coyly, she gives* ESME *a push from behind.* ESME *slumps forward across her own knees : there is a knife in her back.*

DIXIE *screams and crosses herself.* FLINT *cannot move.* VICTORIA *is laughing.* DIXIE *and* FLINT *look at each other.* DIXIE *rushes offstage. Slowly,* VICTORIA *quietens down. All the time,* FLINT *has remained stockstill. There is a long silence.*

FLINT. My poor Victoria.

VICTORIA. Yes. You'll not waste any pity (*Points at* ESME) on this one I should hope.

Pause.

FLINT. I don't pretend to feel anything for Esme. But I never wished her dead. (*Pause.*) And I pity you.

VICTORIA. You've *often* wished her dead! (*Sing-song.*) In my *bed* you wished her dead. (*Pause.*) Stupid virgin. And it was she fired the church my darling Ossy. (*Pause.*) And I have loved you all your filthy obscene years. (*Grimacing.*) You'll inherit her money, now.

She comes forward to FLINT *and stands quickly in front of him.* (*In a dead voice.*) She thought I was in league with her against you, Ossian. Imagine that, the bitch!

FLINT *puts his arms round her.*

She bullied me cruelly. And she called me mad and thought me mad. Then secretly she'd say . . . time and time again . . that I am sane and you are out of your mind. (*Pause.*) Over and over again: You're sane, Victoria, you're sane. (*Pause.*) We had long giggles about your wedding night. But she was insincere that way – she drove me easily to hysteria, until I laughed and laughed.

FLINT *gently moves her away from him, keeping his hands on her shoulders.*

FLINT. I never wished her dead.

VICTORIA. You'll be free.

FLINT. Through murder. Not self-sacrifice. Which I abominate anyway.

VICTORIA. You said there are no sins. Then murder isn't a sin. So what is it? And don't you look so pious when there's never been a ripple of holy thought anywhere in you!

She moves away from him, seeming almost triumphant.

There *is* a thick mist in my head *sometimes*, but you roll it away, Ossian. Away and away. So that I can see you. And understand you. (*Pause.*) I have gone further than you ever will, by killing her. (*Pause.*) So you dwindle in my eyes. (*Laughing.*) A soggy little cocky! Put *that* in your Liverpool whore and pump it! Her with her nasty belly tumour!

With a flourish, she grabs the wheel chair, circles with it once, and exits.
Fade out and fade in to

Scene Three

The Church Hall.
ESME'S *coffin stands on low trestles, with a few wreaths. The light is as if from stained glass windows. There are sheaves of corn and baskets of fruit. Loud harmonium music.* FLINT *sits alone, hunched, on a chair. After a moment the music stops.* FLINT *looks up, stands, calls out in an authoritative voice:*

FLINT. Swash. Stop playing that harmonium. And leave this hall.
> *There is a short pause. Then a burst of cacophonic music from the harmonium and silence.* FLINT *sits.*
> INSPECTOR HOUNSLOW *enters, walking slowly up to* FLINT. *He stands beside him.* FLINT *looks at* HOUNSLOW, *then away.*

HOUNSLOW. Paying your last respects, Mr Flint? (*Pause.*)

FLINT. You know better than that, Inspector. (*Pause.*)

HOUNSLOW. One's wife inside a coffin. An unbearable thing. Whether she was loved or hated. (*Pause.*)

FLINT. By the standards of many, she was a virtuous woman. (*Pause.*) Virtuous people are . . . so . . . unassailable. (*Pause.*)

HOUNSLOW. It's tragic, your sister-in-law.

FLINT. No. In her way she'll feel more secure.

HOUNSLOW. Ah, Mr Flint! But a prison for the insane! Madness. To rot away there.

FLINT. No. Victoria's world is indestructible. It can be entered . . . or understood . . . but not shattered. My world on the other hand has always been precarious. Never knew when the whole outrage to respectability would cave in. (*Pause.*) But even fire and murder leave me unawed, Inspector. Moved – but not overwhelmed. (*Pause.*) Victoria's means were terrible. Yet I am their unseeking beneficiary.

HOUNSLOW (*points*). Sheaves of corn. Fruit. (*Pause.*) It smells like the loft where my father used to put his apples.

FLINT. Yes. Last Sunday was harvest festival.

   Pause.

HOUNSLOW. Lucky they can use the church hall. (*Pause.*) Very temporary, let's hope. (*Pause.*) I'm not really a frivolous man. Did you think I was? The day I came, when it happened.

FLINT. No.

   Pause.

HOUNSLOW. My colleagues say I have this little fault . . . I get . . . jocose, sir. In an irritating fashion. Jocose, when I can't get that sense of how things fit. (*Pause.*) I overstep the boundaries of good form. (*Pause.*) Which is not incompatible with being a policeman. (*Pause.*) But I *have* bungled a few interrogations that way. In my time. (*Pause.*) I just called at the vicarage. The young lady said you were here, in the church hall. (*Pause.*) I was moved to pop in, Mr Flint. (*Pause.*) *En passant,* as the French say. (*Pause.*) Not a morbid impulse, I assure you. Or a wish to intrude. (*Pause.*) Even if not grieving, you might be introspective. In that kind of a mood just now I mean. (*Pause.*) I'll take myself off, sir. (*Pause.*) Everything's cleared up. The fire. Everything. (*Pause.*) It made me smile, just the very idea of you as a fire-raiser, Mr Flint! (*Pause.*) I'll shake your hand, sir –

   Pause. FLINT *rises.*

FLINT. You won't be lonely in your retirement. Three children you said, if I remember?

HOUNSLOW. They are very nearly a joy, it's true. And I've taken to astronomy. The sky at night. (*Pause.*) You'll be off away, somewhere, I take it?

FLINT. After the funeral. We have the motorbicycle and sidecar. (*Pause.*) Miss O'Keefe wishes to see St Peter's in Rome. (*Pause.*) And *I* fancy the Acropolis, Carthage. I've not visited the ancient places. It's autumn. My bones ache for sun. For warmth. (*Pause.*) Wine dark seas.

Pause.

HOUNSLOW. And there'll be the child, sir. (*Smiles.*) The pitter-patter of little feet on the Appian Way?

FLINT *smiles. They shake hands.*

FLINT. Jocose!

HOUNSLOW. There you are, you see! I can't resist, can I? Jocose!

HOUNSLOW *exits.* FLINT *goes to the coffin, leans on it with both hands.* SWASH *enters, not quite himself.*

SWASH. You can't order me to leave this hall. (*Pause : nervously.*) I must say, it wasn't the same as having the harvest festival in the church proper. (*Pause.*) Not at all the same. (*Pause.*) Quite a different atmosphere here. (*Pause.*) Rows of chairs, I mean. Instead of pews. (*Pause.*) I find it stinks, rather. (*Pause.*) I mean, the Youth Club boys play handball here. (*Pause.*) Not much left of the Youth Club, is there?

FLINT. Oh, you put a lot of hard work in with that, Eric. (*Pause.*) Very commendable.

Pause.

SWASH. And then – when we have the temporary altar fixed up. (*Pause.*) We'll have it ready for . . . for Esme, you know. To-morrow. (*Pause.*) Well it's a bit unsteady. And it's a funny thing. I look down at the congregation, and I can't take my eyes off the markings for the badminton court. (*Pause.*) I think badminton's getting more popular. (*Pause.*) Something a bit wrong with the harmonium. (*Pause.*) Hodge got it out of the vestry, you know. (*Pause.*) Reliable man, Hodge. (*Pause.*) I'm in digs, now. (*Pause.*) What used to be Miss Biggin's place. (*Pause.*) Gives me an uncanny feeling. (*Pause.*) I . . . I'm deeply sorry about Victoria, Ossian. (*Pause.*) Things shake one, don't they?

FLINT. To conceive of you being shaken, Eric . . . is to have one's faith in you marginally restored.

Pause.

SWASH. I still think you're an unsavoury person. (*Pause.*) To put it mildly. (*Pause.*) But I –

Pause.

FLINT. Yes?
> *Pause.*

SWASH. I have to say before you leave. I have to get it out some-how. (*Pause.*) I feel guilty, Ossian.

FLINT. Haven't you experienced guilt before?

SWASH. Look, there's no need to go on being sarcastic with me. (*Pause.*) Not any more, is there? (*Pause.*) Who doesn't feel guilt, one time or another? (*Pause.*) But it was little things.

FLINT. Yes. I should think your misdemeanours have tended to be puny. It can't be much fun to be on the touchline watching the really strenuous sinners in the scrum! I should ring the Bishop's secretary, Maurice, if I were you. He has some rivet-ingly mammary theories about the origins of one's problems.
> *Pause.*

SWASH. You're aware . . . that in my awkward way . . . I'm trying to apologize to you?

FLINT. For this and that?

SWASH. More or less.

FLINT. But you'd have preferred it if I were the demon church-burner of North Kensington. Wouldn't you?
> *Pause.*

SWASH. I'll leave you with Esme.

FLINT. Esme is not here.
> *Pause.*

SWASH. I am sure she is with God.

FLINT. They certainly deserve each other.

> SWASH *can take no more of this kind of thing. He exits. The lights are dim. The coffin, wreaths, fruit, etc., are removed – whilst* FLINT *stands facing the audience impassively.*
>
> *As soon as* FLINT *is alone on the stage, we hear the staccato roar of a motorbike.* DIXIE *in the saddle, the bike and sidecar roll onstage and stop.* DIXIE *revs the machine up and down a few times, then switches off. She reaches into the sidecar, and offers* FLINT *his crash helmet and goggles. He puts them on. Fade up to*

Scene Four

The Journey.
DIXIE *leaves the saddle and gets astride the pillion.*
DIXIE. Come on, Ossy. For Christ's sake.
   Pause.
FLINT. The money? The maps? The passports? A few spartan
   provisions? A morsel of cheese and a glossy tomato?
DIXIE. The lot.
FLINT. I'm pretty well agog, Dixie. Very all agog with the ex-
   citement of it –
DIXIE. Come *on*, then!
   FLINT *takes the saddle. Declaims, can't resist it.*
FLINT. Ephesians, six twelve: We wrestle not against flesh and
   blood but against principalities, against powers, against the
   rulers of the darkness of this world, against spiritual wickedness
   in high places.
DIXIE. All I want is a quick nip round St Peter's before I drop
   this bloody kid.
   FLINT *adjusts his goggles. Starts the bike. The sound of the*
   engine swells to a roar.
   BACK PROJECTIONS: *of fields, roads, cities, ruins, resting*
   finally on a still of St Peter's in Rome. The engine stops. Bells
   tolling. DIXIE *exits, wrapping a scarf round her head.* FLINT
   dismounts, removing the goggles, wiping his eyes with a large
   red handkerchief. The bells fade, but remain, muted. A WAITER
   brings FLINT *a frothy glass of light beer. He drinks hard, wipes*
   his mouth.
FLINT. I am blest. The little foetus grows and grows. And biffs
   her tum with his totty feet. (*Pause.*) And when you look the
   business fairly and squarely in the face: better she was visited
   by Arthur, that feckless exponent of anarchy. Than an angel.
   (*Pause.*) Which would have played hell with my bleak view of

the cosmos and all its contents. (*Pause.*) Nice, in Rome. (*Drinks and raises his glass.*) To Anglicans, and their spiritual pastors. Everywhere. A continental beer. Light. Weak. Tastes like distilled jockstraps. (*Pause.*) And not only (*raising the glass again*) to Anglicans: But all denominations and their clergy. Everywhere. (*Pause.*) And policemen. (*Pause.*) Holding body and soul together. Looking after all humans, of all sizes and colours and shapes. (*Pause.*) Drawing blood here and there. (*Pause.*) In the name of.

> *Holds out empty glass: the* WAITER *enters, takes it, exits.*
>
> FLINT *withdraws a huge postcard from his inside pocket, and a Biro.*

Dear Bishop? Dear George? (*Pause.*) Dear George I got this card in Pompeii. (*Pause.*) Lock it up in your desk, and steal a glimpse when low or in times of stress. (*Pause.*) P.S. Are you de-beagled? P.P.S. Love is a possibility. With Dixie. (*Pause.*) Yours in blissful exorcism: Ossian.

> FLINT *tucks the card away, as* DIXIE *enters and remounts the pillion.*
>
> FLINT *puts on his goggles and gets on the machine. Switches on engine.*
>
> BACK PROJECTION: *more roads, cities, fields, forests, until an arid rocky landscape – and then the* ACROPOLIS.
>
> FLINT *stops the engine and pushes up his goggles.*

FLINT. Ecco!

DIXIE. Is *that* it?

FLINT. That is *it*.

DIXIE. Ossy, I don't want to have this kid on the *road*, you know.

FLINT. Historically speaking, there's a straight line from that majestic ruin to the Pentagon, No. 10 Downing Street, Buckingham Palace, the Eiffel Tower, the Empire State Building, the –

DIXIE. I don't like it.

FLINT. Then – *avanti*!

> *The engine starts, and the back projection changes once more to an arid landscape. It stops at a scene of oasis-like lushness: green*

trees, water, blue sky, heat. The sound of cicadas is very loud. When the sound of the motorbike engine dies away, we hear DIXIE *moaning loudly.* FLINT *helps her off the pillion: she stretches out with her back to the audience. Her groans subside.*

DIXIE. Fetch somebody.

FLINT. It's three kilometres.

DIXIE. *Fetch* somebody, bugger you!

FLINT. And you alone here?

DIXIE. D'you want me to be dead here?

FLINT *shades his eyes.*

FLINT. There's an army column moving down the mountain. Over there – I can't see properly. The air's shimmering.

DIXIE. Then fetch the bloody *army!* Armies have doctors, don't they? Or *some*thing!

Pause.

FLINT. I'm not even sure where we *are* –

DIXIE. Ossy, I've got a bloody hippo inside me and it's kicking it's way out. Will you not dither, and be *off* man!

DIXIE *begins to writhe and moan. Her struggles become more and more pitiful, her cries louder.* FLINT *gets on the bike and drives off,* DIXIE *is going into labour. We hear the sound of the motorbike receding.* DIXIE *is screaming.*

Behind the cyclorama there is a huge explosion – the silhouette of a rising black column of smoke and flames.

Fade out and fade in to

DIXIE *stands holding her wrapped child in her arms. The stage is empty and dark, with only a spot on* DIXIE.

DIXIE. No, sir. I have no means of support. (*Pause.*) The father? (*Pause.*) No father. (*Pause.*) I had a friend who – (*Pause.*) He was killed in an accident. Drove his motorbike into an army truck full of something explosive. (*Pause.*) Somewhere abroad, you know. (*Pause.*) He couldn't see properly. It was the sun. (*Pause.*) In his eyes. (*Pause.*) And he was old. An old man. (*Pause.*) No, sir, he was not the father. (*Pause.*) Edna Mary Cecilia O'Keefe. (*Pause.*) It was a terrible explosion. Nothing left of my man.

My friend, I mean. In the fire. (*Pause.*) What a fire! They couldn't get near. (*Pause.*) The child's name is Prometheus, sir. That was my friend's idea. No, I've never heard anything like it myself, either. (*Pause.*) But we agreed on it before he was born. (*Pause.*) I agreed with my friend on all matters of importance, though you could not say he was an easy man to understand. And is now, I should think, frying in a greater fire than that so tragically laid on by the army. Whoever's army it was. (*Pause.*) He will be amazed to find himself in hell. Though he had a wicked sense of humour, and I fancy will hold his own in his own quaint way. With the Devil. (*Pause.*) In my ninth month he would lay his hand on my belly and sing. This little song. (*Pause.*) He nicknamed Prometheus here, Prom. (*Pause.*) Prom is quite nice, isn't it? (*Pause.*) I would lie in my night-shift in those hotels in those foreign places. And my friend would sing with his hand on my bulge. In his quavering voice. A poor singer, for a man of the church. But that would be his vocal cords I think. Do the vocal cords go quicker than other parts of the anatomy? Well he would quietly sing, sir. And he brought me a fine, wholesome peace. (*She sings.*)

Pom tiddley om pom – Prom Prom;
Prom tiddley om pom – Pom Pom –
etc.

   Curtain

The Bankrupt

THE BANKRUPT was first presented by BBC Television on BBC 1, on 27 November 1972, with the following cast:

ELLIS CRIPPER	Joss Ackland
GOWRAN CRIPPER	David Waller
ANGELA	Sheila Allen
JAMES	Peter Cellier
ANNE	Alethea Charlton
DOCTOR	John Woodnutt
TAXI-DRIVER	Bob Hoskins

Designed by Richard Wilmot
Directed by Christopher Morahan
Produced by Graeme Macdonald

Scene One. *Interior. Large hall of converted stately home : night.*

The large hall of a stately home converted into ANGELA's *laboratories.*
An expanse of parquet, high ceiling, restored Adam décor. CRIPPER *has painted a pentagram and a silhouette of a male figure with its feet in the ascendant apex.*
Candles are burning at each apex. Present are GOWRAN, JAMES, ANGELA *and* ANNE *by the candles –* CRIPPER *in the pentagram.*

CRIPPER. Welcome –

They raise their heads and look at him.

Any presents? A bauble or two for my half century?

Long pause.

Mean bastards!

Long pause.

I've often suffered for my thin streak of optimism.

Long pause.

For God's sake! We've heard of life imitating art – but must it imitate dreams? (*Pause.*) Well. Whichever is going on, none of you can come into my jolly old pentangle. That's in the rules, isn't it? I mean. Well. Have I sought individuality in mere quaintness? Am I a trifle confused? Mixed up? (*Pause.*) Shall I wake sweating and thankful for the morning light? Alone but safe? (*Pause.*) Lost your tongue, have you? That *would* be unnatural. (*Pause.*) Look. I'm getting frightened. Sphincters loosening, Dad? James? Anne? *Angela?*

One by one they blow out their candles. CRIPPER *seizes the remaining one. They move in on him. He threshes about, waving the candelabrum.* ANGELA *without effort or fuss, blows out his candle. Darkness.*

Blackout.

Scene Two. *Exterior. Country railway station: day*

A MAN *in his late forties exits the station and stands looking around him with an abstracted air:* ELLIS CRIPPER. *He is conventionally dressed in suit and raincoat, carrying only a briefcase with a travel label on it (somewhat faded and torn) – 'Barcelona'. The station itself is on the main line, but serves only a smallish country town. The forecourt is dreary and cindered, with parked cars and two taxis. The* DRIVERS *stand smoking and chatting.*
One or two other PASSENGERS *come past* CRIPPER *and go to waiting* FRIENDS *with cars, or simply walk towards the forecourt exit.* CRIPPER *approaches the* TWO DRIVERS. *One of them looks inquiringly at him.*

CRIPPER. Er . . . taxi?

The DRIVER *turns to his taxi and stares at the lighted sign over the windscreen – 'Taxi'.* CRIPPER's *face acknowledges the put-down.*

CRIPPER. I'd like to go to . . . er . . .

Pause

DRIVER. Where?

Pause.

CRIPPER (*humbly*). Lower Burleigh.
DRIVER. That'll be sixteen mile –
CRIPPER. I know.
DRIVER. Front or back?

CRIPPER. I beg your pardon?
DRIVER. Next me, or in the back?

Pause.

Of the car!
CRIPPER. Oh. Yes. Well.

Pause.

Front, I think.

> *The* DRIVER *sighs, opens the front passenger door and goes round the other side. They both get in.* CRIPPER *at first slams the door on his coat, opens it and pulls his coat in sheepishly.*

Scene Three. *Interior. The car : day*

They are leaving the outskirts of the town and the road begins to wind into the country. CRIPPER *sits tensely, the brief-case on his knees. He stares ahead.*

CRIPPER. You know Lower Burleigh?
DRIVER. You mean – where it is? Be hard luck if I didn't. If you didn't either.
CRIPPER. I meant, do you *know* it? Know the village itself.

Pause.

DRIVER. I know you can drive through it in round about a minute an' a half!

Pause.

CRIPPER. Yes. It's quite small.

Pause.

My father lives there. On Pond Street.
DRIVER. So you'll be wanting Pond Street.
CRIPPER. Alas!

Pause.

DRIVER. Eh?

CRIPPER. Nothing.

DRIVER. When it's a single fare, I prefer a person that sits in front you know.

CRIPPER. I can understand that.

DRIVER. Some gets a kick out of sittin' in the back feeling high and mighty.

CRIPPER. Do they still?

DRIVER. In these parts. Some do. *And* some from London. Like you are yourself no doubt.

CRIPPER. Well. From Paddington Station.

DRIVER. Not from London by way of residing there –

CRIPPER. No.

DRIVER. I couldn't stand London.

CRIPPER's face becomes somewhat blank, trance-like.

CRIPPER. One needs a vision. (*Pause.*) One should have a vision. Of some kind. (*Pause.*) It's bleak when you're more than half way through life. No vision.

The DRIVER gives him a sideways look, thinking he's got a nutter.

DRIVER. Oh yer. You need a vision all right. (*Pause.*) Like what's-her-name? Bernadette? Like Saint Bernadette, you mean? I bet her little visitation's brought in a bob or two. Over the years. For somebody.

He concentrates very hard on his driving, though moistening his lips nervously.

CRIPPER. You mustn't think I'm crazy. My mind was wandering. (*Pause.*) It tends to wander.

He turns to look at the DRIVER. Behind the wheel he sees an OLD MAN in dark glasses, wearing evening dress. CRIPPER suddenly ducks his head, his hands over his eyes. Peering again cagily, it is the DRIVER as before.

DRIVER. You all right?

CRIPPER. Fine. Yes. Fine, thanks –

> DRIVER: *his face is set, tight-lipped.* CRIPPER: *he closes his eyes.*

Scene Four. *Exterior. Country house. Drive gates: night*

CRIPPER *stands clutching the locked gates tightly, shaking them. The* OLD MAN *in dark glasses and evening dress stands expressionless. A pack of dogs rushes up behind him. They press barking and yelping against the gates.* CRIPPER *turns and runs away.*

Scene Five. *Exterior. Village street: day*

A road rather than a street, on the edge of the village. To one side trees and fields. To the other, detached cottages – whitewashed and thatched. The taxi draws up outside one of these and CRIPPER *gets out. The taxi pulls away immediately.* CRIPPER *stands a moment looking at the cottage. It gives directly on to the pavement, with a narrow border of flowers along the wall. There is a gate to one side and* CRIPPER *makes for the gate.*

Scene Six. *Exterior. Cottage garden: day*

We see CRIPPER *come round the house slowly. He wanders round the garden, looking back once at the house. There is a long, wide lawn bordered with flowers.* CRIPPER *goes to one of the borders and looks down. He is clutching his brief-case to his chest. Between some flowers, on the soil – a fat worm.*

CRIPPER. Oh, worm!

> *He crouches looking at it.*

Limited amnesia is not a bad thing. It leaves spaces in the mind for humble concentration. (*Pause.*) And dreams.

> *Pause.* CRIPPER *straightens up.*

What *is* a vision? What do they mean by the word. (*Pause.*) Worm. Where is your owner? Where my father? Where the deadly Gowran Cripper? (*Pause.*) For I must confess to nefarious doings on the Costa del Sol. If I can remember. You know? Travel agencies and things. Property deals. Non-existent plumbing. No sea view. Charter flights not up to the standard of . . . of anyone. (*Pause.*) So I am told. (*Pause.*) Fifty. Not an age for a man so parsimonious with his enthusiasm for life to begin again. What say, worm? You and your mates will have fun with me one day.

He turns to the cottage and shouts.

Father –

He firmly makes his way to the side door of the cottage.

Scene Seven. *Interior. Cottage: day*

A large, white-painted sitting-room – the furniture is from GOWRAN CRIPPER's *council house in the north. Sideboard. Glass-fronted china cupboard. Table with folding leaves. Three-piece suite. Brasses. Too much space for the humble contents.* GOWRAN CRIPPER *sits watching TV – horse racing. He is the man* CRIPPER *hallucinated in the car, but is now in baggy trousers, shirt, braces, no glasses.* CRIPPER *enters. The* OLD MAN *takes no notice.* CRIPPER *taps him on the shoulder.*

CRIPPER. It's me, dad –
GOWRAN. I know.

Pause.

CRIPPER. Nowhere else to go.
GOWRAN. I know.
CRIPPER. Welcome, I hope?
GOWRAN. Welcome enough.

CRIPPER *goes to sit on one of the chairs near* GOWRAN. *He keeps his brief-case on his knees.* GOWRAN *concentrates on the*

TV – stiff-backed, his thick heavy hands on his knees. He is like a big old root. CRIPPER *coughs.*

CRIPPER. Dad. I propose to blow up a biological warfare station and then commit suicide.

GOWRAN. Oh aye?

CRIPPER. Dad. I have come here to murder my sister. Possibly you as well. And get a life sentence.

Pause.

GOWRAN. You know, lad. That nag I put two bob each way on – I think it's gotten a leg missing.

Pause.

CRIPPER. It's a good job I'm not Hamlet. *You'll* never bloody well die.

GOWRAN. Look at it! Yon one miles behind all t'others. Any minute now it'll topple over.

CRIPPER. Dad. I'm suffering from loss of memory. Known technically as amnesia. (*Pause.*) And delusions of persecution.

GOWRAN. I wish somebody'd persecute yon feller as tipped me that horse. See you? Down it goes. They'll need a bloody tractor to get it off t'course.

CRIPPER *puts down his brief-case, takes off his raincoat and throws it down. He stands between* GOWRAN *and the TV set.*

CRIPPER. Why don't you switch over to wrestling?

GOWRAN. I shall, by God. (*Pause.*) In a minute.

CRIPPER *stares wearily at the ceiling.*

CRIPPER. No daddy ghost. No Hamlet. The world would have been deprived of a masterpiece. In my case – no such luck, since I cannot put two sentences together.

GOWRAN. Are you planning on staying long, Ellis?

CRIPPER. Only until the murder or murders.

GOWRAN. I wish you wouldn't talk daft. I can't see TV for you, neither.

CRIPPER *moves to one side.*

CRIPPER. Where else to go? Bankrupt. Penniless. Unemployable. What's more, this house may be in your name but I paid for it. (*Pause.*) My sole vicarious asset. I won't say resting place, since you're here.

GOWRAN *gets up and switches the TV to wrestling. He sits down again.*

GOWRAN. There's been talk about you. It's all over t'village. Somebody saw summat in a newspaper.

CRIPPER. Yes, dad. I was told about it in court. But, you see, *I* have forgotten. To me it is hearsay. I've learned it all by heart but have failed to regain my actual memory. See?

GOWRAN. Cheating folks!

CRIPPER. Oh yes!

GOWRAN. Fiddling wi' money not your own!

CRIPPER. That too. (*Pause.*) What's more, I employed a shady architect to build a block of flats in Portugal and it fell down. (*Pause.*) One dog was killed, two passing mules covered in dust and may well by now be suffering chronic bronchitis. (*Pause.*) A water main was splintered, and happy children played in the resulting fountain.

Pause.

GOWRAN. A cruise ship sank, so I'm told by your sister –

CRIPPER. Not before each human life was saved. I can't speak for the fate of the rats.

GOWRAN. They call this wrestling! It's all a fake, you know.

CRIPPER. I admit, father. I have engaged in the filthy work of capitalism. And to compound the crime, worked at the visibly dishonourable end of the system. (*Pause.*) What a way to spend and lose one's wartime gratuity. From a grateful country.

(*Pause.*) Oh dear.

GOWRAN. I will say. The air down here, after t'north – you've got to breathe it it's that clean.

CRIPPER. *Do* you have to? Do you really?

GOWRAN. Like wine.

CRIPPER *sits, his head in his hands.*

CRIPPER. Spitfires, Hurricanes, Mosquitoes, and once a stolen Messerschmitt. Just for the joke. (*Pause.*) That's when I got shot down – flying the Messerschmitt. (*Pause.*) By a Spitfire. (*Pause.*) I parachuted into a ditch full of British infantry. They gave me a cup of tea and a cigarette. (*Pause.*) I think I must have banged my head on something. I was never the same after. (*Pause.*) Do head injuries lead to subsequent crimes of fraud etcetera etcetera? Piling off thousands of happy English to their doom-laden holidays? (*Pause.*) I was betrayed, father. Dad. By my partner. Whose name I cannot remember but appeared in court as Gomez y Some-thing-or-other.

Pause.

GOWRAN. Foreigners!

CRIPPER. Crossing the Channel, dad, one finds the world is full of them. (*Pause.*) God made it so. And His work cannot be maligned or spited. (*Pause.*) If you believe in Him.

GOWRAN. England for the English!

CRIPPER. I don't know. I'd say Bradford has been improved by the Pakistanis. You might say they add colour to the place. For people like you to disapprove of. (*Pause.*) A maverick son isn't enough. You *need* foreigners, dad, or you'd have a coronary through insufficient outlet for your prejudice.

Pause.

GOWRAN. I wonder why they don't put bankrupts in prison? You know? To protect honest folk.

CRIPPER. I'm in prison, dad.

He taps each side of his head.

This thing. Skull. Can't get out. Food and liquids in – yes? By all means. Down the oesophagus and so to be metabolized into the other bits of me. Waste products eliminated. All systems go. Except the interior of the skull. (*Shouting*.) Which is prison, God damn you! (*Pause*.) Who ever devised a better one, after all?

Pause.

GOWRAN (*grinning maliciously*). You can always do yoursen in, can't you?

CRIPPER. Ha ha! Ho ho! Ha ha! (*Pause*.) The matter has been in my Pending Tray for years. (*Pause*.) God! Look at your feet!

Baffled, GOWRAN *lifts up his outsize clumsy shoes.*

GOWRAN. What's up wi' my feet?

CRIPPER *goes to the door, laughing. Opening it, he turns.*

CRIPPER. They're on the end of your legs!
We hear him laughing as he leaves the room, closing the door. Close-up of GOWRAN. *Close-up of wrestlers on TV.*

Scene Eight. *Interior. Cottage bedroom: afternoon.*

CRIPPER *sits on the bed in shirt and trousers, his tie hanging loosely down his shirt. The bedroom is furnished like the rest of the cottage, with pieces from* GOWRAN's *council house.* CRIPPER *takes from his brief-case a small bottle and shakes out two tablets. He has a glass of water on the bedside table and washes down the tablets. He lies back on the bed.*

Scene Nine. *Interior. Cottage living-room: afternoon.*

GOWRAN *sits with his head thrown back. His mouth wide open, snoring. The TV is still on; a* NEWSCASTER *mouths silently, and there is a cut to streams of Bangla Desh refugees hopelessly making their way through monsoon rains.*

Scene Ten. *Interior. Cottage bedroom : afternoon.*

CRIPPER *is asleep, tossing and turning, still in his clothes.*

Scene Eleven. *Interior. A space in the studio.*

At a desk sits CRIPPER, *in suit and raincoat. His brief-case is on the desk in front of him. Some yards in front of the desk stands* GOWRAN *in his hallucination/dream aspect – the dark glasses, the evening dress. He pulls a cord and a large chart descends showing a five-pointed star (pentangle) with one point in the ascendant. Within the pentangle is the silhouette of a man, upright, his head in the upper point of the star.* GOWRAN *speaks in a cultured voice.* CRIPPER *listens attentively, but looks frightened.*

GOWRAN. And this is the pentangle I spoke of in your last dream. Pay attention. A five-pointed star which can be drawn without taking pencil from paper. (*Pause.*) The sign signifies the domination of the mind over the elements. Demons of the air, spirits of fire, phantoms of water and ghosts of the earth are enchanted by this sign. That is, spellbound by it. (*Pause.*) By its means, spirits can be forced to appear in vision. It represents order or confusion according to the direction of its points. The Divine Lamb of the Accursed Goat. Star of the Morning or Evening. Victory or Death. Day or Night. (*Pause.*) A pentagram with the human figurehead downwards represents a demon; that is, intellectual subversion, disorder or madness.

   Pause.

CRIPPER. I wish you'd keep your bloody dogs off me.

   Pause.

GOWRAN. My dogs?

CRIPPER. Yes. That slobbering pack. I even had them in the taxi from the station.

   Pause.

GOWRAN. I have no dogs.

CRIPPER *points at the pentangle chart.*

CRIPPER. I reject all that rubbish.

Pause.

GOWRAN. Just so –
CRIPPER. There's no need to be bloody enigmatic!
GOWRAN. But there are enigmas!
CRIPPER. No news to me!

Pause.

GOWRAN. Your mind has rejected everything else, Ellis –
CRIPPER. Yes. Right. I'll settle for peevish bewilderment, then.
O.K.?

Pause.

GOWRAN. Very well –

GOWRAN *exits frame.* CRIPPER *sits staring at the pentangle chart. Close-up of diagram.*

GOWRAN'S VOICE. When conscious of failing will, the Magus turns his eyes towards this symbol. Takes it in his right hand. Feels armed with intellectual omnipotence, provided that he is truly a king. Worthy to be led by the star to the divine cradle of realization. Provided that he knows, dares, wills and keeps silent. Provided that he is familiar with its usages. Provided that the intrepid gaze of his soul corresponds with those two eyes which the ascending point of our Pentagram ever presents open. (*Pause.*) A man called Eliphas Levi wrote that in 1896 Ellis. (*Pause.*) You have read Levi.

Close-up of CRIPPER. *He opens the brief-case and takes out a revolver. He holds it.*

Scene Twelve. *Interior. Small converted farmhouse: evening.*

The house of ELLIS's *sister* ANNE, *and her husband,* JAMES. *They are obviously well off. The ground floor is a large split-level kitchen and living-room with modern furniture which is tastefully design-conscious in every way.* ANNE *is a textile designer, and one corner of the living area is taken up by her drawing-board, materials, files, etc.* JAMES *is a lawyer. He sprawls on a large white leather couch, with a drink.* CRIPPER *sits hunched in a similar leather chair whilst* ANNE *passes him a drink.* ANNE *and* JAMES *are in their mid-forties.*

ANNE. You look nervous and defensive, Ellis –

CRIPPER. Possibly. These days I sometimes forget *not* to look like what I feel.

> ANNE *moves away and pours herself a drink. She sits on the arm of another chair.*

JAMES (*languidly*). *I* think he wants a row.

> *Pause.*

CRIPPER. Why would I want a row?

JAMES. It's one of those banal paradoxes. If we showed disapproval, you might feel less guilty.

> *Pause.*

CRIPPER. Guilty of what? You mean the bankruptcy bit?

JAMES. Oh, nothing so vulgar!

> *Pause.*

CRIPPER (to ANNE). He'll be making me *want* a bloody row in a minute.

ANNE. Oh, come on, you two.

JAMES. I meant, darling, your brother's sense of failure. Everything gone. Law Court. Nursing home. Middle-aged depressive. (*Pause.*) He's kept his numerous faculties, one must admit – but clearly has nothing to apply them to. (*Pause.*) Nothing to live for.

CRIPPER. Yes. That's good. Pretty good. Keep at it, James. You'll begin to drool with self-satisfaction if you persist. (*Pause.*) What's worse than a cultured lawyer, with one of those aloof, dissecting minds?

JAMES. You've become . . . seedy, Ellis.

CRIPPER (*almost brightly*). Wasn't I always?

> ANNE *crosses to* CRIPPER *and plants a kiss on the top of his head, moving away swiftly.*

ANNE. *I love* my brother.

CRIPPER. Do you love James?

ANNE (*turning to him swiftly*). Of course –

JAMES. Don't mistake me Ellis. I'm very fond of you. (*Pause.*) But what on earth are we to do about the mess you're in?

CRIPPER. What are *we* to do? *We?*

ANNE. Don't you want us to help you, darling? Isn't that why you came down here?

JAMES. Don't you see, Ellis? I mean, well, of course, you are literally a bankrupt. But the business has its symbolic side, wouldn't you say?

CRIPPER. Funny phrase, really. The 'Bankruptcy Business'. Has me in fits. And as for 'symbolic'. Digs like that just bounce off me. They're just your pathetic way of trying to entertain yourself.

ANNE. What about Father? Do you really intend to live down there at his place?

CRIPPER. Dad?

JAMES. I remember at the time. I thought it somewhat aggressive of you to buy him a house in our village.

ANNE. Alright, then. *Dad.*

JAMES. What a pity you two didn't *inherit* something. Instead of of all that painful business to *achieve!*

CRIPPER. I regret to say, the old man has planted cabbages where I would have preferred, say, hydrangeas. Yes. He's a problem. He's made up what passes in him for his *mind*, about me.

(*Pause.*) I do my best. I spill tea on him. I trample on his feet as I go past. I burn his toast. I did cunning things with the TV controls that seem to have foxed him. (*Pause.*) This morning I threw a bucket of boiling water over his rhubarb patch. (*Pause.*) Can't get any sort of reaction. (*Pause.*) I am a blight that the Lord has visited on him – and that's that. He isn't just an old working man. He's a chunk of the bloody West Riding landscape. Transported down here to exist as a living reproach to all that is *southern*. Cabbages apart, and rhubarb, his garden looks like something cultured to screaming point by a retired bank executive in the Reading area. Mind you. You'll have noticed. He's got a wee slag heap at the bottom. Only three feet high. But it looks like the real thing alright.

   Pause.

JAMES. Ought to get yourself a woman, Ellis.

CRIPPER. I lost two, when things fell asunder for me around the coasts of Spain, Portugal and Greece. (*Pause.*) So I'm told. People *will* try to bring things back for anybody so unco-operative as to have amnesia.

JAMES A mature woman. A confident creature. A woman who respects your secrets but won't be a slave to your behaviour. (*Pause.*) She would need, of course, some kind of private means.

CRIPPER. Can a man who's lost his memory be said to have secrets? And *what* behaviour are you talking about? (*Pause.*) The private means I have no objection to.

   JAMES *turns to* ANNE, *smiling.*

JAMES. We have one for you. Haven't we Anne?

   Pause.

ANNE. A possibility.

JAMES. A certainty.

CRIPPER. You haven't given me much to go on yet. But she sounds like an obscenity.

JAMES *lounges to his feet, carrying his drink, and crosses to stand over* CRIPPER.

JAMES. Brother-in-law, you've decided to re-enter our lives. Our world. You've been idiotic in business and perverse about the cure of your mental aberrations. Your lonely father no doubt grieves for you one quarter of a mile from this very room. Your sister disturbs my sleep with her anxieties about you. What about a spot of discipline? A sense of values? A few social co-ordinates? (*Smiling.*) So that you might live peaceably – or at least without too much friction – among us?

    Pause.

CRIPPER. Grieves for me does he? (*Pause.*) Dad? (*Pause.*) What's her name?

ANNE. Angela?

CRIPPER. That sounds ominous. What does she do?

JAMES. A Cabinet Minister.

    Pause.

CRIPPER. What sort of government do we have at the moment?

JAMES. Does it matter? Have you any political positions? And if so – are they consistent with what you've learnt about these last fifteen fraudulent years of yours?

    ANNE *joins her husband, looking down at* CRIPPER.

ANNE. Ellis. Doesn't it matter more what she's . . . what she's *like*? As a person?

JAMES. Come round for cocktails. Sunday? About half-past twelve? (*Pause.*) Get to know each other, old boy –

    Pause.

CRIPPER. I must say. I'm taken aback, you know.

JAMES. Angela will take you forward, Ellis.

    Pause

CRIPPER. But I'm a sort of derelict!

ANNE. That's the whole point, darling Ellis!

JAMES. Angela needs a derelict.

CRIPPER. She has time for one? Outside of her obligations at the Ministry?

JAMES. It's a small, rather pointless Ministry really. No need for worry on that account.

Pause.

CRIPPER. But I'm an *intractable* derelict!

JAMES. So much more the challenge to Angela.

Pause.

CRIPPER. On the train. From Paddington. I had the fantasy that I was coming here to murder my dad. (*Pause.*) And it's becoming an obsession.

JAMES. Your father inspires similar feelings in all of us, Ellis. We are ashamed of them. We obviously wouldn't dream of acting on them. He is a harmless, if unconsciously brutal old man. He is innocent, I'd say. No awareness. He possesses only the minimal requirements to move, breathe, feed. We're quite used to him by now. And so will you be.

CRIPPER. You wouldn't dream of? But sometimes I do, you know. What I mean . . . I tend to dream that either he or I wishes to see the other one violently propelled into the void. It could be anything; savage dogs, a revolver, a dose of weedkiller in somebody's Ovaltine one night –

ANNE. There's no need to mock James and me, Ellis!

CRIPPER. I read some strange books in the nursing home. About the occult, etcetera. You familiar with pentangles? pentagrams? Spirits, demons and phantoms?

JAMES. No wonder you've been having bad dreams! I thought that sort of thing was more in the line of dropped-out youth, these days –

ANNE *turns to* JAMES.

ANNE. He frightens me.

JAMES. He *wants* to!

CRIPPER. I certainly do not. Things just . . . pop out of my mouth *these days*. Where do they come from? What goes on *inside*?

JAMES. Books on the occult?

CRIPPER. I was only passing the time.

Pause

JAMES (*looks at his watch*). Yes. Time. Afraid we have people coming to dinner, Ellis –

ANNE. Ellis, *do* take care –

CRIPPER. I'm not unhinged, you know!

He stands, ready to leave. They look at him, smiling. CRIPPER *seems to shrink down into the crumpled collar of his shirt, his disarrayed tie.*

ANNE. You *have* had a bad time, haven't you?

JAMES. He certainly has.

CRIPPER. I even talked to a worm, the day I arrived.

JAMES *and* ANNE *laugh –* ANNE *somewhat hysterically.*

JAMES. Good God, Ellis! I talk to all kinds of inanimate objects –

CRIPPER. I believe the worm was animate.

JAMES. But you know what I mean –

CRIPPER *lurches towards the door, the other two following.*

CRIPPER. I think I might try to find it again in the morning. Cheerio –

He quickly goes out, closing the door behind him. JAMES *and* ANNE *stand frozen, looking at each other with masked faces.*

Scene Thirteen. *Interior. Studio.*

On a large white marble-looking floor, CRIPPER *is inscribing a five-pointed star in gold, with a brush.*

GOWRAN'S VOICE. The circle surrounding the star should be

nine feet in diameter. Candles around the outside of the circle should be encircled by wreaths of vervain. (*Pause.*) Once inside the circle, the person conjuring up the spirits is safe.

CRIPPER *looks upwards over his shoulder.*

CRIPPER. *I* know how to do it!

Scene Fourteen. *Cottage garden: day*

CRIPPER *is digging in one of the flower borders. There are small mounds of earth all along, where he has been previously digging.* GOWRAN *comes lumbering up and stands watching.*

GOWRAN. Now Ellis. What's tha up to?

Pause.

CRIPPER (*digging*). Looking for a worm.

Pause.

GOWRAN. Goin' fishing, are you?

CRIPPER (*irritably*). A *special* worm.

GOWRAN. One wi' your name on it, then? Like they say about bullets –

CRIPPER *stands up to face his father.*

CRIPPER. A worm with which I . . . I mean, I should say *to* which . . . I talk.

GOWRAN. Eh, Ellis! What's to be done?

CRIPPER. About me?

GOWRAN. Who else?

Pause.

CRIPPER. I'm harmless, you know –

GOWRAN. Talking on murder?

CRIPPER. A figure of speech, merely. (*Pause.*) In a sense, an untruth, dad.

Pause.

GOWRAN. That bottle of brandy I keep for when I have me bronchitis –

CRIPPER. Yes?

GOWRAN. It's gone down.

CRIPPER. Gone down where?

GOWRAN. Down an inch –

Pause.

CRIPPER. Ah. Yes. *That* inch went down *me*. After I'd been to see our Anne and James last evening. (*Pause.*) You were in bed.

Pause.

GOWRAN. I still don't hold wi' drinking.

CRIPPER *is studying the ground. He points.*

CRIPPER. Look! Worm. Could be mine –

Pause.

GOWRAN. What you got against me, Ellis?

CRIPPER. Nothing personal, dad. I am the victim of a condition, that's all.

GOWRAN. What condition?

CRIPPER. Very widespread. Utter lack of communication with a parent or parents. (*Pause.*) Incurable. (*Pause.*) Try worms instead.

GOWRAN. I could never make thee out!

CRIPPER. The condition *does* affect both sides. Don't get worked up. It's normal. There you are. There's a nice word that you like: normal.

Pause.

GOWRAN. Tha talks gibberish, lad!

CRIPPER. And what does your daughter talk? Your son-in-law?

GOWRAN. They speak as I can understand –

CRIPPER. Do you *like* them?

Pause.

GOWRAN. Any man loves his own –

CRIPPER. They don't speak to worms. They waste no time on humble fauna. Yes. They must have learnt your *language*, dad. That's where I'm deficient. You'll have to give me time. Meanwhile I shall hold discourse with worms, unless thrust into some situation which compels an appearance of sociableness. (*Pause.*) One learns to be cunning dad.

GOWRAN. Tha always was!

CRIPPER. I *wish* you'd leave me to it!

Pause.

GOWRAN. Nay, I'll leave you to owt that tha likes –

GOWRAN *trundles away down the garden towards his shed.* CRIPPER *looks down: worm.*

CRIPPER. Damp red curly worm! Pin back your ears. Ellis Cripper speaks. A man of yearning, if not much learning. Whose soul creaks. (*Pause.*) Using the term soul very loosely, of course. (*Pause.*) Whose days are vacant and whose mental night life seems to be carrying the burden. Of what? Don't ask me. Fifty years' wreckage? From pram to middle-aged humiliation. No politics. No religion. No philosophy. (*Pause.*) No love. No family of my own. No desire, now. (*Pause.*) Nor money either. (*Pause.*) Self-pity might help – though disgusting to others. But I seem to have missed out on that as well. Cripper is the last one to pity Cripper. Neither can he dish out the blame on others. Refuses to hold anyone responsible for *anything*, preferring to accept the consequences of their random passage through life. (*Pause.*) But. (*Pause.*) Where my anger? Where my yell of rage? *Am* I wounded? Or not? (*Pause.*) Who cares if their unconscious is busy – when the achingly conscious man lacks will and purpose, direction and allegiance?

Pause. Close-up of CRIPPER's *face.*

CRIPPER. There you go, worm. Sliding back into the earth. (*Pause.*) Bored? (*Pause.*) What if I should marry a Cabinet Minister then? Eh? (*Pause.*) See all kinds of doctors first, Cripper! Get yourself some X-rays, a cardiogram, encephalogram. Have the pancreas and liver probed. The thyroid. The stomach, guts and gonads. (*Pause.*) Assert yourself at least as a functioning specimen. Anyway, blind the woman with one thing or the other – health or disease! I'd settle for creeping debilitation. Typical. And why? Because it hints at some form of quiet, undramatic departure – and at the same time implies one is heading there slightly faster than luckier men. Touch this Angela's heart, but not without medical documentation. Remember that. Because hypochondriacs make poor clowns!

He grips his spade firmly, and starts smoothing out the soil where he had been digging.

Scene Fifteen. *Interior. Doctor's surgery: day.*

CRIPPER *sits in his underpants on the examination couch morosely swinging his legs. The* DOCTOR *sits at his table, writing.*

CRIPPER. Nothing at all, then?
DOCTOR. Nothing.

Pause.

CRIPPER. Of course, these medical technicians can make mistakes –
DOCTOR. Naturally.

Pause.

CRIPPER. A bit overweight, though? No?
DOCTOR. A bit.

Pause.

CRIPPER. I assure you. I have treated this body badly. Doctor.
DOCTOR. It's come through your abuses remarkably well, then.

Is all I can say. (*He looks up with a spark of interest.*) Exactly *what* have you done to it?

He looks CRIPPER *up and down.* CRIPPER *looks himself up and down.*

CRIPPER. Oh, the usual, I suppose. I don't want to make a fuss ... to seem exceptional in that respect, you know.

DOCTOR. What? Smoking? Drinking? No exercise? Overwork? Lack of sleep? (*Pauses.*) *Decades* of it?

CRIPPER. Yes. And a great deal of psychosomatic spadework by my *unconscious.*

DOCTOR. Look. I'm just an average, over-worked GP. Your sister and brother-in-law are registered with me – now you. (*Pause.*) It makes a GP's stomach sink, when the patient uses the word psychosomatic. I expect you realise that? (*Pause.*) An intelligent man –

Pause.

CRIPPER. I was teasing.
DOCTOR. Thanks be to god.

He carries on writing. CRIPPER *is naturally unsatisfied.*

CRIPPER. I hope, doctor – I hope you know your Freud, Stekel, Adler, Klein and so forth? Up to – shall we say – those of our contemporary chaps who are subverting the lot? And especially behaviourism –

Pause. The DOCTOR *gets up, goes to his window.*

DOCTOR. Mr Cripper. We have worked over you from scalp to toenails, practically. (*Pause.*) In the meanwhile, thousands less fortunate than yourself have died from everything from accidents to plain ordinary despair. Imagine the spectrum, the range of awful possibilities for the human body to sicken and perhaps die. (*Pause, turning.*) Should we be chatting? (*Pause.*) I'll concede you the amnesia. The doubtless troubling period in the nursing home. But all that's outside my province. (*Pause.*) I fear you are healthy. (*Pause.*) Is that really bad news?

CRIPPER. Well. In a way.

DOCTOR. You wish to be ill?

CRIPPER. Something to focus on, you know –

DOCTOR. Why not focus on twenty to thirty more years of fruitful existence?

Pause.

CRIPPER (*pleased*). There you are! You've hit on it! That's my trouble. I can't.

Pause.

DOCTOR (*wearily*). The report from your psychiatrist in the nursing home is resonant with despair, Mr Cripper. Not apropos the amnesia, I hasten to say. That one was obvious. Crime, discovery, indictment . . . and withdrawal from recollection of the matters involved . . . these fit together with a tedious frequency, Mr Cripper. (*Pause.*) No. I fancy you had the man – your psychiatrist – fretting to get to grips with more serious cases. (*Pause.*) I fancy you *bored* him, Mr Cripper.

CRIPPER. Does one have to be yelling and screaming? Rushing about with an axe? Menacing young children? Or *what*?

DOCTOR. Obviously not! (*Pause.*) *Do* get dressed now. *Please* –

CRIPPER *begins to dress at once.*

CRIPPER. My brain?

DOCTOR. Organically sound.

CRIPPER. My nerves?

DOCTOR. Self-inflicted.

CRIPPER. My hostility to Dad?

DOCTOR. Healthy.

Pause.

CRIPPER. My unhappiness?

DOCTOR. Understandable.

CRIPPER. My apathy?
DOCTOR. Reassuring.

Pause.

CRIPPER. Reassuring?
DOCTOR. What a fix we'd all be in if you were indulging yourself more energetically than you are!
CRIPPER. You wag! You joker! You awful cynic!
DOCTOR. I'll prescribe a mild tranquillizer.
CRIPPER. But dammit. I *am* tranquil. To the point of vegetating –
DOCTOR. Very well. Something to pep you up?
CRIPPER. I didn't mean to be rude –
DOCTOR. I'm sure your situation is upsetting –

CRIPPER *is now nearly dressed and looks at the* DOCTOR *craftily.*

CRIPPER. What's my situation? You think I've got one?
DOCTOR. Hasn't everybody?
CRIPPER. I was trying to shake another concession out of you. That's all.
DOCTOR. I admit defeat. Are you prepared to give way now? To a young woman with a query malignant tumour of the breast? For example?
CRIPPER. Don't batter me! Don't shame me! Leave it to my relatives, will you?
DOCTOR. I certainly will –

He opens the door. CRIPPER *slips out with a dazed look, struggling with his jacket.*

Scene Sixteen. *Interior. Studio space.*

CRIPPER *sits at the desk with a ledger, inside the pentangle. Candles burn at its points. Beyond their flickering shadows, darkness. A* FIGURE *steps forward – also* CRIPPER, *naked.*

CRIPPER (*pen poised*). Name?

FIGURE. Tacitus.

CRIPPER. Message?

FIGURE. Everything unknown is taken as marvellous. But now the limits of Britain are laid bare –

CRIPPER. You look like me!

FIGURE. It is a characteristic of the human mind to hate the man one has injured.

The FIGURE *moves away into the darkness.*

CRIPPER. *That's* a point well taken.

Another FIGURE *comes forward – again* CRIPPER *naked.*

Name?

FIGURE. Alexander the Great.

CRIPPER. Message?

FIGURE. I am dying with the help of too many physicians.

The FIGURE *moves away.*

CRIPPER. Begod, I multiplies and multiplies –

Another FIGURE *– the same.*

Name?

FIGURE. Aristotle.

CRIPPER. Message?

FIGURE. A plausible impossibility is always preferable to an unconvincing possibility.

The FIGURE *moves away.* CRIPPER *laughs to himself. He writes, speaking as he writes.*

CRIPPER. Dear Dad: I like these pentangles. I am raking history like an ashtip. See self everywhere but mostly in dead men. (*Pause.*) No *real* clue· yet.

Scene Seventeen. *Interior converted farmhouse. Dining alcove: night.*

CRIPPER, GOWRAN, ANNE, JAMES *and* ANGELA *are dining.* GOWRAN *has his face lowered over his plate, almost touching his food.* ANGELA *is laughing. She is an attractive rather sharp-looking woman about forty-five.*

ANGELA. But, of *course*, I'm not a Cabinet Minister, Ellis!

CRIPPER. Don't think I wouldn't have found it absorbing –

ANGELA. James! What a ridiculous thing to have told him!

JAMES. He likes being told ridiculous things.

CRIPPER. When I know that that's what they *are* –

ANNE. I must say. *I* kept quiet. But I didn't think it was very funny. Not funny at all. (*Pause.*) I'm sorry Ellis –

CRIPPER. No cause for sorrow –

ANGELA. Really, James!

CRIPPER. What *are* you, then?

ANGELA. A biologist.

CRIPPER (*to* ANNE). Your bloody husband's got a tortuous mind. (*Pause.*) Where *I'm* concerned, you know. (*Pause.*) I know I shouldn't have come back to Lower Burleigh. But three days on Paddington Station was quite enough.

GOWRAN *puts down his knife and fork and blinks round at the others.*

GOWRAN. He talks in his sleep, Ellis does. Paper thin, them walls. I can hear him jabberin' half the night. (*Pause.*) Call it peaceful retirement wi' our Ellis round t'place? It's more like a bloody asylum. (*Pause.*) Course, I'm t'first to make allowances –

JAMES. With Anne and me hot in pursuit –

GOWRAN. In pursuit on what?

JAMES. Allowances. Yours. *We* make allowances for Ellis too. What else? His brain may be infirm, but his idiosyncrasies continue to entertain.

CRIPPER. My *brain* as you call it, is alert to all forms of human sorrow, sadness, hollowness, loss, grief. Behind the eyes, it contemplates itself with wry astonishment. What about *yours*?

ANNE (*pettishly*). They will *bicker* –

JAMES. Ellis once referred to me a long time ago as being upper-class. And naturally, he's never quite got over it.

GOWRAN. His *mother* worked her fingers to the bone for gentry!

JAMES. Mercifully, she didn't live to hear of her son flying a Messerschmitt.

Pause.

ANGELA. I feel quite out of the conversation.

CRIPPER. Tell us about biology. I was talking to Darwin in a dream last night. In my pentangle. He said: We will now discuss in a little more detail the struggle for existence.

Pause.

ANGELA (*firmly*). I'm in *molecular* biology.

JAMES. And what did you say to Darwin, Ellis love?

CRIPPER. I said. My struggle for existence is over. (*Pause.*) You see, I always write it all down the following morning.

JAMES. Did your remark induce gloom in Darwin?

CRIPPER. Not at all. He simply said: The highest possible stage in moral culture is when we recognize that we ought to control our thoughts.

Pause.

JAMES. And our dreams? Eh?

CRIPPER. Yes. I chipped in with that merry riposte. But he faded out and Freud faded in.

JAMES (*deliberately, to* ANNE). The man dreams like a sodding film!

GOWRAN, *who has been eating again, slams down his knife and fork.*

GOWRAN. I'll not have such language!

JAMES. It slipped out. I do apologize.

GOWRAN *points his knife at* ELLIS.

GOWRAN. *He* used that word once. In front of his mother, an' all.

CRIPPER. I don't think she minded.

GOWRAN. *I* nearly *killed* thee!

CRIPPER. What a noble way to die, that would have been, at forty odd. Not to mention the reason. (*He gets up.*) I must leave. No hard feelings. I can't eat at the same table as any of you. Shall *wend* my way. *Wend*! (*Pause.*) I wonder if the evening's warm enough though?

ANGELA *also gets up.*

ANGELA. Let me drive you.

CRIPPER *inspects the sole of one shoe.*

CRIPPER. I *do* need some shoes. And God knows, there is a certain amount of gravel between here and there.

ANNE. Well then?

JAMES. Oh, let the miserable sod go!

GOWRAN. That's what I say. Chucking folk's hospitality in their ·faces –

CRIPPER. No, dad. (*Pause.*) I take back what I said before. We do, in fact, communicate after all. (*Pause.*) Hideously well. Thought, word and etcetera. (*Pause.*) Angela, if you'll drive me, I shall be a bog of gratitude.

JAMES. Do you know what you're doing, Angy?

ANGELA. I like him.

JAMES. She likes him!

GOWRAN. Watch out, young woman!

ANGELA. Why?

GOWRAN (*cackling somewhat*). Might find thisen digging for worms!

CRIPPER. He refers to a strange habit I've acquired. You suddenly found yourself a sense of humour, dad?

GOWRAN. Nay, I've never been short on seeing t'funny side. *He* wants to learn to see t'funny side, Ellis does. Then happen he'd pull his self together.

CRIPPER. I'm held together by my skeleton dad. It's doing a good job.

CRIPPER *declaims to* ANGELA.

Let us go then, you and I when worms are flying in the sky – like spaghetti aetherized upon a table. (*Pause.*) Or should it be gable? Down at the old church? Where yesterday, a small skull rolled gently out from among the graves and came to rest at my feet. Child of seven or so, I should say. Must remind the vicar to keep a sharp eye on the movements of his tenants.

ANGELA *firmly takes his arm.*

ANGELA. *Ellis –*

They make to leave. ANNE *suddenly bursts into tears.*

JAMES. You see what I mean? He's turning my wife into a nervous wreck.

CRIPPER. What have you been turning her into all these years, James? What am I? No more than a colourful expression of my interior poverty. You are a straw, a reed. But doubt if you would sing gently in the wind, no. Suppose for years you have been digging my sister's psychic grave? Eh?

ANNE *is still crying.* CRIPPER *gently touches the top of her head.*

Quote:
If thou didst ever hold me in thy heart,
Absent thee from felicity for a while,
And in this harsh world draw thy breath in pain,
To tell my story –

Looking round the table he speaks lightly.

Alas poor Anne! She knew her Shakespeare well –

ANNE *looks up at him, shouting.*

ANNE. Bugger off! *Brother!*
GOWRAN. Nay, nay –
CRIPPER (*to* ANGELA). Didst hear? My father is a horse and neighs –

JAMES *leaps round the table and hits* CRIPPER *very hard. He is felled, and lies still.* JAMES *looks down unmoved.* ANGELA *kneels beside him.* ANNE, *now sobbing loudly, is led out of the room by* GOWRAN. JAMES *follows them. Close-up of* CRIPPER'S *face. After a moment his eyes open and slowly scan the room.*

One appears to have jolted James somewhat. Out of his customary sneering superiority. (*Pause.*)
ANGELA. And your sister? (*Pause.*) And your father?

Pause.

CRIPPER. Being loved by me is a nasty, unwholesome experience –
ANGELA. Can you get up?

He does so, reeling a little.

CRIPPER. Bells between the ears. The brain is, dammit, suddenly a clapper in my skull. James has the punch of a professional, when he's man enough to get down to it. (*Pause.*) Angela, does compassion still niggle somewhere?
ANGELA. For you?
CRIPPER. Aye. For me.
ANGELA. You were cruel to Anne.
CRIPPER. Yes. But at the same time I respected her distress. Lack of orientations, you know. What's the point of disguising from the poor sods that their problem in me is a really big one. A bleeding colossus of a problem. (*Pause.*) Either that or they should exile me altogether. Face the facts, father, sister and awful brother-in-law!

ANGELA. Awful you.

CRIPPER. Do I attract you somehow?

Pause.

ANGELA. I don't know.

CRIPPER. You were simply then – shall we say – ready to be kind?

Pause.

ANGELA. I don't know. You don't love your family at all, I should say.

CRIPPER. Past it?

ANGELA. Sitting on your rubbish dump –

CRIPPER. Just striking out at them now and then?

ANGELA. More or less.

CRIPPER. Hum.

ANGELA. An ordinary man – trying to strike extraordinary postures?

CRIPPER. Take me away, Angela –

ANGELA. For good?

CRIPPER. I wouldn't be so presumptuous.

ANGELA *goes to the door, closed by* JAMES *when he left it. She opens it and looks at* CRIPPER, *smiling.*

Scene Eighteen. *Interior. Studio space.*

CRIPPER *lies flat on his back in the pentangle. Candles burning. Another naked* CRIPPER *approaches.*

CRIPPER. You can't come *inside* this thing, you know.

FIGURE. I know.

Pause.

CRIPPER. Name?

FIGURE. Oscar Wilde.

CRIPPER. Message?

FIGURE. Women represent the triumph of matter over mind, just as men represent the triumph of mind over morals.

There is a long silence. CRIPPER *sits up, possibly annoyed by this one.*

CRIPPER. You disapprove of Angela? There was no fornication, for example. At her place. Or indeed anywhere. (*Pause.*) I don't lie.

FIGURE. And I once said somewhere or other: It is a terrible thing for a man to find out suddenly that all his life he has been speaking nothing but the truth.

CRIPPER. Now *that* doesn't apply to me, for God's sake!

FIGURE. Who knows?

CRIPPER. I think *you* had better go away. Go on! Begone! I banish you –

The FIGURE *moves away into the darkness.* CRIPPER *puts his fingers into his mouth and whistles. A pause, he shouts.*

Dad? (*Pause.*) Gowran Cripper?

Pause. GOWRAN *comes out of the shadows in his evening dress and dark glasses.*

One thing –

GOWRAN. Yes?

CRIPPER. Why do you dress and talk posh on these occasions? Why the dark glasses?

Pause.

GOWRAN. There may be a submerged aristocrat in many of us –

Pause.

CRIPPER. There's a conspiracy going on here!

GOWRAN. If so – it's one of your own invention.

He turns smiling back towards the shadow.

Like your distinguished visitors.

CRIPPER. I didn't invoke you!

GOWRAN. No. I invoked you.

CRIPPER. What riddles! What conundrums!

We pull back and high up from CRIPPER *squatting in the pentangle.*

Scene Nineteen. *Interior. Car: afternoon.*

ANGELA *is driving.*

CRIPPER *beside her.*

CRIPPER. How far is it to the sea Angela?

ANGELA. About twelve miles from here.

Pause.

CRIPPER. Take me to the sea –

ANGELA. Any special reason?

CRIPPER. I think it would be nice to wade out and just sink. Maybe with a nice book, you know? (*Pause.*) Peter Rabbit? A fat biography of Tolstoy? (*Pause.*) Wuthering Heights? You know? Just till the seabed shelved away –

ANGELA. And I sit and watch?

CRIPPER. You could drive away.

Pause.

ANGELA. I could love you instead –

CRIPPER. People have tried that.

Pause.

ANGELA. How's your worm? And your dreams?

CRIPPER. Thriving. Both.

ANGELA. I won't take you to the sea.

CRIPPER. Where then? Brighton Pier?

ANGELA. Something will bring your memory back. One day.

CRIPPER. But I told you. The past has been fully researched and recounted.

ANGELA. What about the future?

CRIPPER. That's what that bloody doctor said!

ANGELA. Reasonable enough, though –

CRIPPER. You see. I'm not, so to speak, like a person. I'm like something that's been tape-recorded. And I think the great Cosmic Recorder of Tapes has run out of cassettes.

We see ANGELA's *face in the driving mirror. She smiles. She stops the car and turns it in the road. Starts driving back the way they have come. As she does so,* CRIPPER *tones expressionlessly*

CRIPPER. No more tapes . . . no more tapes . . . no more tapes –

ANGELA. You should never have relied on your family. For anything.

CRIPPER. But I didn't. I didn't *rely* –

ANGELA. Hoped?

CRIPPER. No!

ANGELA. Wanted?

CRIPPER. *No!*

Pause.

ANGELA. *I* think . . . you've been very aggressive. (*Pause.*) Your sister's in a state of nervous collapse. James half ready to kill you. Your father no recourse but to assume you are out of your mind –

Pause.

CRIPPER. Not bad going – eh –

ANGELA. Not bad going at all.

CRIPPER. So?

ANGELA. Leaving only the awkward question –

CRIPPER. Of?

ANGELA. Of *why*.

CRIPPER. Why do you think?

Pause.

ANGELA. *I* want you to make love to me..

Pause.

CRIPPER. Oh. Oh fart!

ANGELA. How did they say you were in that line?

CRIPPER. Well. A girl who said she was once my secretary in Valencia . . . said I had her across my desk. (*Pause.*) There I was one minute costing a new package holiday deal – the next minute, *pounce!*

ANGELA. With her collaboration?

CRIPPER. She said she was taken by surprise at first. Notebook in one hand. Pencil in the other. Then she concluded my way was a better one of spending the time.

ANGELA. And you?

CRIPPER. I, apparently, was utterly taken aback at my behaviour. So there we were, she said. Her feet drumming my kidneys and me looking as if I wondered what on earth my body thought it was doing. (*Pause.*) If the body itself, mark you, could be said to think.

ANGELA. But did she say she liked it?

CRIPPER. The comment was, I believe: known worse, except for the expression on your face. (*Pause.*) She thought my *expression* failed to do the occasion justice.

Pause.

ANGELA. Any other examples? I mean with other women?

CRIPPER. Oh, a few. Nearly always the same story. One or two lived with me for a bit. Then they left because of my *expression* during what one of them called 'intercourse'. It disturbed them. It interfered with their orgasms. It sometimes induced tears, and vehement accusations. (*Pause.*) Things are worse now. I get thunder-struck with amazement that my body can do anything at all. You know? Even getting a mouthful of tea it seems a curious thing for it to be doing.

ANGELA. I see (*Pause.*) *It.*

CRIPPER *holds up his hands; pulls his nose; scratches an armpit.*

CRIPPER. What do you call *it* then?

Pause.

ANGELA. Ellis Cripper –
CRIPPER. Christ! Now that *is* the way out!
ANGELA. Language impossible without naming things, Ellis –
CRIPPER. Many things have become a sort of philosophical puzzle for me.
ANGELA. I see. Now hold on. I'm going to drive fast.

Scene Twenty. *Interior. Angela's bedroom: evening.*

A very simple room – low divan bed, dressing-table, a few rugs. Nothing else. A door leads to an adjoining shower room. CRIPPER *lies in bed looking at the ceiling.* ANGELA *comes out of the shower in a towelling robe.*

CRIPPER. I didn't know you lived in a stately home.
ANGELA. Well, it isn't now. It's a research station.

She goes to a cupboard in the wall, takes out glasses and a bottle of scotch.

CRIPPER. I like that big empty hall. Sunday tomorrow. Could I borrow the hall tomorrow evening?

ANGELA *gives him a drink and serves herself.*

ANGELA. Borrow?
CRIPPER. I mean use. For an hour or two. (*Pause.*) A little surprise for you all. Dad. James. Anne. (*Pause.*) You.

Pause.

ANGELA. Nothing sinister?
CRIPPER. An entertainment. It's my birthday. But no fuss. No catering. A few small props.

Pause.

ANGELA. I don't see why not. (*Pause.*) Will they come?

Pause.

CRIPPER. I rely on you for that.
ANGELA. Oh, my ingenuity.
CRIPPER. Yes.

Pause.

ANGELA. How about my ingenuity this past hour?
CRIPPER. Memorable.
ANGELA. You must start having memorable experiences, Ellis.
CRIPPER. Fill up the vacuum?

He taps his head.

ANGELA. That's right.
CRIPPER. Yes. One shouldn't die without a few *concrete* memories knocking about.

ANGELA *sits on the bed, sipping her drink.*

ANGELA. I see what they must have meant about your expression. When making love.

Pause.

CRIPPER. How was it? From your point of view?
ANGELA. Just as you described it from yours –
CRIPPER. Being?
ANGELA. Disbelief that you were engaged in being at what you were at.

CRIPPER *points at his chest.*

CRIPPER. That *it* was –
ANGELA. All right that *it* was at what it was at.

She grins, wags a finger at him.

Your *mug*, dear Ellis, was contorted with disbelief. (*Pause.*)

But you got on with it just the same and I hope you liked it.

CRIPPER. Ecstatic.

Pause.

ANGELA. *I* nearly passed out.

CRIPPER. From pleasure?

ANGELA (*pointing*). *It* seems to function quite rabidly well. Despite any mental problems you might have about it.

CRIPPER. Jesus! What a split! What a crack! What a division of a labour!

Pause.

ANGELA (*calmly*). I'd say it's not uncommon. (*Standing.*) The jolly old mind–body problem whizz-banging away and never to be resolved.

Pause.

CRIPPER (*sullenly*). You must be very clever. Most perceptive. Something of a genius, eh?

ANGELA (*smiling*). *Silly!* But I did get a first in philosophy before going into science. I *packed in* philosophy for science, Ellis. (*Pause.*) I hope you find me formidable enough for the fact to tranquillize you. Calm you. (*Standing.*) Relaxing. (*Pause.*) Because you see, you can't outwit me!

CRIPPER. I suspected that, you know –

Pause.

ANGELA. Convalescence, Ellis? (*Pause.*) Convalescence with Angela?

CRIPPER *pulls the sheet over his head, frightened; she rips it off him.*

Well?

Pause.

CRIPPER (*blankly*). Right. Yes. Definitely.

ANGELA. Good.

CRIPPER. And can I move in then. With you?

ANGELA. I should expect you to. (*Pause.*) What's more you should see the grounds this place has. Fields. A lake. Woods. (*Pause.*) Must be swarming with worms. Or you can even bring your own. In a little box. On a layer of soil –

CRIPPER. Ah, Angela! Sarcasm from the word go?

ANGELA. Shall we say . . . piss-taking as a form of prudence? Of caution? maybe self-defence?

CRIPPER. I can't *work*, you know –

ANGELA. I wouldn't have thought so.

Pause.

CRIPPER (*diffidently*). Money?

ANGELA. I've got plenty.

Pause.

CRIPPER. So. (*Pause.*) You've got me into your laboratory – ?

ANGELA. In a manner of speaking.

CRIPPER *begins to laugh.* ANGELA *laughs, raising her glass to him. Fade out on this.*

Scene Twenty-One. *Interior. Large hall of the 'stately home' converted into Angela's laboratories: night.*

An expanse of parquet, high ceiling, restored Adam painted. A pentagram – and a silhouette of a male figure with its feet in the ascendant apex. He is lighting candles at each apex.

CRIPPER (*entering pentangle*). Happy birthday to me . . . happy birthday to me. Happy birthday, dear Ellis . . . happy birthday to me. (*Pause. Looking round him.*) Not a bad place. The ticking counters, computers, incubators and other apparatus and so forth. Excellent fate. Like a rat in one of those mazes. Come one, come all. Angela! Study the mournful Cripper. But why?

Out of sadism? Curiosity? Disbelief? (*Pause*.) Will there be punishment and reward therapy as designed by Ange?

GOWRAN, JAMES, ANNE and ANGELA come forward slowly out of the shadows. Each takes up a position by one of the candles – leaving the fifth, so to speak unoccupied. They stand silently watching the flames. Close-up of each of their faces in turn, ending with ANGELA.

Welcome –

They raise their heads and look at him.

Any presents? A bauble or two for my half century?

Long pause.

Mean bastards!

Long pause.

I've often suffered for my thin streak of optimism.

Long pause.

For God's sake! We've heard of life imitating art – but must it imitate dreams? (*Pause*.) Well. Whichever is going on, none of you can come into my jolly old pentangle. That's in the rules, isn't it? I mean. Well. Have I sought individuality in mere quaintness? Am I a trifle confused? Mixed up? (*Pause*.) Shall I wake sweating and thankful for the morning light? Alone but safe? (*Pause*.) Lost your tongues, have you? That *would*, be unnatural. (*Pause*.) Look. I'm getting frightened. Sphincters loosening Dad? James? Anne? *Angela*?

One by one they blow out their candles. In a panic CRIPPER seizes the remaining one. They move in on him. He threshes about, waving the candelabrum. ANGELA, without effort or fuss, blows out his candle. Now they grab him. Darkness. A long, drawn-out scream.

Fade out.

An Afternoon at the Festival

AN AFTERNOON AT THE FESTIVAL was first presented by Yorkshire Television, on 6 May 1973, with the following cast:

LEO	Leo McKern
DANA	Adrienne Corri
HOWERD	Donald Pickering
ANITA	Rosalind Ayres
JACK	Jason Kemp

Designed by Eileen Diss
Directed by Donald McWhinnie
Executive Producer Peter Willes

Scene One. *Exterior. Garden: afternoon.*

A large walled garden behind a big house in a West European capital. There are tall trees, bushes, flowers, an ornamental pond. A boy of fifteen or so, in Victorian dress, is idly pushing himself backwards and forwards on a swing suspended from a tree branch. A woman of forty, also in Victorian dress, slowly crosses the garden behind the boy's back. It is a hot day. She holds an open parasol negligently across her shoulder. In her other hand – a pistol. Calmly, she raises the pistol and shoots the boy, who tumbles off the swing. The woman stands looking down at him for a moment, then walks back towards the house.

Scene Two. *Interior. Bedroom: afternoon.*

Present time: the room was once rather grand but now there is a sense of decay – broken mouldings, peeling paint here and there. A large bed with a canopy and a silk cover. In one corner a washbasin and a bidet. Along the wall parallel to the large bed there is a divan, with clean white sheets turned back. High windows, open, sunlight streaming in through thin lace curtains. By the central window, a round mahogany table and two comfortable chairs. The parquet flooring is dull and stained. On the walls one or two fly-blown prints. A young woman of nineteen – ANITA *– enters, followed by* LEO BRENT, *who is around fifty.* ANITA *is very good-looking, with long straight blonde hair. She wears a white shirt and a very short yellow skirt. Leo wears a thin cotton shirt and levis. He carries a safari-style jacket over his shoulder. He is overweight, sweating, and looks tired. A middle-aged woman, who has let them in, closes the door.* LEO *stands looking round the room.* ANITA *puts her leather wallet on the table by the window, her back to him.*

ANITA. She will bring the wine –
LEO. *Cold?*
ANITA. Yes. Cold, of course.

> LEO *walks – almost hobbles – to one of the chairs by the window and sits down.*

LEO. How *well* do you speak English?
ANITA. I'm bilingual.

> *Pause.*

LEO. Oh hell!
ANITA. Why?
LEO. Oh, I don't know. I expect I was hoping you were exclusively native. Or mute. Or had your vocal cords removed at birth or something.
ANITA. Why?
LEO (*looking round*). Well. It isn't Brazil. But it's four walls and a place to sit down –
ANITA. Brazil?

Scene Three. *Exterior garden: afternoon.*

As in Scene One, except there are one or two pieces of cast-iron garden furniture painted white, a swinging couch, and also the rough wooden swing from the first scene. On this sits the boy – JACK – but now dressed in shirt and jeans. He is holding a coke bottle and reading a book. Nearby, at a table, sits LEO's brother HOWERD. He is smoking and typing, with a large pile of letters beside him. He and the boy are absorbed in what they are doing. After a moment a woman comes down from the house – the same woman as in Scene One, but now dressed in a light trouser suit. Her name is DANA. Approaching quietly she points two fingers at the boy.

DANA. Bang bang!
JACK. Oh, Gawd! Look who's here –
DANA (*sweetly*). Insolent little bastard.

> HOWERD *gets up and goes to shake her hand.*

HOWERD. Dana! I thought you were in Brazil –

DANA. I was. I thought I'd just . . . you know . . . jolly well jet over for the film festival. (*Pause.*) Anything to annoy Leo. Where is he, by the way?

JACK. Out.

DANA. Can't you shut him up? It was bad enough when we were making the picture.

She sits down near HOWERD, *who has resumed his place at the typewriter.*

JACK. Oh, Christ!

He throws down his book and heads for the house.

DANA. You must admit, Howerd. He's the most awful little sod. What's he still doing here?

HOWERD. He isn't exactly 'still' here. Leo brought him over for the première.

DANA. What on earth for?

HOWERD. Well, I suppose if *you* were a kid] of fifteen who'd been scooped out of a London slum into a feature film . . . you know?

DANA. How sweet of Leo! Nice for the Press too.

Pause.

HOWERD. Why did you come, Dana?

DANA. My God! I'm only the bloody star, after all.

HOWERD. Which is why you vanished to Brazil two weeks before the festival! And why each of your replies to my frantic cables said 'get stuffed'. I wonder if the Brazilian postal people knew what it meant –

DANA. *Leo* didn't ask me to come.

HOWERD. The distributors did. So did I. I mean, why *Brazil* for one thing. When you bolt, you usually head for St Tropez.

DANA. I walked into the airport. Looked at the next scheduled flight – and Brazil it was. I can promise you I shall never go there again. Not bloody likely. (*Pause.*) What a pity Jack only got shot in the film. He rather tempts one to shoot him for real.

Scene Four. *Interior. Bedroom.*

As in Scene Two.

LEO. I *would* get somebody bilingual. My wife's bilingual too. Born in Poland and raised – if that's the word for it – in England. (*Pause.*) Are you talkative by nature? Curious? Like to get to know people?

ANITA. I'm – whatever you pay me to be.

LEO. Ah! Yes. Let's get that one out of the way. How much?

ANITA. For me, fifty. For the woman, ten.

LEO. And the wine?

ANITA. Ten.

LEO. Which means you come for the price of five bottles.

> ANITA *shrugs.* LEO *takes out his wallet and counts some notes on to the table.* ANITA *picks out a ten and a fifty.*

ANITA. Thank you.

> *The woman comes in with a tray – a bottle of wine in an ice-pail, and two glasses.* ANITA *hands her a ten, then another off the pile. The woman goes out.* LEO *mops his face with a handkerchief. The wine bottle is open, and* ANITA *fills two glasses, handing him one.*

ANITA. There you are, you see – it is cold.

LEO. And damned hot out there –

> ANITA *sips her wine, then begins to remove her shirt.*

LEO. Now *wait* a minute –

ANITA (*pulling her shirt down*). As you wish.

> LEO *takes out cigarettes and a blue French 'stick' lighter. He offers her a cigarette. She shakes her head. He lights one and picks up his glass. She smiles diffidently.*

ANITA. What is it about Brazil?

LEO. Nothing to worry about. The place just obsesses me. Yes, I'm hung up on Brazil, you know. I wish you'd sit down. (*She does so.*) And tell me your name, eh?

ANITA. Anita.

LEO. Mine's Leo Brent. I'm here with a film at the festival. (*He looks at his watch.*) They're having a projection this afternoon at four. (*Pause.*) It's all bloody nonsense. It always is.

Scene Five. *Exterior. Garden.*

As in Scene One, except that DANA *sits alone in the garden, dozing. She wears a white Victorian afternoon gown.* JACK *creeps up behind her. He stands looking round for a moment then suddenly squeezes her left breast and runs away.* DANA *jerks upright and sees him vanish towards the house. Her face is expressionless. She looks down at her breast and begins to massage it.*

Scene Six. *Interior. Bedroom.*

As in Scene Four.

LEO. Now, about this getting undressed –

ANITA (*standing*). You want me to now?

LEO. Look. Are you in a hurry or what?

ANITA. No –

LEO. Let's get something clear. Crystal clear. I came up off the street with you for three things: one, a cold drink. Two, to sit down. Three, to take my bloody shoes off. (*Pause.*) It's an expensive way of going about it, but then I don't care about the money and anyway I couldn't have walked another ten yards.

   Pause.

ANITA. And that is all?

LEO. Those are my sole requirements.

   Pause.

ANITA. I am not attractive to you?

LEO. I think you're ravishing!

> *Pause.*

ANITA. You are afraid I am not . . . clean?

LEO. I hadn't thought about that, since it's beside the point.

> *Pause.*

ANITA. You want something . . . different?

> LEO *bends down to pull off his suède casuals.*

LEO. Just to get my bloody shoes off. (*He wriggles his toes.*) There you are. That's all it is. Just two hot feet. Burning like cinders. (*He prods his stomach.*) And all this weight marching about on top of them in ninety-odd degrees Fahrenheit.

Scene Seven. *Exterior. Garden.*

As in Scene Three. HOWERD *is typing and* DANA *sits listlessly staring in front of her.*

DANA. When I came through the house I asked the maid to bring out some cold wine –

HOWERD. Still on the Chablis?

DANA. Still on the Chablis.

HOWERD (*looking at his watch*). There's a projection at four. I'm supposed to meet Leo at the theatre, with his notes. They're having a sort of forum after the showing. You know how he hates those things.

DANA. Poor Howerd! Still trotting round after brother Leo. Making sure he's got his brief-case, his notes, his bloody air ticket, his this that and the other.

> *Pause.*

HOWERD. That's what he pays me for. If it weren't for Leo I expect I'd still be slaving my guts away for the Inland Revenue.

DANA. Lovely old successful Leo!

HOWERD. Well, you married him!

DANA. *And* left him –

HOWERD. And what's more, I think all things considered it was very decent of him to have you in his last film!

DANA. Come, come, Howerd. He's no altruist. It was just damned good casting. Except for that demonic boy with his cokes and his comics!

HOWERD. Jack's *marvellous* in the film. You should have seen *some* of the cream puffs we auditioned. Little boy prima donnas from breakfast food commercials!

DANA. Yes! And didn't he enjoy the scene where he had to creep up and take a squeeze at my left breast!

HOWERD. Who wouldn't? Especially a ripe and bursting adolescent –

Pause.

DANA (*quietly*). Would you, Howerd?

HOWERD. What?

DANA. Enjoy doing that –

Pause.

HOWERD. Now look here, Dana –

She begins to unfasten the jacket of her trouser suit.

DANA. Would *you* like to look *here*?

HOWERD. *Please!* Come off it –

She laughs, refastening the button.

DANA. I sometimes used to think I'd married the wrong brother –

A maid comes down the garden with wine and glasses on a tray. HOWERD *clears a place for it on his table.*

DANA. Let's be naughty and get completely sloshed – what about it?

Scene Eight. *Interior. Bedroom.*

As in Scene Six. LEO *stands by the window, holding his glass.*

LEO. You know. I once came down that street in a tank. (*Pause.*)
Nothing but rubble. (*Pause.*) I'm amazed this house is
still here. Silly bugger I was. Tanks, I thought! Yes, tanks –
that's it. Your feet off the ground and plenty of armour
plating. (*Pause.*) There are some very nasty ways to die in a
tank.

> *Pause.*

ANITA. I am glad I was not born then –
LEO (*turning*). So am I. (*Pause.*) Why do you do this?
ANITA. Going with men for money?
LEO. Exactly. *Prostitution.*
ANITA. I only have for one month. (*Pause.*) And not often.
(*Pause.*) I am a student – and I need the money.
LEO. Of course, there's only about a hundred *other* ways of making
a bit extra!

> *Pause.*

ANITA. Why does it annoy you so much? It is my own choice.
LEO (*angrily*). It *doesn't* bloody well annoy me –

> *Pause.*

ANITA. I suppose you paid for your wife?
LEO. My now separated wife is an *actress.*
ANITA. And she used always to pay everything for herself? So
her going to bed with you was different for that!
LEO. Of *course* it was!

> *Pause.*

ANITA. Why did you separate?
LEO. Because I'm too bloody awful to live with. I've had three

wives and they all fled after they'd punished me with their martyrdom long enough to leave a few scars.

Scene Nine. *Exterior. Garden.*

As in Scene Seven. DANA *and* HOWERD *are drinking the wine.*

DANA. Where do you think Leo is?

HOWERD. I've no idea. He told me he was going to walk around a bit before the projection.

DANA. In this heat?

HOWERD. I expect he's sitting in a café with a nice cold lager or something. (*Pause.*) You didn't just turn up here for the première – did you?

DANA. Not quite. (*Pause.*) I don't think I like Leo's films anyway.

HOWERD. Oh no? He's only about one of the top twenty-odd in the entire bleeding world!

DANA. I didn't say he isn't good. I said I didn't *like* his movies.

Scene Ten. *Exterior. Garden.*

As in Scene One. This time the garden is empty. JACK *comes shuffling out of the house and starts kicking at some flowers.* DANA *comes rushing after him. As he turns to her she slaps his face hard. He kicks her shin.*

Scene Eleven. *Interior. Bedroom.*

As in Scene Six. LEO *stands looking moodily at the big bed, then the divan, then back to the bed. Pointing.*

LEO. I assume that large bed is not for customers? I mean, otherwise – why the divan? Sheet's turned back. Ready and waiting.

ANITA. I am not to use it.

LEO. Does *anybody* use it? Special customers, for example? What are the qualifications? Who gets the *luxurious* romps?

ANITA. I know very little about this house. Or the woman who keeps it. I ask nothing.

Filling his glass, LEO *crosses to the bed and carefully lowers himself on to it. He swallows half the wine and balances the glass on his chest with one hand.*

LEO. You look as if she's going to come bursting in here with a pack of wild dogs!

ANITA. Of course, she won't come. But I am timid. (*Pause.*) In everything.

LEO. Well. Fear *me* not.

ANITA *crosses and sits on the edge of the bed.*

ANITA. Are you famous?

LEO. Let's put it this way. In the last fifteen years I've made eight films. Two of them made a lot of money. One was hailed as a masterpiece. The others had more complicated destinies.

Pause.

ANITA. Have you never been with a . . . prostitute?

LEO. Twice, when I was a young man. The first time I ran away. The second time she put her hand on me and started singing. I was paralysed. There we were – she on my knee staring out of the window and trilling like a canary. Me sweating with humiliation.

ANITA *laughs.*

LEO. Oh, it was funny all right. About as funny as a humming bird trying to excite a walrus. Needless to say, she was hoping I'd pay up and get out. Meanwhile a cantata or two. Keep your hands on his privates to show willing, and yodel away –

ANITA. Maybe when she was looking out of the window, she was day-dreaming –

LEO. She certainly didn't have her mind on her work.

ANITA. Was she naked?
LEO. In an offhanded sort of way –

Pause.

ANITA. Where was it?
LEO. Cyprus. Near a place called Famagusta. (*Pause.*) I was born
in Cyprus. Father in the army. First words I ever uttered were
in Greek. There's nothing like a classical education. What
finer than to look up into your old nanny's lined face and
declaim a syllable or two in the language of Homer? (*Pause.*)
Well, not really like Homer but what the hell. (*Pause.*) You look
bored.

Pause.

ANITA. What's your film about?
LEO. A woman who shoots her stepson. A fifteen-year-old
monster. Bang bang, she goes. And there he is – dead.
ANITA. It sounds horrible.
LEO. It was both passionate and logical.

Scene Twelve. *Exterior. Garden.*

As in Scene Nine. DANA *and* HOWERD *are sitting on the swinging
couch, both holding glasses of wine.* DANA *looks round the garden.*

DANA. I always liked it here.
HOWERD. Until Leo shot the film here –
DANA. Didn't *you* think it was creepy?

Pause.

HOWERD. Yes . . . I suppose I did.

Pause.

DANA. Why don't you leave him?
HOWERD. You know, I don't *mind* being his paid secretary-cum-
everything else. (*Pause.*) It's a very comfortable life, all things
considered.

DANA. And comfort is all?

Pause.

HOWERD. Of course it isn't!

DANA. Well then?

Pause.

HOWERD. Why *did* you come here this afternoon Dana?

Pause.

DANA. Leo's degenerating fast. I wanted to see how far the process had gone.

HOWERD. I don't know what you mean, degenerating.

DANA. He's physically sick, emotionally demoralized . . . and his talent –

Pause.

HOWERD. His talent what?

Pause.

DANA. Arid.

> HOWERD *gets up and walks away from her. At the table, he fills his glass.*

HOWERD. No sign of it in this last film –

DANA. We'll see what the world thinks.

HOWERD. Since when did it matter what the world thought?

DANA. To Leo? (*Pause.*) Always.

HOWERD. I wish you'd piss off!

> *She waves her arm languidly at the garden.*

DANA. This place belongs to me too, you know.

HOWERD. Legally!

> *He sits down at the table and begins to type.* DANA *gets up and walks about in front of him, still holding her glass.*

DANA. You don't wish I'd piss off. You wish I'd come upstairs with you.

He stops typing, keeping his fingers on the keys. She puts her hand across his two.

DANA. I'm *not* degenerating, dear Howerd!

HOWERD *pulls his hands from underneath hers.*

HOWERD. It's time I was going to the film theatre –
DANA. With little Jack? You'll make sure he's presentable, won't you? (*Pause.*) And if Leo's drunk?
HOWERD. He won't be.
DANA. I admit it's often hard to tell. On these occasions, I mean. Especially with a foreign audience. (*Pause.*) All the same. I'm surprised you let him wander off on his own this afternoon.

Pause.

HOWERD. He said he was depressed – and he wanted to be on his own.
DANA. Ah! *Depressed!*

There is a long silence. HOWERD *stands up, looking her straight in the eyes.*

HOWERD. *Come* upstairs then –
DANA. A quickie before the projection?

He turns away and walks towards the house. Smiling, DANA *fills their glasses and carries them after him.*

Scene Thirteen. *Interior. Bedroom.*

As in Scene Eleven. LEO *is asleep on the large bed, snoring gently.* ANITA *sits by the window. After a moment she goes to him and shakes his arm. He wakes disoriented.*

LEO. What? What's the matter.

ANITA. You have no more time –
LEO. *Haven't* I?

> *Pause.*

ANITA. I mean with me. Unless you wish to pay more?

> *He sits up, furious.*

LEO. You *what?*
ANITA. For fifty, it is half an hour.

> *He looks at his watch, then points at the money still left on the table.*

LEO. All right then. Pick one of those notes off the table every ten minutes. How about that?

Scene Fourteen. *Exterior. Garden.*

As per the set-up for LEO's *film. The garden is littered with apparatus for filming – lamps, sound equipment, lights, and a single camera.* LEO, *in sweater and parka, stands by the camera.* DANA *in large Victorian hat and outdoor costume is laying about* JACK's *shoulders with a wrapped parasol.* LEO *calls out:* .

LEO. Stop!

> *She does so.* JACK *moves sulkily to one side.*

LEO. It's a rehearsal, Dana. Not a real beating, for God's sake! You're hurting the boy –
JACK. Bitch!
LEO. I did what you asked. I sent the crew away. You said you wanted to *rehearse!*
JACK. She wanted to bloody carve me up –
LEO. Jack – clear off for a bit, will you?

> .DANA *turns and stands with her back to them.* LEO *gestures towards* JACK *with his thumb, towards the house.* JACK *slouches away. Silence.* LEO *lights a cigarette.*

LEO. Dana –

DANA (*turning*). It's in the bloody screenplay!

LEO. There's real and real! You *wanted* to beat the poor little sod –

Pause.

DANA. I'm leaving, Leo –

LEO. Not with *your* contract you aren't!

Pause.

DANA. I meant – leaving you. (*Pause.*) I hate the film. I hate the boy. And I hate *you* –

Pause.

LEO. Do you *understand* this scene?

Pause.

DANA. I'm his stepmother. He loathes me. I don't know how to get through to him. He's violent. He brings out *my* violence. (*Pause.*) Yes? (*Pause.*) And all in lovely Victorian technicolour – yes? (*Pause.*) And meanwhile, back in one of the bloody colonies my husband is being a true-blue officer. Yes?

Pause.

LEO. *Right!*

Pause.

DANA. I want a drink.

There is a table near the camera, with bottles and glasses on it.

LEO. Come and sit down, then –

He pours them each a drink. They both sit by the table. LEO *looks utterly depressed.* DANA *closed and unyielding.*

DANA. You amaze me, that's all –

LEO. Would you care to elaborate?

DANA. You could be making an original on the same subject. Set *now*. And with a damn sight more relevance. (*Pause.*) So why are we screwing about with all this period bit? (*Pause.*) You and Robert Kelvin are about the only two people who can see the point – if there *is* one!

> *Pause.*

LEO. Robert can hardly see the point of the film when he's *dead!*

DANA. All you wanted to do was film Robert's last novel –

LEO. It's by no means a valedictory gesture!

DANA. No? Are you sure?

> *Pause.*

LEO. Did you hate Robert Kelvin too?

DANA. Not *hate* him! Despised, maybe –

> *Pause.*

LEO. Why?

DANA. For the same reasons he despised himself. He didn't booze himself to death because he was an alcoholic. Anyway, what's an alcoholic? (*Pause.*) No. (*Pause.*) He realized he was a particular kind of *breed* –

> *Pause.*

LEO. Why do you think he called this novel . . . this film . . . 'The Last Days of Buster Crook'?

DANA. Because lacking the guts, the passion or the courage . . . he took wind of fashion. Didn't he? Edwardian England. Victorian England. Collapse, disintegration and decay – whilst the chaps still stride out of the cricket pavilions with their bats and play the game with the locals. Yes?

LEO. I wish you'd . . . shut up . . . about Robert.

DANA. I'm not going to shut up about you and me.

> *Pause.*

LEO. Are we going to rehearse this scene or aren't we?

DANA. Oh, we'll rehearse it! We'll finish the film. And you'll trot out your 'boy star' discovery at the Press conferences. And they'll lick your feet at Cannes, or Venice, or wherever. (*Standing.*) And I shall *blow* –

> LEO *stands up and strikes her across the face so hard that she falls. She lies on the ground looking up at him. He walks away towards the house.*

Scene Fifteen. *Interior. Bedroom.*

As in Scene Thirteen. ANITA *has resumed her seat by the window.* LEO *gets off the bed and goes to her.*

LEO. A student? What do you study?

ANITA. The 'cello.

> *Pause.*

LEO. Whilst the chaps still strode out of the cricket pavilions with their bats and played the locals –

ANITA. I don't know what you are talking about.

> *Pause.*

LEO. The bleeding blasted bloody *'cello?*

ANITA. Why not?

LEO. Oh, it's a beautiful instrument!

> *With an enigmatic look,* ANITA *takes another banknote from the table and puts it in her purse.* LEO *watches dazedly.*

LEO. Nothing like the old themes. (*Throatily singing.*) Dreizig dollar! (*Pause.*) Fünfzig dollar! (*Pause.*) I wonder how they're doing over there in Brazil? Amazonion Indians dying of this and that. Political prisoners being made to watch their women being violated with broomsticks. (*Pause.*) The screams of the maimed and dying in various cellars. (*He goes to the window and*

taps the glass.) Over there – Private Yardley brought me a boot.
A German soldier's boot with the foot and part of the leg still
in it. (*Pause.*) He was grinning –

ANITA. Whilst you were asleep I got more wine –

LEO. Did you hear what I was just saying?

ANITA. Of course –

LEO. But you *aren't* hooked on reflections about Brazil!

> *Pause.*

ANITA. I have my own thoughts –

LEO. Do you? Do you *really?*

> *Pause.*

ANITA. You have some kind of terrible violence in you.

> LEO *pours more drink. Sipping wine with one hand he points
> two fingers at* ANITA *with the other.*

LEO. Bang bang! You're dead.

> *Pause.*

ANITA. What is your film really about?

LEO. My son. His stepmother loathes him. He doesn't know how
to make her love him. She's aggressive. She brings out *his*
aggression. He shoots her. (*Pause.*) I took the precaution of
setting the whole thing in a Victorian context.

ANITA. *Your* son?

LEO. Well, naturally not in the *film*. But I put my own son in the
film, playing the part of the boy who does the hit job on his
stepmother.

ANITA. But –

LEO. Look. Why don't you take your clothes off after all?

Scene Sixteen. *Interior. Howerd's bedroom.*

*A large room, sparsely furnished in a nondescript modern style.
Books and hi-fi equipment, records scattered on the floor.* HOWERD
sits on the (double) bed, unfastening his shirt. DANA *enters walking*

carefully. She carries two glasses of wine, and a bottle under one arm.
There is a divan and a small table by the window. DANA *puts down*
the bottle and glasses, and sits on the divan. HOWERD *avoids her*
gaze.

DANA. Are you undressing, Howerd?

> *Pause.*

HOWERD. Well –
DANA. Well don't.

> *With obvious relief, he buttons up his shirt. She takes him a*
> *drink.*

DANA. After all, you *are queer* – aren't you?

> *Pause.*

HOWERD. I don't know.
DANA. *Don't know?*
HOWERD. I . . . don't.
DANA. There was never once a time when – ?

> *Pause.*

HOWERD. Oh, there've been times –
DANA. *When?*

> DANA *sits on the bed.* HOWERD *crosses to the window with his*
> *glass.*

HOWERD. Did you know that Jack is Leo's bastard son?

> *Pause.*

DANA. No.
HOWERD. It doesn't seem to affect you very much!
DANA. Leo is the kind of person who gradually drains away one's
capacity for surprise. (*Pause.*) The question is: are you evading
the point, or making one?

HOWERD. Did Leo ever talk to you much about the past?
DANA. Childhood? Youth? Early manhood, or etcetera?

Pause.

HOWERD. Anything at all.
DANA. Never. He's always had enough trouble coping with his confusions about the present!
HOWERD. We were both very happy, when we were young.
DANA (*singing acidly*). We were poor . . . but we were happy –

Scene Seventeen. *Exterior. Garden.*

As in LEO's *film,* DANA *and* JACK *are sitting on a white rug. In front of* JACK *is a case of specimen butterflies. She is fanning herself with a delicately painted fan, and looking bored whilst* JACK *pores over the butterflies. Suddenly he looks up.*

JACK. Mother –
DANA. Yes, dear?
JACK. What's the point of having such a nice garden, and sitting in the middle of it on a rug?
DANA. It's more comfortable.

Pause.

JACK. Do you know what happened to my *real* mother?
DANA. She drank herself to death.
JACK. You're *lying!*
DANA. It's your father who lies –
JACK. Not to *me!*
DANA. Well, what does your father say happened to your *real* mother?

Pause.

JACK. He says: another day, old chap. Another day.
DANA. *I* believe in telling children the truth. When they ask for it.

JACK. I'm *not* a child! I'm fifteen –

Pause.

DANA. Your mother couldn't stand the climate –

JACK. But –

DANA. Or the life of a regimental officer's wife –

JACK. But –

DANA. Or your *father* –

JACK. She *loved* my father –

DANA. You'll discover one day that that is beside the point. One can love and abominate a person at the same time. The problem is to reconcile the two emotions, and at the same time struggle for aloofness from both. I should imagine that in her way your mother was quite heroic.

JACK. I don't like the way you talk to me.

DANA. *I* don't like your constant references to your 'real' mother!

LEO's *voice. Cut!*

> LEO *enters frame. He is wearing dark glasses and holding a drink.*

LEO. Dana –

DANA. Yes, dear –

LEO. You don't understand a damn thing about this film –

DANA. What did I do wrong *now?*

LEO. You forgot the butterflies –

DANA. I forgot *what?*

LEO. When he says: I don't like the way you talk to me . . . you're supposed to get off your damned arse and *stamp* on the *case of butterflies!*

> *Pause.*

DANA. I didn't *feel* like doing it just then –

LEO. God help we sons of bitches who put our *wives* into our films!

> *Pause.*

DANA. Doesn't it make any difference our being separated?

LEO. Separated? *Separated?* You wouldn't know a separation from a bad skin graft!

DANA. I don't think that remark makes sense.

JACK (*getting up*). Screw the pair of you –

> JACK *exits frame.* DANA *stands up and stamps on the case of butterflies.*

DANA. *There!* If only you'd been shooting instead of complaining – you could have edited that in.

Scene Eighteen. *Interior. Bedroom.*

As from Scene Fourteen. ANITA *lies naked between the sheets on the divan.* LEO *sits by the window waving his glass at her.*

LEO. I told you. I have no intention of making love to you. (*Pause.*) I don't even want to see you *naked.*

> *Pause.*

ANITA. What do you want?

LEO. I want to abandon the film-showing this afternoon . . . and go home to bed . . . and stay in it for ever.

> *Pause.*

ANITA. You have a house both here and in England? In London?

LEO. Till the Income Tax people catch up with me. (*Pause.*) And about a million dependants, including dogs, cats, goldfish, tortoises and so on. (*Pause.*) Do you think I could manage another woman and a 'cello as well?

ANITA. I wasn't thinking –

LEO. I don't *care* what you were thinking.

ANITA. But I wasn't.

LEO. Why don't you go to sleep? I'll count out the ten-minutely payments until it's time for me to go. Go on. Shut your eyes. (*Pause.*) Dream.

> *Pause.*

ANITA. About your film – first you said the woman shot the boy. Then you said he shot her.

LEO. Did I?

ANITA. Why did you?

LEO. I wasn't concentrating.

ANITA. *Have* you a son?

LEO. Amongst several others – a bastard. I never knew until his mother died. Last year. She was extremely poor. They lived in a damp basement. She got pneumonia. (*Pause.*) Banal though it sounds, the story is *true*. (*Pause.*) Fourteen-year-old boy – a potential fascist, I'd say, after getting to know him a bit.

ANITA. And she never told you or asked you for help?

LEO. No. (*Pause.*) I put the boy in this last film. He was exactly what I wanted: sullen . . . resentful . . . anarchic . . . loveless . . . the classical deliquent.

ANITA *turns to him with a dry expression.*

ANITA. For classical reasons!

Pause.

LEO. He's bloody good in the film –

ANITA (*sitting up with the sheet round her*). And now it is finished? Will he join the cats and dogs and goldfish?

LEO. And prostitutes and 'cellos?

ANITA. I am for one afternoon!

LEO. That's true. One more dreary afternoon at one more film festival –

He takes another banknote from the pile and places it beside her wallet on the table. ANITA rolls on to her stomach, facing him.

ANITA. I believe you are afraid to be in bed with me –

LEO. Like all sentimental people you have a staggering talent for clichés.

Pause.

ANITA. I don't like you at all!

LEO. Why should you? People don't pay you to *like* them, in any case.

ANITA. I suppose you think you know all about what they pay me for?

LEO. Yes.

ANITA. Thank God they aren't all fat, sweating, cruel-minded film directors!

Pause.

LEO. *Fat?*

Pause.

ANITA. *Overweight.*

LEO. *I've* a good mind to start charging *you!*

ANITA. You can take all your money back, if you like –

LEO. Your 'cello never did *me* any harm. Why deprive it? (*Pause.*) At least I don't have to put up with hearing you *play* it!

ANITA. I play very well.

Pause.

LEO. Naked? Where is it? Have you got it here?

ANITA. It is downstairs. I have a lesson when you have your film showing.

LEO. What about a demonstration then?

Scene Nineteen. *Interior. Howerd's bedroom.*

As in Scene Sixteen. DANA *lies on the bed with her wine-glass full.* HOWERD *is sitting by the window.*

HOWERD. Did you ever tell Leo much about *your* childhood?

DANA. Everything. He'd begin by calling me a bloody Polish fantasist – then proceed to drag every detail out of me. Getting out of Poland in the war. Palestine. England. Nice rich Polish cousin with a business in London. Becoming 'anglicized' as Leo so contemptuously called it.

Pause.

HOWERD. I'm not queer.

Pause.

DANA. But you wouldn't have an *affair* with me!

Pause.

HOWERD. I think Leo wants you back.
DANA. Yes. And I can imagine some of his sadistic reasons for it too –

Pause.

HOWERD. I wonder why he provokes women into leaving him – then mourns them?
DANA. Oh yes – it's quite a ritual!

Pause.

HOWERD. I . . . *have* . . . often wanted you, Dana.
DANA. From time to time?
HOWERD. I mean – I've loved you.
DANA. But naturally, since I am your brother's wife –

Pause.

HOWERD. I don't know about naturally. (*Pause.*) Necessarily.
DANA. It used to be rather amusing . . . watching you maintain such vigilant . . . *distance.*
HOWERD. I'm not at this moment –
DANA. Well, of course! I leave Leo – the taboo begins to lose its power. And – *ping!* – at the same time I fly down out of the sky into your bedroom. (*Pause.*) What do you think of my timing?

Scene Twenty. *Exterior. Garden.*

As in Scene Seventeen – but LEO *is alone. He squats on the rug, holding the smashed butterfly case.* JACK *comes through the garden towards him. Still in Victorian clothes.*

JACK. I think the crew are getting fed up with you –
LEO. They are?
JACK. The number of times you've stopped shooting – for her!
LEO. Look. It's *my* job to bring the film in on schedule. They get paid anyway. And I didn't stop just now for Dana.

Pause.

JACK. I think you're sick.
LEO. You're not exactly untwisted yourself!
JACK. I wish you'd take those bloody dark glasses off. They make you look real poncy –

LEO *puts down the case and takes off his glasses. He lies back on the rug with his eyes closed.*

LEO. Can you see my drink anywhere?

JACK *looks round and sees the glass near the rug. He takes it to* LEO.

LEO. Thanks –

Pause.

JACK. Christ, I look weird in this Victorian gear!
LEO. Not in the film, you don't.

JACK *sits down some distance from* LEO.

JACK. The film's what I mean about your being sick. Gawd! Your bastard and your third wife playing stepmother and son! Especially in *this* one!
LEO. *This* one came on my scene before you did.

JACK (*also lying on his back*). Well. It's good bread for sweet f.a. (*He assumes an affected voice.*) How mother would have laughed! (*Pause.*) Howerd tells me they're going to have the première over here. (*Pause.*) I expect you'll want me well out of the way for that!

LEO. I shall want you here.

JACK. Don't count on it.

   Pause.

LEO. You know. Despite the many revolting aspects to your character – I rather *like* you, Jack.

JACK. Thanks!

LEO. Don't thank me. I'd have preferred not to.

JACK. My mother should have told you about me and screwed you for every penny she could get –

   Pause.

LEO. So she should.

   Pause.

JACK. I wonder why she didn't?

LEO. Your mother was pathologically independent. She raised independence to the status of an almost religious self-mutilation. (*Pause.*) Ah, those failed actresses crouched over gas-rings in Notting Hill Gate! (*Pause.*) An egg in the saucepan. A brassière drying on a chair-back in front of one of those oil-stoves. (*Pause.*) An occasional job selling something at an exhibition – you know? Olympia and so on. (*Pause.*) A stint in some bloody coffee-house or other. (*Pause.*) Nowadays she'd be trying to kick the hell out of Equity and working her guts out for some political rally at the Empire Pool.

   Pause.

JACK. Course – *you* couldn't give her a job.

LEO. I hadn't got going myself, in those days. (*Pause.*) Till I made 'The Quiet Frontier' nobody knew I existed.

Pause.

JACK. Wasn't that from one of Robert Kelvin's books as well?
LEO. It was, by the grace of Robert.
JACK. Dana sure does her nut about *him* – (*mimicking* DANA). 'That seedy old armchair communist!' (*He rolls over, laughing.*)

Scene Twenty-one. *Interior. Bedroom.*

ANITA *has taken a chair close up to the large bed. She sits naked, playing the 'cello, her back to the window where* LEO *stands looking at her. She is playing a classical piece, extremely well.*

Scene Twenty-two. *Interior. Howerd's bedroom.*

HOWERD *is sitting up in bed naked, the sheet pulled up to his stomach.* DANA *sits by the window, drinking.* HOWERD *looks very bleak.*

DANA. You know, Howerd. From the look on your face you ought to be doing it for money.
HOWERD. Yours or Leo's?
DANA. *Very* sharp! You're coming on, Howerd.

Pause.

HOWERD. Go away, Dana –

She crosses to the bed.

DANA. I'm coming to bed with you –

Scene Twenty-three. *Interior. Bedroom.*

The 'cello lies on the floor. ANITA *kneels by the bed, her face buried in the cover, sobbing. She is still naked.* LEO *stands motionless at the window.*

LEO. Anita –

She continues to cry.

LEO. Anita –

She stops crying and half turns her head to one side.

ANITA. Yes?

Pause.

LEO. Come home with me –

Scene Twenty-four. *Exterior. Garden.*

As in LEO's *film. A laden tea-table has been set out in the shade of a tree.* DANA *and* JACK *come down the garden towards it. She waits for him to pull her chair out. He does so, and as she sits pulls a face at the back of her head.* JACK *sits opposite.*
A credit title: The Last of Buster Crook.
DANA *pours tea.* JACK *sits with his eyes down towards his plate.*

DANA. Well. It's three weeks before you return to school Edmund. (*smiling.*) We can get to know each other a little better.

JACK *raises his eyes to her impassively.*

JACK. I know you.

Pause.

DANA. It was sad for me too today, you know. Watching your father's regiment leave. (*Pause.*) But didn't they look fine in their uniforms? So proud. So distinguished.
JACK. I don't believe in this war.

Pause.

DANA. Do you *understand* it, Edmund?

She offers him a plate of sandwiches. He shakes his head.

JACK. Do you?

Pause.

DANA. Your father told me they call you 'Buster' at school. Why is that, Edmund?

JACK. Because I smashed three chaps' noses in fights.

DANA. How very pugilistic, for a boy who doesn't believe in war!

JACK. I didn't say all wars. I said this one.

DANA. I'm quite unorthodox myself, you know –

JACK. *Are* you – ?

Pause.

DANA. A little advice, dear Edmund. Let me be . . . how shall I put it? Your Polonius. You remember Polonius?

JACK. He stinks.

Pause.

DANA (*taking a sandwich delicately*). Always pursue a sense of revenge – provided that its results accrue to you some definite self-interest unrelated to the motive. (*She takes a small bite.*) Bear malice only to the point where the victim can still yield you further satisfaction. (*She sips her tea.*) Regard acquisition vulgar – but gain honourable. Show contempt for deviousness, but never underestimate its tactical possibilities. (*Another bite.*) Remember that nothing belongs to you by right – only by the same token neither does it belong to others. (*Pause.*) Never take on an opponent superior to yourself, either out of pride or the defence of some ideal or other –

JACK *gets up from the table looking at her defiantly.*

JACK. Excuse me, Ma'am –

He begins to walk away. DANA *turns to watch him go, smiling.*

DANA. *Mother*, Edmund dear. *Mother.*

And she takes another sandwich.

Scene Twenty-five. *Interior. Bedroom.*

As from Scene Twenty-three, a few minutes later. ANITA *is dressed, and putting the 'cello in its case.*

LEO. To hell with the forum. My brother Howerd'll be there. He'll make some excuse –

> ANITA *closes the 'cello case.*

ANITA. I'm sorry I spoiled your little moment of sensual comedy by crying.
LEO. Anita –
ANITA. Damn and damn and damn and damn.

> *Pause.*

LEO. I won't say it wasn't . . . erotic.

> *She turns round and punches him hard in the stomach. He doubles up, wheezing.*

ANITA. No? And when you came over to me and put your finger on my eyes, my lips, my breasts, between my legs? And say: these shouldn't be for sale! (*Pause.*) You are gross. You are a hypocrite. You are self-pitying –

> LEO *flops into a chair still struggling for breath.*

LEO. All very true.
ANITA. So I should go back to your house with you for what?

> LEO *heaves himself out of the chair and lumbers towards her. He presses her hair round her face. She jerks back a step. He does the same thing again – this time she stands still, looking at him.*

LEO. Come and live there.

> *Pause.*

ANITA. How?

LEO. On any terms you like. Any way you like –

>   *Pause.*

ANITA. So that I shall not be a prostitute?

LEO. I'm not so magnanimous. I'd have a coronary with self-ridicule if I did that!

>   ANITA *picks up the 'cello case, crosses to the door and opens it.* LEO *gets his wallet and hers from the table, leaving the money where it is. He squeezes into his shoes and picks up his jacket.* ANITA *goes out –* LEO *follows her.*

Scene Twenty-six. *Exterior. Garden.*

The garden as it was when HOWERD *and* DANA *went into the house.* JACK *wanders about, drinking now and then from a coke bottle. He goes to the swing and picks up the book he had thrown down on the grass earlier. He begins to swing gently backwards and forwards.*

JACK (*singing softly*). If I had the wings of a sparrow:
>   And the arse of a dirty old crow.
>   I'd fly right up in the treetops –
>   *And . . .* crap on old *Leo below.*

Scene Twenty-seven. *Interior. Howerd's bedroom.*

HOWERD *and* DANA *lie side by side in bed.*

HOWERD. I shall have to tell Leo –

DANA. For God's *sake*, Howerd!

>   *Pause.*

HOWERD. *And* leave him.

DANA. Not for me, I should hope!

HOWERD. No.

DANA. Nor *because* of me?

HOWERD. No.

>   *She turns and gently kisses him.*

DANA. For you?

HOWERD. That's about it.

Pause.

DANA. So you *have* resented him all these years –

HOWERD. Maybe. But I think not.

DANA. Then?

HOWERD. I just want to be . . . away from him. (*Pause.*) Now.

Pause.

DANA. I doubt if he'll ever make another film –

Pause.

HOWERD. So he won't need me. And I shan't want to be around to watch.

Pause.

DANA (*quietly*). Why do we *both* think he's finished?

HOWERD. He's not finished in the way people usually mean it. (*Pause.*) He's tried to tell me several times lately. (*Pause.*) I quote Leo: The sheer magnitude of the offence committed by the species *against* the species . . . and all else . . . leaves me in a condition of silent awe.

Pause.

DANA. That sounds queasily grandiloquent!

Pause.

HOWERD. He means it. (*Pause.*) He'll pack up and shut up. (*Pause.*) I've never watched such terrible resignation grow in a man.

Pause.

DANA. Where shall you and I go?

HOWERD (*half smiling at her*). Brazil?

DANA. St Tropez?

JACK bursts into the room, speaking as he comes in.

JACK. It's time we were off to the – (*he stops short when he sees them.*) I was going to say: to the film theatre!

Pause.

DANA. Don't let the shock paralyse you Jack. Come on in –

JACK. *You two!*

We hear LEO's voice calling as he approaches along the corridor outside HOWERD's room.

LEO'S *voice.* Howerd? Howerd?

And LEO enters. JACK turns to look at him. LEO stands stock still. JACK goes and sits at the window, with his back to it. There is a long silence.

DANA. Everyone always *did* make a habit of charging in on Howerd without knocking. Don't you think it's time he had some privacy?

LEO. Don't you think it's time he spoke up for himself?

Pause.

HOWERD. That's fair, Leo. I never *have* – have I?

LEO. Do you think you can cut me down with this? It doesn't *mean* enough to me!

JACK. You sock it to 'em, Dad –

LEO turns on him shouting.

LEO. *Shut up!*

Even JACK is cowed by LEO's manner. He hangs his head.

HOWERD. If it doesn't *mean* much to you Leo – I'm glad.

LEO (*quietly*). And if it did?

Pause.

HOWERD. That would be less painful, I should think – it might mean you were less far gone.

Pause.

DANA (*quietly*). I wouldn't be surprised if we didn't . . . all three of us . . . love you Leo. In some peculiar fashion –

JACK. Not you two bastards!

DANA. Oh yes! And you too, little bastard!

LEO. What's your love? Enlightened self-interest?

DANA. I was hoping you'd treat us to some spectacular rhetoric!

LEO. She'll chew you into little pieces, Howerd –

HOWERD. You haven't a bad track record on that yourself –

> LEO *crosses behind* JACK *to the window. He stands looking out with his back to them.*

LEO. Get out of that bed.

DANA. Turn around, Jackie –

> JACK *stands beside* LEO *at the window. Close-up of* LEO'S *face whilst they dress.*

LEO. I'm aware I've always been hard to live with. I've always felt doomed. It isn't conducive to gentle living. Gentle loving. As for redemption through love, I've been too isolated – or egoistic if you like – to experience it. (*Pause.*) And friendship? (*Pause.*) I've never been able to give more than loyal acquaintance. (*Pause.*) Fear? Certainly. (*Pause.*) All these things and others add up to the hardened devil of a director you see on the film set. (*Pause.*) Working and behaving in the world almost furiously, through an inner sense of complete inauthenticity. One, therefore, accumulates a personality which lacks the essential core of a *person*. (*Pause.*) People sense it. One senses them sensing it. (*Pause.*) If you are in some worldly fashion successful – so much the worse. That affords people the consolation of reminding themselves that nothing can alleviate the moral squalor of human emptiness –

His voice tails off. We hear the sound of a 'cello outside – the same classical piece ANITA *played earlier.* JACK *leans out of the open window and then withdraws. To* LEO.

JACK. What the bloody hell?

LEO smiles at him. The music continues. HOWERD *and* DANA *come to the window, and look out.*

Scene Twenty-eight. *Exterior. Garden.*

ANITA *sits serenely playing her 'cello.*

Scene Twenty-nine. *Interior. Howerd's room.*

DANA. Now what on earth is *that* all about?

Pause.

LEO. That is all about my next film. (*Pause.*) I think I shall call it 'An Afternoon at the Festival'.

He exits.

Scene Thirty. *Exterior. Garden.*

ANITA *playing.*

Duck Song

DUCK SONG was presented by the Royal Shakespeare Company on 5 February 1974 with the following cast:

HERBERT SHANKLIN	David Waller
EDDIE BONE	Brian Croucher
MAURICE SHANKLIN	Mark Dignam
JANE SHANKLIN	Carole Hayman
WHEELER	Arthur Whybrow
ELEANOR JIMENEZ	Elizabeth Spriggs
LEE MCGUIRE	Gareth Hunt

Directed by David Jones
Designed by Hayden Griffin

ACT ONE

SCENE ONE:
A summer evening. The large studio room in Maurice Shanklin's London house.

SCENE TWO:
The same. The next morning.

ACT TWO
The same. A moment later.

ACT ONE

SCENE ONE

A large studio in a London house. It is no longer used as a studio, but seems more a combination of study, sitting-room and library. There is a high window which becomes, in the slightly sloping roof, an even larger skylight.

The general decor gives an impression of age and leathery comfort, with distinct overtones of a 'Bloomsbury Group' atmosphere. There are several large easy chairs and two big, comfortable couches. One wall consists entirely of crammed bookshelves. There is a desk, covered with bills, papers, a crystal bowl full of pens and pencils, books, an art-nouveau lamp. The paintings on the walls are in English styles prevailing in the Twenties and Thirties. The room is somewhat cluttered with small tables, one or two with maquettes on them. Right of the desk, a wall safe. Left of it on the floor, propped against the wall, a cuckoo clock. Facing the clock at a distance of several feet, sits HERBERT SHANKLIN – *a thin, dry-looking man of sixty. In his lap, a stoneware dish of walnuts. Behind him, on a couch, lies* EDDIE BONE – *a man of twenty-six in denim shirt and Levis.* EDDIE *has his hands behind his head and is staring vacantly at the ceiling.* MAURICE SHANKLIN *is asleep in a chair.* MAURICE *is seventy-one, large, heavy-featured. He snores slightly.*

HERBERT *is holding a walnut poised in his right hand, looking at the cuckoo clock. After a moment it begins to chime seven; and as the yodelling stuffed bird pops in and out,* HERBERT *furiously hurls walnuts at it.* EDDIE *takes no notice.* MAURICE *twitches in his sleep. Whether or not* HERBERT *scores any hits, when the clock goes silent he sits back looking pleased with himself.* HERBERT *now shifts his chair round to look at his brother.* MAURICE – *still asleep, but now with his mouth open.*

HERBERT. The trouble is, you only stand a chance when the bloody thing's hooting after four o'clock at least.

> *Pause.*

EDDIE. I clobbered it at three p.m. yesterday.

HERBERT. It's still working!

EDDIE. Yeh. I reckon there's a tiny little vet inside that clock. Specializes in cuckoos.

> *Pause.*

HERBERT. I wonder what kind of silly bugger made the first cuckoo clock?

EDDIE. Your daughter won't like it. You hammering away with them walnuts. (*Pause.*) When she finds out.

HERBERT. She could hardly object *before* she found out.

EDDIE. Right on!

HERBERT. What's more, Eddie, it's *my* game. You bloody well stay out of it.

EDDIE. Funny how your brother can sleep through any kind of racket.

> HERBERT *glances disparagingly at* MAURICE.

HERBERT. He always could. Maurice doesn't like the world. He tries to have as little to do with it as possible.

> *Pause.*

EDDIE. A man of ambition.

HERBERT. Merely sensitive.

EDDIE. Always been like that has he?

HERBERT. Practically since birth, my father once told me.

(*Pause.*) He came slithering out, opened his wrinkled little eyes once – and devoted the rest of his life to keeping them closed whenever circumstances permitted. (*Pause.*) And it gets easier when you get older, you know.

EDDIE. Lucky he never had to work for a living!

Pause.

HERBERT. None the less he did work. There was his painting –

EDDIE. With his eyes closed? Fast a-bloody sleep?

HERBERT. Maurice did *not* regard his painting as being anything to do with the world. The common business of things *existing*.

Pause.

EDDIE. What the hell did he paint, then?

Pause.

HERBERT. His inner world.

Pause.

EDDIE. His pictures must have been a riot.

HERBERT. He had his vogue, Eddie. He had his vogue. All over the world . . . Toronto, Paris, New York, Philadelphia, Turin . . . and so on . . . here and there you'll find a Maurice Shanklin in some art gallery or other. Not to mention private purchase.

EDDIE. Time I got me finger out and did a bit of educational travelling then. Isn't it?

Pause.

HERBERT. Time you got your finger out in every respect, Eddie. (*Pause.*) Maurice can get mean, you see. And it's Maurice who pays for everything. (*Gesturing.*) This house. Me. My daughter. (*Pause.*) And now you.

EDDIE. It's hardly my fault I'm unemployed.

HERBERT. Being a radical, I agree. But Maurice now! Maurice takes a dim view of political explanations for inactivity.

EDDIE. You a radical? The only difference between you and him is you keep your eyes open during the day. He's blinded with sleep – you're blinded with fucking curiosity.

Pause.

MAURICE. I wish you'd both stop blathering about me –
EDDIE. Shut your peepers, Maurice, there's a war on.

> EDDIE *closes his eyes.* MAURICE *slowly hauls himself out of his chair and crosses to* EDDIE. *He stands looking down at him.*

MAURICE. I wish someone would explain how we got an un-employed person into the house –
HERBERT. Jane told you. He's her lover.
MAURICE. That isn't an explanation. It's an insult to my credulity. Even *my* imagination baulks at certain things, Herbert. (*Leaning over Eddie.*) Mr Bone! Open your eyes and concede my presence face to face –

Pause.

MAURICE. How did you get into this house?

Pause.

HERBERT. Don't you mean into Jane's bed?
MAURICE. Your daughter's bed is as accessible as the very air we breathe, Herbert.
HERBERT. Oh, come now!
MAURICE. I say it in no critical spirit. It is a simple fact. Jane has already informed me that I must adopt no moral postures towards it. Jane is always telling me that I mustn't do things I had no intention of doing in the first place. (*Pause.*) Has *he* gone to sleep?
HERBERT. I think it's just that he's decided to ignore us. (*Pause.*) Don't you think you should sit down?
MAURICE. Why? Do I look as if I'm about to keel over?

Pause.

HERBERT. I thought you looked tired.

MAURICE. I see you've been at the cuckoo clock again –

HERBERT. I bought the walnuts myself.

MAURICE. What have you got *against* that wretched clock?

HERBERT. I've always hated them. Time itself is bad enough. But to compound the offence by having it bleated at you by some stupid mechanical bird – that is too much.

> MAURICE *slumps into a chair near* HERBERT *and glances towards* EDDIE, *shouting.*

MAURICE. Wake up, Mr Bone!

> *Pause.*

EDDIE. I'm concentrating on my inner world.

MAURICE (*to* HERBERT). Is it conceivable that he *has* one?

HERBERT. Jane seems to think so.

MAURICE. Where is she? What's she doing? Why don't people keep me *informed?*

EDDIE (*sitting up*). Listen, dormouse – nobody's got to tell you *anything* –

> *Pause.*

MAURICE. It seems we have more than one cuckoo in the house. And your blunt form of address doesn't improve my temper, Mr Bone.

> EDDIE *gets up and goes threateningly up to* MAURICE.

EDDIE. You know what?

MAURICE. What?

> *Pause.*

EDDIE. I think I'll go and mow your lawn.

MAURICE. Do you imagine that will placate me?

EDDIE. I don't care what it does to you. I'd just rather cut a bit of grass than get mixed up in any aggro.

EDDIE *exits.* MAURICE *turns to* HERBERT *in consternation.*

MAURICE. Aggro? (*Pause.*) *Aggro?*
HERBERT. I fancy it means aggravation.

Pause.

MAURICE. I wonder what he meant by saying there's a war on?
HERBERT. That's one of the problems with Eddie. He seems to
require constant interpretation. I usually consult Jane. (*Pause.*)
I suppose it's good for us you know, Maurice. Stretching our
poor old minds. Introducing us to prevailing manners, language
and concepts.
MAURICE. I find it damned wearing.
HERBERT. You don't like young people anyway.

Pause.

MAURICE. Don't I?
HERBERT. Well I wouldn't exactly say you're prejudiced. No.
I think you resent them for *being* young.

Pause.

MAURICE. The proximity of death, Herbert. The proximity of
death –
HERBERT. At least you've had your seventy-one years. What's
their life expectancy, given one thing and another?
MAURICE. Look here. *I* think I rather approve of them. (*Pause.*)
I'm selfish, that's all. On the verge of being snuffed out, one
tends to become self-preoccupied. And what with my kind of
painting having been consigned to the historical rubbish dump,
I can't even leave behind the odd masterpiece of old age. Not
the merest jolly old swansong, eh? I'm a blasted anachronism.
I've even lost the privileges of privilege!
HERBERT. You haven't lost your money or your property!

Pause.

MAURICE. Still rancorous because father left me control of the estate, Herbert? Let us not reopen old wounds. Personally I thought it embarrassing to inherit a fortune accrued from the sale of things like pots of marmalade and pickled onions. Who'd have thought there'd be enough people in the world masticating such things to finance a whole family's vulgar idleness? Mind you, I've never actually *resented* not having to work. And I think father was quite right to put your future in my care. The money may have reeked of the canning factory but it was still money. And what would you have done with it? You'd have squandered it on personal hedonism and political fatuity. Which reminds me –

HERBERT. What?

MAURICE. I hope you won't be offended –

HERBERT. You know perfectly well you don't care!

Pause

MAURICE. Well. (*Pause.*) That last job you went to prison for –

HERBERT. I've been waiting three years for you to raise that question.

MAURICE. One doesn't like to turn knives in wounds, Herbert –

HERBERT. Doesn't one? (*Pause.*) *One* disowned me for nearly thirty-five years!

MAURICE. Having a brother who blows safes for a living doesn't exactly nourish family pride –

HERBERT. And what about the three years I spent during the war blowing safes all over Europe for those dimwits in Intelligence?

Pause.

MAURICE. During that period, Herbert, I never said a word against you. I was delighted that you were out of prison and doing something for your country. Very brave you must have been too!

HERBERT. And you know sodding well that was why they *let* me out of prison! Christ! Jumping out of aeroplanes, waiting with your guts churning for submarines! Not to mention the Gestapo –

MAURICE. But, dear boy, the Gestapo didn't catch you until nearly the end of the war –

HERBERT. I'll tell you this much. I'd willingly have given those two months in Buchenwald for ten years in Wormwood Scrubs!

MAURICE. What I couldn't understand was why you resumed your nefarious occupation again *after* the war –

Pause.

HERBERT (*almost shyly*). Only once –

Pause.

MAURICE. Which brings me back to my question.

HERBERT. Let's have it.

MAURICE. Odd, really. There's something about Eddie Bone which turns the mind back to these delicate matters.

HERBERT. There you go again! He's young and he doesn't do any work – and what does that remind you of? *My* last five year stint in the nick!

Pause.

MAURICE. The judge was pretty lenient, for an old lag like you, Herbert –

HERBERT. Wasn't he just! (*Pause.*) 'Taking into account your amazing if somewhat bizarre war record, Herbert Shanklin –'

MAURICE. You have to admit. Those chaps at the War Office to whom you refer as 'the dead and the dying' . . . they didn't let you down, Herbert. (*Pause.*) It *could* have been a very long sentence.

HERBERT. The bloody war'd been *over* for nineteen years! What do you think the other cons inside made of *that*?

Pause.

MAURICE. *Why* did you have to go and do it again, Herbert?

HERBERT. One never quite loses the nostalgia for it, Maurice. The small thrill, you know – of robbing the robbers. I was a childish sort of villain. Politically motivated criminals often are. It wasn't so much that I wanted to help finance some revolutionary cause. I never did that. No, it was a kind of glee at nibbling chunks out of the parasites. If I couldn't be up somewhere on the barricades, I could at least be down somewhere in the money vaults. (*Pause.*) Anyway. Even the boodle I picked up on the side during those secret service capers couldn't last forever –

Pause.

MAURICE. And where's the . . . the 'boodle' you snatched on your last little effort? Where is *your* swansong? Considering, I mean, that you live entirely off me . . . setting aside the occasional bag of walnuts.

> HERBERT's *daughter* JANE *enters. She is thirty-two, sharply attractive, dressed in an old leather jacket and jeans. She has a large, bulging bag made of some carpet-like material. She throws the bag on to the floor and flops on to the couch vacated by* EDDIE. *There is a long silence. She looks from one to the other, speaks with a slight American accent.*

JANE. Well. Come on. What about 'Hello, Jane? How are you, Jane? Did you have a good day at the clinic, Jane?'

HERBERT. Hello, Jane –

MAURICE. How are you?

HERBERT. Did you have a good day at the clinic?

Pause.

JANE. I suppose you were dissecting Eddie –

Pause.

MAURICE. Not at all. We were . . . er –

HERBERT. Chatting about old times.
JANE. Where *is* Eddie?

Pause.

HERBERT. Mowing the lawn.
JANE. He's *what?*

Pause.

MAURICE. Something to do with aggro, my dear –
JANE. Yours or his?
HERBERT. I don't think your uncle Maurice *intended* to offend him, Jane –
MAURICE. Oh, I wouldn't say that –

> JANE *springs off the couch and confronts the two men. She also takes in the walnut-bespattered floor around the cuckoo clock.*

JANE. Uncle Maurice. Will you stop *persecuting* Eddie? And Dad. I've told you before. Will you lay off the goddamn cuckoo clock?
HERBERT (*querulously*). Eddie was throwing walnuts at it yesterday. He told me so.
JANE. So that lets *you* off the hook?
MAURICE. I haven't *been* persecuting Eddie –
JANE. I'm getting real pissed off with you two old bastards –
MAURICE. Who planted him on us?

> JANE *goes to her bag, rummages about in it and holds up a letter.*

JANE. Wait till you hear who's going to get planted on you *next!*

Pause.

MAURICE (*mildly*). You know, Jane – for a psychiatrist you do seem to go about in a temper much of the time –
JANE. What's being a psychiatrist got to do with it?
MAURICE. In all humility, I assure you . . . in all humility I often

ponder whether you couldn't apply the skills of your profession to yourself? You know? Insights, and so on?

JANE. I'm an *angry* psychiatrist –

MAURICE. That's precisely the condition which leaves me so bewildered.

JANE. Didn't you know the externalisation of aggressive feeling is *healthy?*

Pause.

MAURICE. It seems to have led to an awful lot of bother over the centuries –

JANE takes the letter over to HERBERT *and slings it into his lap.*

JANE. Slide your rheumy old eyes over *that!*

HERBERT. Jane! *Please!* I'm only sixty, and my eyes are in splendid fettle –

JANE. Okay. Fine. Now glue them to those pages will you?

Pause.

HERBERT. Why don't you just give me the gist? I abhor letters.

JANE. You asked for it. *Mother* is coming.

Pause.

HERBERT. *Who?*

JANE. *You* know Mother! The woman you married and packed off to America in 1939 with *me* in her womb –

Pause.

HERBERT. Oh God!

Pause.

MAURICE. What about a large whisky?

He totters over to a drinks-table and pours a stiff one. Takes it back to HERBERT.

JANE. I think I'll join him.

She gets herself a drink and sips it smiling maliciously at the two men.

HERBERT. I could have sworn we were divorced –

JANE. You are. (*She grabs back the letter.*) That doesn't undo the deadly business of your having knocked her up. Does it? (*Pause.*) What's more, her third marriage having sunk, it looks like you and Uncle Maurice are going to have to do the Samaritan bit.

MAURICE. See here . . . I mean to say. Would anyone care to give a thought to *me?*

JANE. I guess not, Uncle Maurice.

Pause.

MAURICE. I suppose there's always the chance she might take a dislike to Mr Bone –

JANE. Or even you. Or even Dad. But no. I'd say she's a woman of stamina. Like you know, subtly wilful? (*Pause.*) Who else but my mother could have dumped me in a town called Eureka at the age of three and split with a Chilean tycoon? Jesus! Eureka! There's a perverse sense of humour for you.

HERBERT. *I've* always done my best for you, Jane –

JANE. Sure. Redneck foster parents, a fat allowance from England. I even made Sarah Lawrence, didn't I? (*In heavy American.*) 'What does *your* father do, Jane? *My* father? He makes his money in gelignite.'

MAURICE. There's nothing wrong with the odd euphemism, Jane –

JANE. Nothing at all. Some of those dummies even used to call me Nobel Shanklin. I wet my pants at the comic irony of it all.

MAURICE. I do insist. We must encourage your young man to display his most unsavoury qualities at all times. Indefatigably. (*Pause.*) How old is she, Herbert?

HERBERT. Oh, must be about fifty.

MAURICE (*to* JANE). There you are. She's probably still rapable. I think it's the least he could do, for free board and lodging –

JANE. What if she liked it?

Pause.

HERBERT. I regret to say, Maurice. You still haven't caught on. Even ladies of fifty, nowadays –

MAURICE. I wish you wouldn't make me out such an old fool! I am up to date on *nowadays*. Fashions in hypocrisy may change, but human lust is a constant whatever image of itself society is pumping out.

At this point, EDDIE *enters, pulling a small thin wiry man by the collar of his coat – this is* WHEELER. EDDIE *trails him across the room towards* JANE, *and kisses her.* HERBERT *and* MAURICE *are transfixed.* WHEELER *is white and paralysed with fright.*

EDDIE (*after kissing* JANE). Hello, love –

JANE. Where did you find *him?* In the grass?

EDDIE. Not quite. Coming over the wall.

HERBERT (*standing*). *Wheeler!*

WHEELER *opens his mouth to speak but* EDDIE *slams his palm over it.*

EDDIE (*to* HERBERT). You know him? You want him in, or out?

MAURICE *crosses to the phone and begins to dial.*

JANE. What are *you* doing?

MAURICE. Ringing my housekeeper in Cornwall, if you don't mind. I plan a rapid and sullen departure.

EDDIE. Not much to him, is there? Good job I didn't catch him under the mower.

EDDIE *gives* WHEELER *a not unfriendly shake and lets go of him.* WHEELER *points a shaking finger at* HERBERT.

WHEELER. We does the same job, right? He gets five years and I get nine.

> HERBERT *sinks back into his chair.* MAURICE *stands with the phone burring.*

MAURICE. Can't your friends use the bloody doorbell, Herbert? Or should I say your *accomplices?*
HERBERT. Oh, Wheeler!

> MAURICE *slams the phone down.*

MAURICE. Bloody woman's out. She's telepathic. She always knows when I'm beleaguered. *Nothing* is permitted to interrupt that woman's slothful existence. (*Pause.*) Now what? Soothing drinks all round? We all know I can afford it! I presume you too are unemployed, Mr Wheeler?
WHEELER. Fresh out the nick. (*Pointing to* HERBERT.) And Shankers here – Shankers either pays me off or gets done, see?

> MAURICE *goes to pour himself a large whisky.*

MAURICE. How splendid! Shankers! I like it! Herbert, you shall henceforth be forever Shankers –
WHEELER. Where's the justice in it? Five for him and nine for me!
EDDIE. Shall I throw him back over the wall, Herbert?
HERBERT. I wish you would. I'd be most grateful.

> WHEELER *makes a rush at* HERBERT. *As he does so,* EDDIE *grabs him once more by the collar, another hand over his mouth and hauls him out of the room.*

MAURICE. Needless to say . . . he was after his share of what you call the 'boodle'. Was he not, Shankers?
HERBERT. I expect so.
JANE. Well why don't you give it to him? (*Pause.*) *Father?*

> *Pause.*

HERBERT. I buried the money in a field –

MAURICE. Then what's to prevent you digging it up, and paying *all* of us what you owe? I mean, I *have* been keeping you, Shankers. *And* Jane. Then recently Mr Bone –

HERBERT. I wish to God you'd stop calling me *Shankers!*

MAURICE. I'm surprised they didn't think of it at your prep school. Not to mention Harrow – (*Pause.*) Let us away to yonder field, with picks and shovels.

Pause.

HERBERT. They built a housing estate on it. When I was inside.

MAURICE. Suburban rabble! Or was it human effluent from the slums of London?

Pause.

HERBERT. I shall go upstairs and lie down –

He slowly makes his way out of the room, his shoulders bent.

MAURICE (*to* JANE, *wickedly*). Should you go and comfort your old father?

JANE. Let's get one thing straight, Uncle Maurice.

MAURICE. Can anything be *got* straight around this house? Thank God my health isn't failing or I'd be in my coffin –

JANE. When I get my first cheque from the clinic, I'll start paying you. Then Eddie and I'll move out as soon as we can find somewhere.

Pause.

MAURICE. Jane. My dear girl. I don't *mean* all those remarks about money and keeping you and so on.

JANE. Then why keep rubbing it in?

MAURICE. I'm in a chronic state of tension. Irritation. Irascibility. Surely it all makes sense? The way I keep dozing off, then waking up in a querulous frame of mind. (*Pause.*) I'm so afraid of death that everything else loses perspective. And imagine coasting to oblivion in the presence of your father, your lover, the imminent threat of your mother . . . ex-convicts creeping over the garden wall. (*Pause.*) The strain would be bad enough if I were alone. (*Pause.*) God! Things were at least *peaceful* when Herbert was in jail . . . and you in America . . . and Mr Bone was wherever he was. (*Pause.*) In those days I could even toy with the idea of suicide. You know? Get the blasted business over with? (*Pause.*) Somehow you've all managed to rake up my blissfully dormant sense of *responsibility!*

Pause. JANE *goes to sit on the couch.*

JANE. Come and sit down, Uncle Maurice –

He sits at the further end of the couch from JANE.

MAURICE. I hope you're not going to start analysing me!
JANE. You did say you were *physically* healthy –
MAURICE. That doesn't prevent one being struck down at my age! No warning. Some sudden capitulation of a vital organ. Then again, one tends to potter about absentmindedly, you know. All those buses . . . cars . . . taxis . . . prams –
JANE. Would you rather *be* alone then?

Pause.

MAURICE. What would poor old Herbert do? Especially when his swag's entombed under a housing estate. I mean, it's worse than the bloody pyramids – isn't it? Even all that Tutankhamun muck got excavated in the end! No such luck for Herbert. (*Pause.*) He's always been feckless. *I* wouldn't have packed your pregnant mother off to America. I can tell you.
JANE. It was to get her away from the bombing raids, Uncle –
MAURICE. On the proceeds of ill-gotten gains! What a funny expression. Do they still use it? I only met your mother once, and I had the impression bombs would have sheered away from her like rats from a dose of arsenic!

EDDIE *comes in, dusting his hands together.* MAURICE *regards him glumly.*

MAURICE. I think I'll follow your father's example. (*Rising.*) *If* I can make the stairs –

He gets up and shambles past EDDIE, *out of the room.*

EDDIE. He'll make the stairs all right. There's no built-in obsolescence in your Uncle Maurice!

JANE. Isn't there? What about biology? Ageing. (*Pause.*) Terror –

EDDIE. Look. I've been shit-scared of dying since I could toddle. Who hasn't?

JANE. And supposing you live to a ripe old age? When you *know* it's close?

EDDIE. At least he's fading away in comfort. My old man got killed in a factory pulling in the handsome sum of nine pound a week. And me mother gassed herself after her second conviction for shoplifting. With *my* luck I get born into the sort of statistical situation you see getting debated on the telly!

JANE. What did you do with Wheeler?

EDDIE. Took him down the street. Threw him on to a passing bus. Going to Chiswick, I think it was. (*Pause.*) He didn't half squawk –

Pause.

JANE. Chiswick isn't far –

EDDIE. What you expect me to do? Get him to the airport and smuggle him on to a plane for Siberia?

Pause.

JANE. Did you go to the Labour Exchange this morning?

EDDIE. Didn't I! (*Pause.*) *Nothing!* Surprise surprise. (*Pause.*) Do you think I don't *want* work? (*Pause.*) Gawd! And people like your Uncle Maurice still carrying on in the same old way. The bleeding world coming to bits round his head and he don't *notice!* (*Pause.*) And come to think of it, what sent Herbert into villainy? Blowing safes and doing bird –

JANE. Socialism.

Pause.

EDDIE. Would you give me that again?

Pause.

JANE. Socialism.

Pause.

EDDIE. Communist Party?
JANE (*shaking her head*). Nah!
EDDIE. Trotsky?
JANE (*shaking her head*). Nah!

Pause.

EDDIE. You don't mean to say – *Labour?*
JANE. He may have been eccentric, but he wasn't round the twist!
EDDIE. Robin Hood?
JANE. *Nah!* (*Pause.*) You idiot.

Pause.

EDDIE. Just – socialism!
JANE. That's right.

Pause.

EDDIE. I can't get it together.
JANE. Neither can I. Because he's never explained what he meant by it. You ask him – his eyes glaze over. He gets a faraway expression. He smiles . . . not patronizingly. No. Smiles as if he's got some cosmic secret. You know? Some kind of political equivalent of Om.

There is a small handbell on a table beside her end of the couch. She lifts it, smiling, and gently tinkles it.

Om. (*Pause.*) Om Om Om.

Pause.

EDDIE. Not exactly what you'd call dialectical materialism!

JANE. *Om.* (*She laughs.*) You're *almost* as enigmatic yourself, Eddie. (*Pause.*) You seem to know bits and pieces about a lot of things but it's all . . . unconnected.

Pause.

EDDIE. Well I read, don't I? Try to make sense of things. (*Pause.*) But there isn't a beginning a middle and an end is there? Not in anything. Result is, I'm chock full of random information without any *links*. I'm like a bloke scuttling round a bloody great house peering through all the windows . . . but I can't see the *house*. (*Pause.*) If there *is* a house. (*Pause.*) And then coming here . . . you lot make me mind reel. I go all dizzy sometimes. (*Pause.*) No sense here at all.

JANE. There's nothing mysterious, though –

Pause.

EDDIE. Far as I can make out, the absence of mystery doesn't mean the presence of *sense!* (*Pause.*) It tires me out. I tell you. I could flop down somewhere and never get up again. Never lift a finger. Never take another step.

Pause.

JANE. You're not like that in bed!

EDDIE. I'm *demoralized* – not *paralysed*. A bewildered man can still fuck, can't he? No contradiction there at all. (*Pause.*) Mind you. *You* tend to increase the confusion. *I* don't know why I'm here at all. In this house. I just know *how*. (*Pause.*) *You* must have known what you were doing I imagine. (*Pause.*) I sneak off the street through this wide open door into a posh party crawling with *intellectuals* . . . I snatch a plate of prawns and a glass of champagne . . . slink into a corner. Before I can crack me first prawn and have a drink – *you're* standing in front of me. (*Pause.*) You might as well know here and now – I felt aggravated.

Pause.

JANE. I thought you looked nervous.

EDDIE. Have you ever shelled a prawn with *complete* self-confidence? (*Pause.*) Why couldn't they have goulash? If they'd had goulash I mightn't be where I am today.

JANE. They had boeuf stroganoff as well as the prawns.

EDDIE. I didn't see it. And if I had – would I have recognized it? Is it less nerve-wracking than prawns?

He stretches out on the couch, his feet within inches of JANE's *thigh.*

JANE. Are you accusing me of picking you up?

Pause.

EDDIE. I wouldn't say that. No. I'm a great pioneer in the struggle for precision. (*Pause.*) I'd say you *collected* me. That's more like it.

Pause.

JANE. I was attracted to you.

Pause.

EDDIE. I know these things *can* happen –

Pause.

JANE. I didn't drag you back here –

EDDIE. I'm not complaining.

JANE. It sounds as if you are –

EDDIE. I don't mind people taking the initiative. I respect initiative. It's on my list with things like drive . . . ambition . . . motivation . . . praiseworthy self-interest. (*Pause.*) *Energy.* (*Pause.*) Some people might say I'm on to a good thing.

JANE. They very well might!

Pause.

EDDIE. Well that's all right then – isn't it?

Pause.

JANE. The question is – am I?

> HERBERT *comes shuffling in. He sniffs tension but ignores it.*
> *He makes for the drinks.*

HERBERT. It's no use.

EDDIE. What's the matter, Herbert?

HERBERT. Can't just lie in my room tortured by thoughts of her
mother's arrival. (*Pouring a drink.*) And Wheeler. And Maurice
drenching everything with that sarcasm of his. I shall have to
get drunk.

JANE. Father –

> HERBERT *takes his drink to a chair and sits down.*

HERBERT. Whenever she switches from 'dad' to 'father' it
means I am about to be rebuked.

EDDIE. Let him *get* pissed if he wants to. If ever I saw a man
with troubles, it's Herbert.

JANE. *I* don't care if he gets drunk.

HERBERT. *What* then, is the nature of the forthcoming criticism?

Pause.

JANE. I just think you shouldn't prejudge Mother –

HERBERT. Good God I don't prejudge her! But I *worry*, you see.
I worry about every conceivable reason she might have for
invading us. And what about Wheeler too?

EDDIE. On his way to Chiswick.

Pause.

HERBERT (*sadly*). Not very far –

EDDIE. You're as bad as your bleeding daughter!

HERBERT (*drinking*). Worse, Eddie my boy. Worse. (*Pause.*) By way of illustration, I'd say that I have dark thoughts about Wheeler. (*Pause.*) I have visions. (*Pause.*) I see *Wheeler* . . . I see him in one of those compressors they use for disposing of old motor cars. (*Pause.*) Didn't we see something like that once, Jane dear? In a James Bond film I think it was –

> *Pause.*

EDDIE. Cool it, Herbert. If he shows up again, I'll take care of him –

HERBERT. I sometimes think you're the only person of innocent goodwill in this house, Eddie. I thank you. (*Pause.*) I wonder when Nemesis – or whatever your mother is called – will arrive?

JANE. Her name's Eleanor – not that we believe you'd forgotten. And she's flying in tomorrow morning. From New York. (*Pause.*) Come on, Eddie –

EDDIE. What?

JANE. Come *on!*

EDDIE. Where?

JANE. Out.

EDDIE. Why?

JANE. You haven't seen him drunk yet –

HERBERT. She's quite right, Eddie. It is a mournful spectacle. And occasionally tiresome for those on the sidelines.

EDDIE. Meaning?

HERBERT. Oh, *you* know! I sing. Sometimes break things. Practise my old skills on that safe over there. (*Pause.*) Maurice once got terribly singed when I miscalculated with one of those new plastic explosives –

> *Pause.*

EDDIE. I couldn't take the singing.

> HERBERT *pours himself another large drink – he has taken the bottle with him.*

Where did he *get* all that about explosives?

HERBERT. Cambridge.

Pause.

EDDIE. I'm grubbing about for *links* again. Can't seem to find one at all.

HERBERT. Maurice to Oxford and classics – which he subsequently renounced for the visual arts. And I to Cambridge and chemistry, ten years later. (*Pause.*) You must never be a younger brother, Eddie.

EDDIE. For Chrissake I'm an only child and me parents dead!

Pause.

HERBERT. You must try to keep it that way, Eddie.

Sings.

Sitting on, the bridge at midnight –
Throwing snowballs, at the moon.
She said, she was a virgin –
But she spoke, too fu-hucking soon.

Pause.

HERBERT. Flit away, children. *Flit* away –

He amiably waves his glass at them, spilling from it. JANE *and* EDDIE *exchange glances. They get up from the couch and leave. As the lights fade,* HERBERT, *sings, trilling to the universe at large.*

Her man, he was a soldier –
With his trousers, round his knees.
When he foully, sprang upon her –
She whispered, please . . . please please please please.

Blackout.

SCENE TWO

The following morning. WHEELER *is firmly bound to a chair, and* gagged. EDDIE *sits drinking a cup of coffee and eating a banana. Occasionally,* WHEELER *struggles at the ropes – but soon subsides.*

EDDIE. When I put a villain like you on a bus to Chiswick, Wheeler – I expect him to get my drift. To make a new *life* for himself in Chiswick. (*Pause.*) You know what I mean? (*Pause.*) Find a job. Settle down. Wife and kids. (*Pause.*) You're not *realistic*, Wheeler. (*Pause.*) I get restless during the night. A bit of an insomniac. (*Pause.*) And there you are . . . in this *room* I should say you are . . . clomping about like a bloody dinosaur. (*Pause.*) Aren't they giving you any prison after-care? Encouraging you to adjust to society? (*Pause.*) There isn't the money though is there? Not enough by any stroke of the imagination, for that kind of thing.

> WHEELER *makes a strangled, groaning noise.*

EDDIE. Didn't you know we're in a grave economic crisis, Wheeler? Capitalism with its back to the wall and its arse in the face of the workers? And *you* come here whining for your investments! (*Pause.*) It's no secret round here, Wheeler, that Herbert's boodle has been *ploughed back*. Yes it has. Literally ploughed back. In the national interest. (*Pause.*) Thousands of people are *living* on that boodle, Wheeler. *You* are a problem we can do without. (*Pause.*) Getting hungry? Thirsty? What about a bacon sandwich and a mug of tea? (*Pause.*) Help yourself, by all means. I'm no sadist.

> HERBERT *and* MAURICE *wander into the room, each of them absorbed in a newspaper.* EDDIE *idly plays with his banana*

skin, waiting. WHEELER *gurgles. Startled, both men lower their papers and look round the room.* HERBERT *gives a yip of dismay.* MAURICE *drops his paper and claps a hand to his forehead.*

EDDIE. Caught him breaking and entering at four twenty a.m. Lashed him up. Thought you might want a conference after breakfast. Don't be shocked. The bugger will *not* stay in Chiswick. Low I.Q. if you ask me. (*Pause.*) Speechless are you? *Both* of you?

MAURICE. *Mister Bone –*
HERBERT. *Eddie –*

Pause.

EDDIE. That, Wheeler, is what is known as differentiation of character. Maurice is one for the old standards, you know. Formalities and so on. Malicious politeness it is, when directed at me. (*Pause.*) Herbert on the other hand is definitely one of the chaps. No class distinction. No barriers. Straightforward communication, man to man.

Pause.

MAURICE. Was this necessary?
HERBERT (*whispering*). *Was* it, Eddie?
EDDIE. You want him running around the place? Wearing out the carpets? Breathing *your* air?

Pause.

HERBERT. He looks awfully miserable.
EDDIE. I'll untie him then –
MAURICE. You certainly will not!

Pause.

HERBERT. Well maybe not *yet*, Eddie –
EDDIE. There you are, Wheeler. There you've got it. The conflict

of humanism and self-preservation. What do *you* make of it? Whose side are you on?

> HERBERT *sits down.* MAURICE *warily goes up to* WHEELER *and stands with his hands clasped behind his back, rocking up and down.*

HERBERT. And I've got such a hangover!

MAURICE. I shall ring the police. Have it removed.

HERBERT. You can't do that, Maurice. One doesn't *shop* a man. It isn't done.

MAURICE. Then what *does* one do?

> MAURICE *retrieves his newspaper, sits down and shakes it open.*

I knew I should have gone to Cornwall. Slattern or no slattern. Even Mrs Tretharney doesn't have to be actually *tied up*. No need for that with her. She is immobile by nature. Kindly sort the whole thing out, Herbert, if for no other reason than deference to my blood pressure. (*He looks over the paper.*) Not that you wouldn't like to see me *dead!* All of you.

HERBERT. That's a *shameful* thing to say, Maurice!

MAURICE. Don't be hypocritical. Brothers we may be – but care for each other we do not. I tolerate you and your little horde out of indolence. It's always been my vice. You're welcome to exploit it, but don't pretend you have *positive* feelings about me.

EDDIE. *I* think he's shocking, Herbert. He really is shocking.

> WHEELER *gurgles and groans, quite loudly this time.*

EDDIE. His gag's getting wet. Shall we change his gag?

> *Pause.*

HERBERT. Has that chair got castors on it?

EDDIE. Freshly oiled. Did it meself once I'd got him comfortable (*Pause.*) I *thought* you might want him castored –

Pause.

HERBERT. Then perhaps you could . . . perhaps you could wheel him out? (*Pause.*) Eddie?

EDDIE. Wheel Wheeler out? Where to? Not all the way to Chiswick again? I mean. There's a strong chance it might draw attention on the street. Old ladies. Coppers. R.S.P.C.A. They're an interfering lot out there you know, Herbert –

Pause.

HERBERT. I meant . . . the kitchen, say?

EDDIE. Poor old Wheeler. In and out, in and out. And it never teaches him a lesson. (*Pause.*) Any law-abiding citizen would tell you the man is scum, Herbert. What is the world to do with its scum? Launch it forth on a set of well-oiled castors? Can you see it? Can you see them all careering about the planet as if they was on the bloody dodgems? We'd all be run down!

MAURICE's *paper slides to his knees. He is asleep and quietly snoring.* EDDIE *and* HERBERT *stare. Even* WHEELER *swivels his eyes vainly in* MAURICE's *direction.*

EDDIE. You've got to admire him, you know. What time did he get up?

HERBERT. About an hour ago –

EDDIE. Yes. Well. I suppose it *is* a long time. For Maurice.

HERBERT. I feel doomed –

EDDIE. I know a bloke with a van –

HERBERT. I don't quite see that –

EDDIE. We get the van to the back door, see? Whizz old Wheeler out and in – as is becoming customary. Slam the doors. Let in the clutch – (*He bends towards* HERBERT.) My *mate* will let in the clutch and before you can say cuckoo they'll be off. How's that? Cost Maurice a few quid of course – but needs must when a mate of mine is doing the dirty driving. (*Pause.*)

Anywhere you like, Herbert. Hundreds of miles if you like. Any place not requiring passage through Customs. My mate would draw the line there. We know Wheeler isn't dutiable, but you can see the problem –

Pause.

HERBERT. What a *splendid* idea! A *brilliant* idea!

EDDIE. Then you can have a nice untrammelled chat with your ex-wife.

HERBERT. God! You know . . . I'd quite forgotten about her.

He puts his hands to his face. EDDIE *goes to* WHEELER'S *chair and begins to push it towards the door.* JANE *enters. As she takes in the scene and opens her mouth.*

EDDIE. Before you open your mouth –

Pause.

JANE (*grimly*). Go on –

Pause.

EDDIE. Mind your own business. We don't want any quick and scathing briefings on the psychology, the morality, the ethics – or anything else of the situation. You have to try to see friend Wheeler here as no more than say a used Kleenex. What would you do with a used Kleenex? What's more, we don't want to upset your mother by the sight of a trussed and gagged villain in the drawing room. Do we? And don't waken your uncle Maurice. He's had a shock and he needs the rest.

JANE *turns to* HERBERT, *advancing on him.*

JANE. *Father –*

HERBERT. Eddie's only trying to help. Isn't that obvious? I'm shaking from head to foot. Spasms. Nausea. Please. No attacks. Sympathy. Love. Comfort. Understanding. (*Standing up.*) Dammit, girl – where are your *priorities?*

JANE (*to* EDDIE). I don't like your attitude to women.

At this, HERBERT *sinks back into his chair exhausted. Pause.*

EDDIE. I thought you was going to start yapping about *Wheeler!*
JANE. So I was.

EDDIE *takes his hands from* WHEELER's *chair and puts them on his hips.*

EDDIE. I've a good mind to *abandon* this bloody menagerie! I mean to say. Out you go every day spending hours listening to nutters, and –
JANE. *Not nutters!*

EDDIE *pushes the chair towards* JANE.

EDDIE. Okay, love. He's all yours. *I* wash me hands. Plenty of so-called not-nutters for you to get to work on here. I've had *enough* lectures on madness and sanity and male chauvinism and the-woman-as-object and all the bloody rest of it. Christ! There's so much whirring round in your bloody head and so much bloody confusion in *mine* – why don't I just split? Eh? *Regress? Revert.* (*Pause.*) What were them other expressions?

There is a long pause. WHEELER, *who has been chewing wildly at his gag manages to dislodge it.*

WHEELER. I want to go to the toilet.
EDDIE. Anybody got Wheeler's urine bottle hidden on their person?
WHEELER. Honest. I'm bursting –
EDDIE. Hear that? We got a piss-bomb here in this very room. Ticking. Tocking –
WHEELER. The humiliation of it –
JANE. He's *crying! Eddie* –
EDDIE. What? Coming out of his eyes, is it?
WHEELER. There'll be an accident. Can't even cross me legs –
JANE. *Eddie!*

EDDIE *gives them all a strange look, almost hopeless. Then he pushes* WHEELER *out of the room. At the door:*

EDDIE. You want me to get the van round or not Herbert?

Pause.

HERBERT. What else?

Exit EDDIE *and* WHEELER. *Pause.*

MAURICE. Does anyone have a sense of apprehension? I mean, a feeling of approaching tragedy – however small and unheroic it may turn out to be?

HERBERT. I don't know, Maurice. With your caustic way of seeing things it might all turn out amusing. And clearly, Wheeler's a persistent fellow. He's capable of outfoxing even Eddie's peculiar ingenuity I should say. (*Pause.*) Wheeler . . . and Eleanor! (*Pause.*) Wow!

MAURICE. What it would have been like . . . to be magnificent . . . just once before one died –

JANE. Death again. Death death death. After a life devoted almost exclusively to inaction I guess you won't notice the difference when you *do* blow, Uncle.

MAURICE *subsides in his chair, closing his eyes.*

MAURICE. You're cruel. Life is so cruel. (*Pause.*) Does either of you remember the very first time you thought: what's the use? What's it all for?

HERBERT. There speaks a man whose only acquaintance with Buchenwald was a guided tour!

MAURICE. Always pulling rank, Herbert. I wish you wouldn't.

JANE *begins pacing up and down.*

JANE. You suffocating old men! This suffocating house!

MAURICE. Soon to be further violated by she who carried you in her womb!

HERBERT. *Please*, Maurice –

JANE. When did either of you venture any further than Sloane Square from here?

HERBERT. ⎫
MAURICE. ⎬ We read the newspapers –
　　　　 ⎭

JANE. Shit you do! Belting your way rapidly through the head-lines, home news, foreign news, letter columns. Till with a sigh of exhausted relief *he (Pointing at* MAURICE.) gets to the cricket and *you (At* HERBERT.) to the chess.

　　MAURICE *perks up somewhat. Turning towards* HERBERT.

MAURICE. Yes you know. I've always considered it affected on Herbert's part. Chess. Did they play it in Wormwood Scrubs?

HERBERT (*defensively*). It . . . it keeps the mind agile.

MAURICE. *Mind? You?* I would laugh, did I not exist in sorrow.

HERBERT. Why is he picking at me again? What's so uplifting about cricket? (*Pause.*) I once went to Lord's –

MAURICE. Oh, bravo! (*Pause.*) *And?*

HERBERT. I got pissed. What with the sun, and those demented people running about. (*Pause.*) It's not a decent way to treat a nice patch of grass, you know –

MAURICE. Indeed? And has the resident psychiatrist any thoughts on such things? For instance. Does a man's preference in games come within the scope of psychopathology? Is it illuminating for you who spend life poring over such recumbent unfortu-nates as confess a passion for a rubber of bridge? A point-to-point. A sweat in the fives court –?

　　JANE *crosses to* MAURICE.

JANE. Uncle Maurice. Do you dislike me?

MAURICE. Goodness no. (*Pause.*) Er . . . I find you a shade pompous sometimes. D'you see? A trifle over-serious. (*Pause.*) Your commendable devotion to the sick leaves you a touch humourless when sporting with the er . . . when sporting with the *well*.

JANE. Who said they were sick? Or us well? I see. (*Pause.*) You?

MAURICE. Do restrain her, Herbert.

JANE. You bloody hidebound narcoleptic!

Pause.

MAURICE. Eh? Narcoleptic? That sounds like something most dreadfully vile –

HERBERT. It's what Eddie calls your 'dormouse syndrome', Maurice. People have always ribbed you about your way of dropping off. They don't like it you see. It must make them feel unwanted.

MAURICE. Oh. Well if it's only that.

MAURICE *picks up his newspaper and spreads it over his face.*

JANE. He shouldn't be frightened of dying. I don't think he ever will.

MAURICE *lifts the paper.*

MAURICE. You'll see –

He puts it over his face again. HERBERT *is sidling towards the whisky. As his hand reaches for the bottle:*

JANE. Are you on a bender, Dad?

Pause.

HERBERT. I thought . . . well a nip or so. Before your Mother – eh?

He pours a drink and heads back to his chair.

HERBERT. After all, Jane dear. You did say that *alcoholism* isn't very amenable to psychiatric ministration. (*Drinking.*) Thank God.

JANE *goes to him.*

JANE. You're as tight as a cat's ass-hole on the subject of Mother. Why did you marry her?

Pause.

HERBERT. It wasn't so much a shot-gun wedding as a safe-blast affair. (*Pause.*) Quite nice though. Lots of champagne.

Pause.

JANE. How come?

HERBERT. Well. Her father had this town house somewhere behind Harrods. (*Pause.*) One weekend they were all supposed to be in the country. Early Sunday morning, in goes Shankers – and wham! A lovely quiet job, really. (*Pause.*) But what's-her-name was up in town for a party and caught me.

JANE. Actually caught you?

HERBERT. 'Discovered' would be more exact. Of course I could have biffed her on the nose and scarpered. But we got to talking, you see. Some of the young nobs were like that in the Thirties. I suppose that's what accounted for that spate of ghastly romantic who-dunnits, with some charming bounder running rings round glum detective inspectors. (*Pause.*) No one could resist a burglar from a really good family in those days.

JANE. Love at first bang?

HERBERT. Oh I couldn't say I love her. What I felt was more like benevolent cynicism. (*Drinks.*) She was pretty good cover don't you see.

JANE. She became your *accessory?*

HERBERT. Put it like this. She joined the struggle against fascism. Bags of people in her set were doing it. Shall we say it was their way of fiddling whilst Jarrow marched.

There is a long, loud snore from MAURICE.

JANE. And Uncle Maurice?

HERBERT. Uncle Maurice . . . (*Strong French accent.*) typiquement . . . was burrowed in the South of France with his back turned to world events. The poor fellow never had a head for politics. Somebody once asked him what he thought about

Trotsky. He said that he, personally, Maurice Shanklin, thought a chap so frequently bowled for a duck in his first over should have taken up politics.

JANE. I'm beginning to like the sound of Mother!

HERBERT. A pretty woman. Fond of parties. She loved making exotic exits. (*Drinking, whilst going to refill his glass.*) She once pulled the German Ambassador's nose and jumped out of a first floor window. (*Pause.*) Naturally, she had some chaps outside holding a blanket. But no one knew. (*Pause.*) Oh yes . . . tremendous exits but dreadful entrances. She never knew how to *enter* a room gracefully.

The door opens and ELEANOR *enters, pushing* WHEELER *in his chair. She is followed by* LEE (*alias* SWIFT ARROW), *a Red Indian. He in turn is pushing* EDDIE *in front of him – bound and gagged.*

LEE *is dressed urbanely, in dark suit and tie, white shirt. He is in his early thirties.*

ELEANOR *is expensively if rather conventionally dressed, and is about fifty-five.*

ELEANOR. How time stands still! You had a glass in your hand the last time I saw you, Herbert.

HERBERT'*s glass falls from his fingers. There is a moment of stunned silence all round.* WHEELER *moves his head from side to side in what one might call questioning disbelief.* LEE *pushes* EDDIE *into a chair.*

ELEANOR. And this is surely our darling Jane! Do give me a kiss, my dear.

She flutters to JANE, *who submits to a peck on either cheek. Then to* HERBERT.

Herbert! (She embraces him.) There! Now you can find another glass and go on drinking.

HERBERT. Er . . . (*He points at* LEE *vaguely.*)

ELEANOR. That's Swift Arrow. Swift Arrow, I want you to meet
my husband – I should say of course *ex*-husband Herbert. And
our daughter Jane. And – well that torpid heap under the
newspaper is my brother-in-law Maurice. A hopeless person.
Not to be woken up if it can be avoided.

LEE. Hi.

JANE. All we need now is the goddamn U.S. Cavalry. Would you
kindly untie my friend Eddie?

LEE. Right on, Sister –

> *He proceeds to remove Eddie's gag and the old clothes line
> which is binding his arms. As he does so, to the room at large:*

Mrs Jimenez gets carried away. Name on my passport's Lee.
Lee McGuire.

HERBERT. Mrs Jimenez? Lee McGuire? It's all most confusing.

ELEANOR. I'll have you know he's a real Red Indian!

HERBERT. Any particular tribe?

LEE. Algonquin.

HERBERT. I thought that was a hotel in New York.

ELEANOR. Precisely where we met – wasn't it, Lee?

JANE. Don't you call him 'Swift'?

> MAURICE *slowly removes the newspaper from his face and sits
> up, looking round bemusedly.*

MAURICE. Would anyone care to . . . dare one ask? To explain?

> ELEANOR *crosses to* MAURICE *and pumps his limp hand.*

ELEANOR. Maurice!

WHEELER. You see, that maniac (*Nodding towards* EDDIE.) had
just taken me to the toilet. And then –

> EDDIE *is now free and very angry.*

EDDIE. Them two freaks comes through the front door, and *this* one (*He glares at* LEE.) grabs me before I can get Wheeler into the kitchen and call me mate with the van. What's it all about?

HERBERT (*quite adrift now*). Jimenez?

ELEANOR. My second two husbands were South American, Herbert. Jimenez had something to do with Bolivian tin. (*Pause.*) Nasty little man, so it turned out. (*Pause.*) Things *here* seem a little complicated –

EDDIE. You walk in here with that bloody Red Indian mugger and *you* call things complicated!

Pause.

MAURICE. They came *through* the front door? You imply they can pass through solid matter, Mr Bone?

ELEANOR. The bell didn't work thirty odd years ago, Maurice, and it doesn't work now. We simply – entered. Despite the bizarre spectacle confronting us, Lee kept his head –

EDDIE. And gagged mine!

LEE. It seemed kind of advisable to immobilize the disturbing elements first.

WHEELER. For a Red Indian, he ain't so red – is he?

ELEANOR. And what (*Pointing at* WHEELER.) is this wretched creature?

HERBERT. Oh he's . . . er . . . a friend of mine.

WHEELER. He's lying.

ELEANOR (*to* LEE). Have they all gone mad?

LEE. I guess so.

MAURICE. Speaking for myself, sir. I am woefully sane. We *do* have a psychiatrist on the premises if you are not feeling well yourself. (*He indicates* JANE.) What you have blundered in on is, so to speak, a not uncommon type of occurrence in this house.

ELEANOR *crosses to* JANE.

ELEANOR. A psychiatrist, dear? What on earth for? I thought it was all old hat nowadays. I thought it was all primal screams, and encountering and things. (*To* LEE.) Isn't that right, Lee? Isn't that what we did at that place on the West Coast? People over *there*, Jane my love, well they seemed awfully *down* on what they called . . . well I should say they referred to my own experiences in a nursing home as 'institutionalised violence'. (*Pause.*) I never quite knew what they meant. But I loved all the stroking and breathing. So did Lee.

JANE (*to* LEE). You did?

LEE. I've done some goofy things in my time for three meals a day.

ELEANOR. Oh *Lee!*

JANE (*to* ELEANOR). Why did you run out on me in Eureka?

ELEANOR. I was bored with you, darling.

JANE. *What?*

ELEANOR. All you did was perform your . . . your natural functions and scream.

WHEELER. Christ! I wish I was back in the nick –

LEE. Can we just work out in what precise way who is sort of related to whom?

JANE. For a start we could find out what she's come here for! Not to mention bringing a goddamn Algonquin Indian from the Algonquin Hotel. What *is* the place these days? A reservation?

LEE. We couldn't make it on Alcatraz.

JANE. What were you trying to make?

LEE. The white man stole our lands. They moved us from the graves of our ancestors. They slaughtered the buffalo.

MAURICE. I shouldn't let it get you down. Till the Norman Conquest, England was continually being overrun . . . then there were all sorts of wars. Bloody old Cromwell, the empire . . . no bloody end to it. (*Pause.*) I thought Alcatraz was a jail –

LEE. We seized Alcatraz Island, making an honourable offer. Twenty-four dollars in glass beads and red cloth. Of course, we know this to be more than was paid for Manhattan Island; but we appreciate that land values have risen over the years.

And what more suitable for an Indian Reservation by the
white man's own standards? That is to say: isolated from
modern facilities; no fresh running water; inadequate sanita-
tion; no health care; no education facilities; the population has
always exceeded the land base – and always been held as
prisoners, kept dependent on others. (*Pause.*) We re-claimed
the island, Mr Shanklin, in the name of all American Indians
by right of discovery.

MAURICE. Bravo! What happened?

LEE. The white imperialists cut off the public utilities. We seek
other tactics now.

MAURICE (*to* ELEANOR). Is he real? What do you do, Mr
Arrow?

LEE. McGuire.

MAURICE. Mr McGuire.

LEE. Anthropologist. (*He looks round.*) Seems like you need one
around here. (*Pause.*) Elly – you didn't warn me.

ELEANOR. Lee, do get the bags up. Would you, darling?

> LEE *stares at her for a long moment, then exits.* HÈRBERT *has
> been consistently drinking throughout. Now he begins to sing in
> a quavering voice.*

HERBERT. Love's last word is spoken, chérie
        Now the spell is broken, chérie . . .

His voice trails away before a barrage of glares.

EDDIE. Do I fix Wheeler or don't I? After the way I been treated –
honestly, Jane. Old Broken Arrow isn't the only one who
wasn't warned!

WHEELER. Here here!

ELEANOR. Are you *laughing* at Swift Arrow? Are you a racist,
Mr – ?

EDDIE. Bone.

ELEANOR. Are you?

EDDIE. No lady. I'm an out of work machinist. An Ireland-for-

the-Irish-an'-everywhere-else-the-same man. An autodidact. A
gate-crasher. An orphan. A –

WHEELER. What's an auto . . . auto – ?

EDDIE (*leaning over him*). I am self-taught, Wheeler. I have also
worked for Wandsworth Borough as a dustman, and I am
definitely going to dispose of you this time. (*He pushes the
chair towards the door.*) You know them new type rubbish
trucks with the grinders, Wheeler? They'll take anything and
chew it out like candy floss.

> *At the door, he stops stupefied as* LEE *enters carrying a buffalo's
> head on a stick.* MAURICE *holds the newspaper just above his
> face.*

MAURICE. Once in Venice I saw a dwarf chasing a cross-eyed
whore through a gathering of anarchists. These persons wanted
to dam the Grand Canal and turn it into a Marina for the sole
use of beggars. Meanwhile, a clutch of nuns was being fired
upon by the police, who were under the mistaken impression
they were communists in drag. A bomb went off in front of the
Doges' Palace. A fountain began to spout sewage. Mussolini
passed by in a large black car, eating water melon and spitting
pips into the hands of waving admirers. (*Pause.*) I can reliably
inform you those were monotonous times compared with now.
I beg your silence, your indulgence and your departure. (*He
lowers the paper onto his face.*)

JANE. Why are you here, Mother?

ELEANOR. I think . . . something to do with light, my dear.

JANE. Divine, Festival of – or electric?

> *There is a huge, blinding magnesium flash.*

Curtain

ACT TWO

The ACTORS *remain in the same positions as the end of Act One. Most of the furniture and props have gone – the buffalo stick remains.* LEE *is dressed in skins – and a headband with a single feather. He has a bow and a quiver of arrows on his back.* WHEELER's *chair lies on its side with him in it.* MAURICE *in another chair, reaches for his newspaper.*

EDDIE. Now what was that bloody great flash?
MAURICE. This isn't The Times!

Nonetheless he puts it over his face.

ELEANOR. I imagine it was a cosmic snapshot, Mr Bone. That was before and this is after. Crisis is no excuse for want of logic. (*Looking round.*) There appears to have been a furniture removal.

LEE *is examining his clothes, his bow and arrows.*

LEE. There appears to have been a change of clothing! And why me? (*He looks at them.*) I guess if some people changed into their rightful gear they'd be wearing coffins! (*Pause.*) Somebody want me to be the joker? The clown? The *Indian* clown? (*Pause.*) I shall meditate on this indignity. (*He squats.*)
HERBERT. They've taken the booze as well –
MAURICE (*moaning from under the paper*). Oh, Shankers . . . Shankers.

ELEANOR. Personally I feel distinctly peculiar and I wish I were back in Vermont. Mr Bone – you might at least set your friend's chair back on its little castors.

EDDIE does so. He also removes WHEELER'*s gag and. unties his bonds.*

WHEELER. I can't see. There's all spots and wiggles in front of me eyes. What the hell was it? Shankers been having a go at the wall safe?

They all turn to look at the safe. A thin trickle of smoke begins to emerge from it.

HERBERT. Of course I haven't. (*He goes to look at the safe.*) If I had – the door would have been off I can assure you. (*He sniffs the smoke.*) It doesn't smell of anything. Just a sort of . . . visible draft.

The smoke stops. From a bowl in front of the buffalo stick, a trickle of incense vapour begins to rise. This is viewed by all with consternation.

WHEELER. Why has everything changed? What's he (*Pointing at* LEE.) dressed up like Geronimo for? What's caused it? (*Pause.*) Nuclear war?

ELEANOR. What an interesting atomic bomb it would be, Mr Wheeler, which was so curiously selective in its choice of things to vaporize!

WHEELER. There's got to be a reason.

ELEANOR. Don't be a philistine. Change without reason or cause may boggle the minds of philosophers. I should think for most ordinary mortals it's a day to day problem. They blunder from birth to death in a state of utter bewilderment about the whole thing. *We* must do the same. (*Pause: thoughtfully.*) No doubt after a revolution, for example, the dispossessed have a very similar problem.

EDDIE. I'll bet things are the same inside that thick head of yours,

Wheeler. It's the outside that's changed. You've got an insecure ego, Wheeler. That's what you've got. Can't adjust. I'm not surprised. If you'd stayed in Chiswick and blended with your surroundings, you'd be fine. (*Pause.*) For one thing you wouldn't be here.

WHEELER. I bleedin' well am, though.

EDDIE. You sure?

LEE *goes to kneel in front of the incense bowl.*

ELEANOR. I think – fortitude would seem to be required.

LEE. Chief Tecumseh, 1812: In view of questions of importance we have met together in solemn council tonight. Nor should we debate here whether we have been wronged and injured, but by what measures we should avenge ourselves. For our merciless oppressors are still making attacks on those of our race who have as yet come to no resolution. Nor are we ignorant by what steps and by what gradual advances the whites break in upon our neighbours. Are we not being stripped day by day of the little that remains of our ancient liberty? Do they not even now kick and strike us as they do their black-faces? How long will it be before they will tie us to a post and whip us, and make us work for them in the cornfields? (*Pause.*) Think not, Brave Choctaws and Chickasaws, that you can remain passive and indifferent to the common danger, and thus escape the common fate. You people too, will soon be as falling leaves and scattering clouds before their blighting breath. (*Pause.*) Shall we wait for that moment or shall we die fighting before submitting to such ignominy? (*Standing.*) On the other hand, folks, some of us will not be 'white nosers' or Uncle Tomahawks. And I must say, having taken in a couple of books and plays on the Indian tragedy in various forms by whites – I kind of laugh. My God the compassion! The insight! The indignant, articulate rage on our behalf. (*Pause.*) I vomit. (*Pause.*) I study anthropology so as to study these people. This tribe of whites which studies *us*. (*Sneering.*) Your time has sure come, white man.

HERBERT. Mr McGuire. I have no ethnic prejudices whatsoever There's no point in making such ominous remarks. Since the occasion when I apologized to a black man in Oxford Street for *him* standing on *my* foot – I've decided against all forms of self-coercion.

LEE crosses to HERBERT and kicks his shin.

You aggressive red bugger!

LEE. Great.

He returns to a kneeling position by the incense bowl.

LEE. No more slob Indians: winos, drop-outs, misfits. (*Pause.*) No more jokers: no clowning. (*Pause.*) No more sell-outs, accepting anything Indian is dumb, usually filthy and immoral . . . so becoming a little brown American. (*Pause.*) No more ultra-pseudo-Indians: proud but phony. No angry nationalists: bitter and abstract. (*Pause.*) Oh, this white kid she came to Alcatraz. Her tight jeans. Her cassette player. Her round intelligent eyes and dumb mouth. Her nosy little tits and Mickey Mouse sweat shirt. (*Pause.*) 'Women' she said, 'women feel just the same you know, man'. (*Pause.*) Wow!

Singing: tune 'Red Flag'

From Alcatraz to Wounded Knee
A red-white chick she followed me.

JANE. Oh, Mommy! You a red-white chick? I'd say a kind of faded blue broiler.

ELEANOR. I shall ignore your vulgarity. The poor girl he refers to is now in prison. (*Turning to HERBERT.*) Perhaps we should ask your father to write her and pass on a few tips.

MAURICE (*standing*). I wish you'd all go away.

They begin to file off-stage.

Er . . . well not all, you know. Somebody might have the compassion . . . I mean, for a dying man? And who's taken my favourite chair? Bring it back at once. (*As the last of them exits.*) Parasites and fools. (*Pause.*) Anarchists? That's the explanation? (*Pause: shouting.*) Come back –

WHEELER *rushes on with a chair and places it carefully.*

WHEELER. There you are. That the one? That's a nice chair. It's a chair to encourage good posture and all that. (*Pause.*) Mr Shanklin –

MAURICE. Wheeler, you remind me of an obsequious ferret. Get out.

WHEELER *exits,* MAURICE *tests the chair, rocking it from side to side with one hand whispering.* Eleanor . . . Eleanor –

ELEANOR *enters with a stool. As* MAURICE *sits on the chair she places the stool beside him and sits.*

MAURICE. This is a crisis.
ELEANOR. As I remarked after it happened.
MAURICE. That bull's head thing –
ELEANOR. Yes?
MAURICE. And that . . . that bowl of incense –
ELEANOR. Yes?

Pause.

MAURICE. Well of course, I'm used to not catching on about what's happening around me. Only –
ELEANOR. What, dear?
MAURICE. All some kind of trick? A jolly jape? A spot of red magic? (*He giggles.*) Oh, I don't want to complain. I've seen some strange enough things in my life.
ELEANOR. Yes we have, haven't we, Maurice –
MAURICE. Er . . . eh? (*Pause: standing.*) I *am* unnerved. I *am* shattered. I've never known things change like *this* before –
ELEANOR Do sit down, Maurice. (*He does so.*) I think it must be people of our class and age, you know. Every now and then one sort of . . . wakes up to new surroundings without having

realized there was anything going on. (*Pause.*) Those of us who
are unworldly, at any rate. We should be thankful we are at
least all still here, with our health and wits.

MAURICE. Wits? People like Herbert? And Wheeler?

ELEANOR. To survive through incomprehensible changes,
Maurice, is a rare faculty. So much of oneself depends on
things remaining familiar. I remember once . . . staying with
friends in a remote place in Bolivia . . . there were shrieks and
howls and gunshots in the night. The house was surrounded by
ragged people, burning and destroying. (*Pause.*) We fled.
(*Pause.*) When we came back in the morning the house was
looted and gutted. (*Pause.*) My hostess took one look and started
screaming. She screamed until they got her into a hospital and
under sedation. (*Pause.*) I sat by her during the night, and in
the morning she said: I might as well be dead, now. (*Pause.*)
Her loss was the loss of things, and it shattered her mind.
(*Pause.*) I thought of the mob who did it. They were angry,
Maurice. Angry and despairing.

MAURICE. By light of magnesium flare?

ELEANOR. Really, Maurice! There's so much one doesn't understand that one might as well accept things and make the best
of them. (*Pause.*) If that seems to you an inadequate cliché in
the circumstances, remember the one with which you parted
from me the morning after we slept together.

MAURICE. Er . . . what?

ELEANOR. 'Ships in the moonlight' you said, as you closed the
door with a most shifty grin. (*Pause.*) Given the neon sign
outside our window, it was more like rowboats at high noon!

Pause.

MAURICE. Here now. Herbert must never know that you and I –

ELEANOR. Do you think he'd be agitated now? It was only once.

Unseen by them, HERBERT *strolls on with a glass of whisky.
He stands in shadow listening.*

MAURICE. Oh God. You made love so condescendingly.

ELEANOR. I was very nice to you.

MAURICE. You sang lewd songs and tickled me when I blushed. (*Pause.*) Mind you, I suppose they were quite good as an erotic ploy –

ELEANOR. Just clever parodies, my dear. I was dotty about Brecht in those days.

MAURICE. I only did it because . . . well, because I envied Herbert. Such a man of action, however eccentric. No morals. Cynical about human nature. A thief. A complete villain. Charming manners. (*Pause.*) What a Prime Minister he'd have made!

ELEANOR. I liked you because you were gentle and dreamy. (*Pause.*) So charmingly inept.

MAURICE. About this crisis –

ELEANOR. I'm as baffled as you are. (*Pause.*) Back in Vermont, you know, I was looking forward to such a peaceful autumn. I *refuse* to call it fall. I don't like the connotations of the word. But then, American is only a panic-stricken substitute for a lost language – isn't it? (*Pause.*) I used to think I wouldn't mind death in Vermont. Perhaps one day in my orchard, in a comfortable chair . . . with a book . . . and the fading sun. (*Pause.*) Don't you think we should retain the moral confidence of our immoral privileges?

MAURICE. Ah – the moral fabric. The sort of ethical warp and weft of things . . . it's vanished, Eleanor. People seem to do anything they like nowadays. Go to dreadful lengths. No more silver spoons from birth. Little girls more likely to be handed a dildo. (*Pause.*) D'you know I'm still half blinded by that damned flash.

ELEANOR. I'm sorry you are so weary, Maurice. My own life has been quite transformed by Lee. (*Pause.*) Dear Swift Arrow.

MAURICE. What was the damned feller doing in the Algonquin?

ELEANOR. He wasn't in it he was on it.

Pause.

MAURICE. Sending up smoke signals?

ELEANOR. He was a construction worker. Some of his people are good at heights, you see.

MAURICE. Vertigo unknown to the Indian? I thought he said he was an anthropologist –

ELEANOR. Yes, and working his way through college for his doctorate. I believe it's called 'Genocide and Guilt – a study of the death agony rituals in the male Caucasian'.

MAURICE (*pointing*). Does he carry that bull's head thing with him everywhere?

HERBERT *goes to the bull's head, pats it and exits.*

ELEANOR. I've never seen it before.

MAURICE. I've always had a sneaking *suspicion* that life is arbitrary. Oh well, no point in brooding. If somebody walks into a room and everybody gets their retinas scorched – that's life, I'd say.

He crosses to the buffalo, touches it gently.

Jolly beasts. Galloping round the prairies. Doing no harm. Virtual extinction round the corner. But I can't stand these sentimentalists who maunder about such things. Everything has to go. And if the bloody business happens piecemeal – well what else is time for? Soon be our turn. That's why I sleep so much. It's a kind of training. A catwink, a nap, a snooze . . . rather puts death in its place for a while. (*Pause.*) If one weren't scared shitless.

ELEANOR. It would have been pleasant, to end one's life in Vermont –

MAURICE. With Lee-stroke-Swift?

ELEANOR. Oh I suppose he would have gone his way soon enough. But at least he isn't mercenary. (*Pause.*) One day quite suddenly I thought to myself: you've enjoyed life so much, but you'll

soon be alone. Go to England. Comfort Herbert. Be kind to
Maurice. Be a mother to Jane. If they will let you.

MAURICE. After thirty-odd bloody years?

ELEANOR. I can see that it is you who perhaps have most need of
me.

MAURICE. Eleanor. What I have need of is immortality. Nothing
grand. Nothing ambitious. Nothing squalidly egotistical. Just
a wee, small but infallible nostrum to stop me actually dying.
Some sort of truce with the Great Cosmic Engineer. Can you
manage that, Eleanor? Get Him to leave me alone and I'll do
the same in return.

ELEANOR. I didn't know you were a believer, Maurice.

MAURICE. It's precisely my trouble that I'm not. If I were, I
wouldn't even get hung up about Hell. After all, who could
have led a more blameless life than a man who quietly snored
his way through it? Of course, people had a nasty way of
waking me up with the latest bad news – but that wasn't my
fault. I'm not exactly one of the levers of history, am I? I could
have cheerfully zizzed my way through any catastrophe –
human or natural.

*He gives a contemptuous push at the buffalo's head. There is a
long, loud roar. For a moment* MAURICE *is riveted with fright.
Then he smiles slyly.*

You hear that bloody great roar?

ELEANOR. I didn't hear anything at all.

MAURICE. I thought not. (*Pause.*) It looks as if they can do
anything, doesn't it? Any kind of trick with tape recorders . . .
lighting . . . gadgets –

ELEANOR. They?

MAURICE. Oh, can't you take a joke, Eleanor? *I* didn't hear
anything. (*Pause.*) I only try to amuse. To get you *properly*
involved –

ELEANOR. You don't think I am? You have no sense of the poetry of life, Maurice. You feel like a mere thing, so you want everything and everyone else to be just a thing.

MAURICE *shrugs and exits.* LEE *enters.*

LEE. The bull roared.

JANE *enters.*

JANE. It – roared?

ELEANOR. Of course it did. Uncle Maurice is much, much preoccupied by death, children. He scares so easily. His nanny must have been one of those things-that-go-bump-in-the-night people.

LEE. It would be easier to face death with dignity if he had lived.

JANE. People aren't worthless because they're sad, and defeated.

LEE. So then. Is he of *worth?*

ELEANOR. *I* can't judge. Who can? (*Pause.*) The silly man. What irks him is precisely that he's done nothing with his life. A few paintings. Well they had their vogue, certainly. But. (*Pause.*) He was so aloof from everything that I could never understand why he *did* paint. Why bother? (*Pause.*) I used to tickle him, and pull his nose, and say: at least have a good time, Maurice! He tolerated me. No more. It is Herbert, he used to say, who has the perverse energy – hah! (*She clicks her fingers.*) The zip! The zing! (*Imitating* MAURICE.) The Shanklins, er er er . . . merchants under Cromwell, bigots under Victoria, and fools under the stars at all times. (*Still imitating.*) Er er er . . . stars, did I say? Large, meaningless, twirling volumes of hot gas. E equals MC squared. Er er er. (*Pause.*) He'd nod off muttering such fancies. (*Pause.*) And now he thinks I'm nothing but a whimsical middle-aged woman. Old, really. For a woman. And so he can dismiss me like all else. (*Pause.*) Dismiss me – yet he's the one who actually walks away.

MAURICE *re-enters.*

MAURICE. A few paintings? They were agony! I hated abstraction and I was bored by life. I was meaninglessly obsessed with altering the surface of a piece of canvas. That's all. Relation, texture, weight, light – I had this insane passion to juggle them about, without knowing why. (*Pause.*) I was quite cynical about my puerile activities.

He exits.

ELEANOR. Now he's hurt.

JANE. Are you surprised? (*Pause.*) Well, I guess you're not, are you, mother? And do you care? Well, I guess you don't. Not if that old man's heart is *shaking!* Put your arms round him? No. (*Pause.*) Listen just how did you walk away from me? I mean, like was I in my cot? My carriage? Was I asleep? Did you cry? Did you make a production out of it or did you go modestly and guiltily? Did you screw the guy you went off with that night? (*Pause.*) Did you *mourn?*

ELEANOR. Come, Jane. Let me put my arms round you. Don't look so fierce. (*Pause.*) Yes, I know. It's unnatural for a mother to abandon her child. (*Pause.*) Darling, you frightened me. Don't you see? You were such an *angry* baby. And I wanted to hit you sometimes. I wanted to beat your screaming head to pulp. (*Pause.*) So I thought it best to go.

LEE *resumes his former position by the stick.* JANE *goes to her mother.*

JANE. Mommy! In Eureka California, goddammit?

ELEANOR. Does it matter where? It would have been equally grave in El Paso.

JANE (*looking round*). Do you have the feeling somebody's manipulating this situation?

ELEANOR. Not at all. No. That's something in life which really annoys me. When people turn round and say: you made me . . . I had to . . . they made me. And so on. Just an excuse for irresponsibility and moral cowardice. (*Pause.*) I wish you'd sit down, Jane. What a tall girl you are!

JANE (*sits, pointing at* LEE). What's he all about? You sail in here and I must say – you expect a lot.

ELEANOR. A lot of what?

JANE. It never occurred to you I might feel violent about you?

ELEANOR. Of course it did. It's quite natural. I suppose you're full of theories about that sort of thing. What does Mr Bone say? I presume you two co-habit? (*Pause.*) Lee, she's crying!

LEE. White squaw, she in pain – huh? You want me make Indian talk? (*In a normal voice.*) Jane, baby – don't cry. It's pointless. There's no consolation to be had.

> ELEANOR *sits beside* JANE.

ELEANOR. Jane dear. Are you inconsolable? I only wanted to take you away from the bombing, child. I wonder *why* people become psychiatrists? (*She taps* JANE'*s knee.*) Dry your eyes and tell me. Can you honestly say it ever helped anyone?

JANE. I could throttle you!

ELEANOR. Honey –

JANE. It wasn't because I was an angry baby – you bitch!

ELEANOR. Honey –

JANE. Honey, it was because you are wholly, and entirely, and without mercy, at the centre of your own fickle disgusting life. The way you talk to us! You're really vain and hard and dull – but intent on glittering. You pronounce on us all in those hypocritically gracious tones. But you're a tight-ass.

ELEANOR. Darling –

JANE. Darling, you're so withered and dry and bile-ridden inside that you need to come out, sweet, don't you? Well, that you're not. And I'd like to see you cut down. Spliced. I'd like to see you skewered. Whilst no doubt that little charmer voice of yours would go tinkling on . . . and tinkling on –

> JANE *seems about to break down, but is containing herself.*

ELEANOR. And you *want* me to feel guilty?

JANE. *Yes!*

ELEANOR. It sounds dangerously unprofessional.

JANE swoops off her chair and throttles ELEANOR, *who submits without a struggle. When she is supine:*

LEE. Well now. How about that?

He goes to ELEANOR *and gently holds her head for a moment. Calling out.*

Herbert –

HERBERT *enters with whisky bottle and glass.*

How about that, Herbert?

HERBERT. D'you know, there's nothing in *my* room either. (*Pause.*) Well, only three very insolent mice. (*Pause.*) Chewing a telegram they were. (*Pause.*) I rescued a fragment – it said 'gum'. Perhaps only the end of a word. How many words end in 'gum'. (*Pause.*) Begum? (*Pause.*) I knew a man in New York whose son was a poet. Stoned out of his mind all the time. Well, this poet had reduced his entire lyrical statement about life to one word. Gum. (*Pause.*) Any connection? (*Crossing to* ELEANOR'*s body.*) Still. Plenty of booze though. (*Musing.*) Telegrams from poets? Not a chance. (*Pause.*) Land values going up. Property rows brewing. (*Pause.*) Well, if they can build a new town on my boodle they can bloody well do anything, I suppose. Shamming, is she? (*He touches* ELEANOR *with his foot.*) Hysterics?

JANE. I just strangled her.

HERBERT. No, no. Impossible. She hasn't had a pee yet. Eleanor always tended to faint when her need for a pee became urgent.

JANE. Father. I had my bloody hands round her throat.

Pause.

HERBERT. Maurice is sitting in *his* room looking quite stunned. Stunned into wakefulness, I imagine. (*Pause.*) It must be a

novel experience for him. (*Pause.*) I think the truth is, Maurice
would like to make some eloquent gesture before he kicks the
bucket. I think he'd have liked to build a pyramid . . . or a
fucking great bridge over some bay or other. (*Pause.*) Some
people just can't go out without a sense of dignity. However
spurious.

LEE *squats beside* ELEANOR.

LEE. I liked her, you know? You know what I mean?

HERBERT. Why are Americans always saying 'you know what I
mean' instead of saying what they mean? It's caught on over
here too. Damned irritating. A substitute for mental effort.
(*Pause.*) You liked her, did you? (*Pause.*) Since Buchenwald
I've got hazy about that word like. (*Pause.*) You'd think to
survive that place would make one thankful to be alive. Grateful.
And I suppose many were. (*Pause.*) For me, the world had
turned into a bad imitation of something I could never quite
remember. Something that lay on the borders of the memory.
(*Pause.*) Do I mean life seemed purposeful before? (*Pause.*)
It's as if one spent the first act of a play getting to the theatre –
and once inside for the second act, one were preoccupied with
trying to imagine the first. Buchenwald was an intervening
disaster of such magnitude that those who couldn't cherish
life afterwards . . . perhaps they could at the most . . . endure
it. Nothing else.

LEE. Herbert. Didn't you ever miss your wife?

HERBERT. Sexually?

LEE. Any goddamn way.

HERBERT. No, I don't think so. Awfully busy during the war.
And then afterwards I couldn't think what she and I had been
all about. I do recall that she wasn't magnificent in bed. Used
to act it, really. Her set had made such a thing of not being
inhibited. The result was, some of them were lustful without
being erotic. When it came down to it, I believe Eleanor
regarded it as the price she had to pay for having other kinds

of fun. (*Pause: he looks down at* ELEANOR.) Possibly an unconscious puritan. What about that, Jane, eh? Unconscious. Right up your street.

He takes a step towards the Prompt Corner and bends his head.

Yes?

PROMPT. Yes.

HERBERT. I meant 'yes' – you wily sod – as what's the line.

Pause.

PROMPT. The line is 'yes'.

HERBERT. Oh, fart! (*Pause.*) Yes?

PROMPT. Do you mean is it 'oh fart' after 'yes'?

Pause.

HERBERT. I think I shall go back to my evening paper.

WHEELER *enters, pushing a pneumatic drill on the sort of trolley used for baggage at airports.*

WHEELER. I'm going after that boodle, Shankers –

HERBERT. I wouldn't, if I were you.

WHEELER. I want a map – see?

HERBERT. A map of where? Peru?

WHEELER. Honest, I'll do you, Shankers, if I don't get me map.

HERBERT. But, dear slug – the money rests beneath a launderette. (*Pause.*) Or is it a pedestrian precinct?

WHEELER. I want it –

HERBERT. Such avarice! (*Pause.*) Come along then. (*He crosses to* ELEANOR'*s body.*) Eleanor – a little drinky? Whilst we trace the location of that crock of gold?

She rises and he takes her hand. They exit, followed by WHEELER. EDDIE *enters.*

EDDIE (*to* LEE). Do you box?

LEE. Some.

EDDIE. Netball?

LEE. Some.

EDDIE. A pretty atheletic sort of chap.

LEE. I guess so.

EDDIE. Well, I wish you'd go after Wheeler. I've a feeling he's done his nut. I think the man's in a panic. Lost his bearings. Unsure of his whereabouts. There's Celtic blood in Wheeler. He's got his fey side. He has to be either forced or carefully instructed. Let him rush off on his own and he's in trouble. Especially with a pneumatic drill. (*Pause.*) I'm beginning to like him. Don't you think that's nice? I'm fond of Herbert. Split me sides over Maurice. I love Jane. And I'm beginning to like Wheeler. (*Pause.*) Have either of *you* any poetry in you?

JANE. I thought I'd just killed my mother. Could have sworn it. Then she got up and left with Dad. He'd got a bottle of whisky and wasn't making much sense.

EDDIE. There's something amiss. (*Lights a cigarette.*) Take . . . (*Pointing at* LEE.) Take him, now. A quick change artist. A change of gear – provocative. But he doesn't give much away. No whoops and war dances. No go in him, really. (*He walks round the buffalo stick.*) I don't believe in mysteries. It's not even a totem pole. Just a stuffed head on a bit of wood. I *hope* it's stuffed. (*Bends to smell.*) Would you care to shed a bit of light, Chief?

LEE (*bowing his head*). My people live in darkness.

EDDIE. Blind as bats are they?

Pause.

LEE. They are sad.

He exits.

EDDIE. Funny sort of cove –

Pause.

JANE. You said a minute ago – that you love me.

EDDIE. So I did.

Pause. JANE *begins to walk slowly in a circle.*

JANE. Do you like this garden?
EDDIE (*looking round*). Yeh. It's quiet. I like the smell of it.
  (*Pause.*) I like them olive trees.
JANE. Come and sit by the stream –

She sits. EDDIE *joins her.*

It's love, then.
EDDIE. That's it.
JANE. Romantic.
EDDIE. Yeh.
JANE. The old kind.
EDDIE. The old kind.
JANE. For always.
EDDIE. Till the grave.
JANE. Fidelity.
EDDIE. Yes.
JANE. Worlds away.
EDDIE. Innocent.

*They embrace and kiss, fondling each other. It must be very
gentle and seem almost slow motion.* MAURICE *enters and
stands watching them.*

MAURICE. I'm not one of those who can love. It isn't a lack of
  feeling . . . the yearning to love. (*Pause.*) What passes for it
  nowadays? On the rare occasions when I meet the young, they
  seem unhappy. As if their very freedom has left them blunted
  and unsatisfied. (*Pause.*) Small, mindless convulsions –

EDDIE *gets up and goes to him. As he speaks,* JANE *exits.*

EDDIE. I displayed no sign of reluctance. I fancied her all right.
  I didn't hang back. People don't waste time these days. Yes or
  no. On or off. Take it or leave it, we can get it anywhere. No
  obligation. Nothing's permanent. (*Pause.*) But the birds still

get sad. You see in their eyes when you nip off afterwards. If they could admit . . . what's in their eyes is: hope. Have you noticed they talk more about their right to sexual freedom – should they raise the subject at all – than their right to anything beyond it? So what I think – all the old stuff is still there underneath. Makes *me* sad, it does. The heart of the male pig in me bleeds.

MAURICE. Well . . . she – she's a vulnerable young woman, Mr Bone.

EDDIE. I feel subjugated. The male as object. Guilty. Conditioned to be what women expect of me. Think of the gross exploitation of my sex by women's grasp of the principles of male domination –

MAURICE. You know, years ago in Bloomsbury –

EDDIE. I feel my cock is an offence against the universe –

MAURICE. The Bloomsbury . . . group? Set? How they pursued their selfish notions of personal freedom! I was just an observer, of course. Whose fault? One almost hated them. Their endless affaires . . . their endless letters to each other. I never felt part of it. I was no asset . . . at a dinner table. I sat aching with shame and resentment.

EDDIE. I get the idea my cock is an offence against the universe. The things it gets up to. Like going *in* – eh? The vicious, arrogant, domineering ways of the organ!

MAURICE. Always been some kind of anachronism –

EDDIE. I speak to it at night –

MAURICE. But anachronism from what period?

EDDIE. Bone, I say to myself. None of that male sneering at women's struggle to throw off the shackles.

MAURICE. That's why I took the place in Cornwall. To get away from the obligation of seeming interesting.

EDDIE. But I must say. Knowing Jane, it's shown me the error of my ways –

MAURICE. I wonder if I was envious of those people? Their writing. Their diaries. Their cunning expertise in society –

EDDIE. I adore that woman. Worship the ground she walks on.

Pause.

MAURICE. I turned my back on it all.

He wanders off to sit beside the buffalo stick. EDDIE *begins to shadow-box.*

EDDIE. That – and that! And that that that! (*He stops still.*) Blows against fascism? (*Recommencing.*) That – and that! And that that that –

JANE *enters.*

EDDIE (*still again*). I adore that woman. Worship the ground she walks on.

JANE goes for him, slapping and thumping. EDDIE *submits, his hands over his head. After some seconds of this:*

Herbert –

HERBERT *enters.* JANE *subsides.*

HERBERT ⎫
         ⎬ *Jane!*
MAURICE ⎭

EDDIE. You see that? You witness that battering? Cor Christ! And I'm supposed to be a woman hater!

JANE. Which is clearly what you are.

EDDIE. Would you say that's true, Maurice?

MAURICE. I haven't the vaguest idea Mr Bone. I haven't thought about it. I've been preoccupied by your other distasteful qualities. (*Pause.*) But my . . . my conscience is stirring. (*Pause.*) Something tells me we must all look at each other again. Ask ourselves what we truly feel. (*Pause.*) For I confess . . . I believe we are all in extremis . . . in some way I cannot define. When will the car come? When shall we be led away tied and hooded? The machines humming, the electric wires put to our bodies. (*Pause.*) We shall cower there, forgetting that we once walked about freely .The absence of pain will be a faint memory, the sunlit world a dream. (*Pause.*) Notice. I warn you. We are at the limits of civilization, and we cannot see into the future.

He appears to go to sleep.

HERBERT. I'm sure you've no reason to attack Eddie, Jane. (*Holds up his whisky bottle.*) Let's all have a drink, shall we?

JANE. He . . . I . . . we –

EDDIE. I do the shopping and the launderette. And I expel wandering villains like Wheeler, don't I?

JANE. He sleeps with me. He lives for free here.

HERBERT. He buys walnuts to throw at the cuckoo clock. Only (*Looking round.*) we don't seem to have it any more. Or walnuts either.

JANE. He reads and thinks and talks about educating himself –

EDDIE. I do the washing up. I mow the lawn. I creep about doing all sorts of chores, trying not to wake up old Maurice.

JANE. And with it all, he's a bigoted, childish, mummy-sucking infant!

EDDIE. But very loving. (*Pause.*) Tender, I am.

JANE. Oh, *hell!*

HERBERT. Try this –

He takes out a revolver and gives it to her. She stands looking at it for a moment, then shoots EDDIE. HERBERT *takes the gun from her hand.*

EDDIE. There. Is that better?

MAURICE *gets up wearily.*

MAURICE. Bangs. Flashes of light. People wandering in and out. (*He makes to go, but turns before exiting.*) You know it's not true that I never exerted myself to care, to pursue civilized pleasures and endure the inevitable pains and heartaches with grace. (*Pause.*) I tried to be human. I simply failed. And there have been insults, ribald jests at my expense. The very people who sniggered at my painting, for example, never hesitated to enjoy my hospitality. They were a harder generation than my own. No doubt brutalized by the collapse of one civilization, and lacking the authentic vision of another. But still. Kindness has gone from the world. And thought for others . . . who appear to be crippled in some way . . . or comic in their vain-glory, their ineptitudes. So much has gone, and one sees why. But I do wish those of us who are, one might say, the decaying hulks . . . stranded with dimming eyes on the shores of *your* wretched monstrous continent of hates . . . one does wish you would permit us the final small privilege of eccentric withdrawal. Dismiss us and leave it at that. Do not humiliate us too. (*Pause.*) The young man is not dead, of course. I know that. I don't know what he *is*, being not dead. But will whoever or whatever is at work kindly withhold it from the consciousness of *this* old man? (*Pause.*) That would be charitable.

MAURICE *exits.* HERBERT *takes a drink from the bottle*

HERBERT. Do you think we could get the furniture and stuff back? If only for Maurice. I don't care for myself. (*Pause.*) I wonder, though. (*He goes to the wall safe.*) One last elegant demonstration, d'you think? Blow it ever so quietly. Minimum damage – maximum access.

JANE *kneels beside* EDDIE.

JANE. Why do we feel so violated? (*Pause.*) We bore you, fed you, soothed your cries and nightmares. (*Pause.*) We watch you put on uniforms and go out to war. (*Pause.*) We heal you and bury you. We grieve you and love you. Desperate with ourselves. Yes. The torn, mangled bodies make us cover our eyes. The starving raise their arms in supplication. (*Pause.*) We hear your martial music. We grimly notice your flags breaking the air with colour. (*Pause.*) It is not we who feed you to your machines, or cause you to blight the very earth . . . the corn . . . the rice . . . the air and water. (*Pause.*) No. (*Pause.*) We must refuse. We *shall* refuse.

EDDIE *reaches up and puts his arms round her. She lies beside him.* LEE *enters during the following song. He moves as if he is walking high up on some construction site – slow, sinuous, graceful.*

HERBERT. (*sings quietly*)
Swans sing before they die –
'twere no bad thing
Did persons die before they sing.

He watches LEE, *who finally becomes still.*

What do you want, Red Man? We are a post-imperial nation. We can always pretend to listen.

LEE. Up on one of those high rises –

HERBERT. I have personally always adhered to socialism and revolution.

LEE. High up over Manhattan –

HERBERT. Not coherently, I regret.

LEE. The wind blows . . . you tread careful –

HERBERT. But neither could I give allegiance to fools and charlatans. And worse, to cynical men with great human ideas between their teeth and lies at the back of their throats.

LEE. All we had from you was lies. Lies . . . and more lies.

HERBERT. What *does* dialectical mean?

LEE. Where my people hunted and fished – I can see no land. Only the city. (*Pause.*) Manhattan festering –

HERBERT. Never could quite grasp ideology. Only my feelings. (*Pause.*) Justice.

LEE. The city weighs heavy on the earth –

HERBERT. Yet I'm not afraid of revolution . . . only of men. (*Pause.*) The price can be terrible. (*Pause.*) When they make their decisions, the logic of history becomes the language of pain. (*Pause.*) What did one visualise? Nothing utopian. No. The transfer of power from one class to another. (*Pause.*) But then?

LEE. I never say much, Mr Shanklin. Sometimes an ancient phrase is breathed out of me.

HERBERT. When they make their decisions –

LEE. Words from vanished men . . . vanished tribes.

HERBERT. When they fill the prisons –

LEE. For centuries you crushed the world. It may be now the world will crush you.

HERBERT (*going to examine the buffalo head*). Funny sort of thing to carry in one's luggage.

LEE. The oppressed will pull a shroud over your incredulous faces. *You* will be cold. *You* will be hungry. *You* will be robbing each other for what remains of that carcass you took to be a living society. (*Pause.*) Yes sir, Mr Shanklin.

HERBERT. And you?

LEE. We shall stand aloof from your tragedy.

Pause.

HERBERT (*looking round*). D'you think we could get a wigwam in here?

He goes to examine the buffalo head. ELEANOR *enters.*

Eleanor – it's yours, is it not?

ELEANOR. What would *I* do with such a thing?

HERBERT. I shouldn't think they're easily come by. I'd even go so far as to say . . . if you hadn't come here, Eleanor, neither would *it*.

ELEANOR. Always blaming other people. You always did. You sent me away to America and then accused me of desertion. Why, even in the beginning you took my virginity and said I seduced you. (*Pause.*) I remember. (*Pause.*) I remember staring at the ceiling, with you on top of me. And thinking: Herbert will say it's all my fault. If I have a child, it will be my fault. And if I had rejected him, well just not wanting him would have been a fault in his eyes. Now Lee here –

HERBERT. Lee there?

LEE. Elly's been kindness itself to me, and I don't blame her for anything. How could I? She harms no one –

HERBERT. You must have been on to a good thing, over there in Vermont.

LEE. Elly and I were good to each other.

HERBERT. Sexually?

ELEANOR. You think it indecent, Herbert? I only take your vulgar question seriously because I pity you.

HERBERT. Can you imagine Wheeler drilling away beneath a launderette? What I didn't tell him was, it's a twenty-four hour service.

ELEANOR. Herbert. There are so many facile sneers about women such as I. My Chilean husband *was* older. He *was* rich. But I adored him and he taught me a great deal. He was even prophetic. He told me that one day a precarious justice would come to his country. And that when it did, it would be stillborn. It would be ruthlessly opposed by families like his own – which he despised. (*Pause.*) With Jimenez . . . the Bolivian . . . I went temporarily insane. Innocently, I repeated some of the things Carlos had taught me. Whenever I did so, Jimenez struck me across the mouth. Sometimes in public. I spent hours whimpering in corners because of his cruelty. He scathed and whipped me with insults. I became thin and hysterical, prone to sudden fits of laughter or screaming. (*Pause.*) One day, he was assassinated. (*Pause.*) I scarcely remember how I came to be in Vermont . . . with a big, gracious house . . . servants. (*Pause.*) On a trip to New York, Lee . . . found me. (*Pause.*) Life began to seem magical. Until the guilt . . . or whatever . . . brought me to your brother's house.

> HERBERT *crosses to her and moves his hand up and down in front of her eyes. She does not respond.*

HERBERT (*to* LEE). Gone into a trance – or what?

LEE. She seeks herself within herself.

> ELEANOR *goes to sit cross-legged in front of the incense bowl.*

HERBERT. Really? I expect it does require a bit of concentration. (*Pause.*) There's a lot of this mystical rubbish about these days.

LEE. You don't care to hear about her life?

HERBERT. Of course I don't. The woman's got no sense of humour. Oh, she used to be lively, you know. Mischievous. Full of pranks and all that. (*Pause.*) You'd think she'd realize that after somebody's been in Buchenwald, they . . . (*Pause.*) It was only a short spell. (*Pause.*) People who were in the camps, they're usually the ones who make the least of it. Anyway, the reasons for my own incarceration were too unlikely for anyone to take seriously.

LEE. My own people were imprisoned by history –

HERBERT. I wish you wouldn't be so solemn, old Arrow. (*Pause.*) Not that one doesn't sympathise. (*Pause.*) You'll be all right. She's keeping you, isn't she? I'd just jog along if I were you. (*Pause.*) God! If you had *my* problems!

> *That seems to remind him of something. He goes off, calling 'Wheeler' and again 'Wheeler'.* LEE *takes his bow and arrow. Just as* HERBERT *disappears into the wings,* LEE *shoots an arrow after him.* MAURICE *enters carrying a blue and white Chinese vase – one of the props from the set in the First Act.*

MAURICE. I caught some uncouth feller *handling* this. Actually handling it. A beautiful piece. I – now where did it go? (*He finds a place for it.*) Mr . . . er . . . if you'd put some less out-landish clothes on and *she'd* get up? Why *is* she squatting there?

LEE. She seeks herself within herself.

> *Pause.*

MAURICE. Oh? (*He walks round and round* ELEANOR.) Bloody incense still puffing away I see. Does it help? Jane used to burn the stuff. In your own room, I said. There, if you must. But nowhere else. The girl's had some mind-bending habits in her time. Of which Mr Bone is perhaps the most unfathomable. (*Pause.*) Can one take after one's mother when one's never known her? Something on the genetic side? Shouldn't think it was much fun, in Eureka California. (*He pinches* LEE's *sleeve* and bends towards him confidentially.) They've got one of my things in a San Francisco museum.

Note: not a gallery. A museum. Four by three. Oil on imprimed hessian. We used to give our things cheeky titles in those days. I do believe the *museum* piece was called: 'Nature Morte Au Mind of Observer'. (*Pause.*) Oh yes, we thought that sort of thing a terrific wheeze. Of course when painters started going *really* dotty the joke was obscured. People made their own jokes about it, if you catch me. We got to feel we'd lost control of the situation. (*Pause.*) Should we wake her up, or whatever you do to people who are seeking themselves?

LEE. I think it would be unkind.

MAURICE. Oh yes. Mustn't be unkind, must we? By the way, I have to ask you –

LEE. Yes?

MAURICE. Were you thinking of staying?

LEE. I wasn't thinking of anything at all.

Pause.

MAURICE. I say. Are you seeking yourself within yourself? With your eyes open? That'd be jolly clever. (*Putting his hand out.*) Shake –

He extends his hand to LEE. *They shake.* MAURICE *withdraws his, to find a broken egg dripping from his palm.*

I see.

He takes out a handkerchief to wipe his hand. JANE, EDDIE *and* HERBERT (*entering*) *gather round.*

Look at that. (*They all start laughing.*) Herbert, shake, will you?

HERBERT. Not bloody likely.

MAURICE. Shake, Shankers! Be done to as Mr Arrow would do. (*As* HERBERT *shakes his head.*) Wheeler then. Where's Wheeler?

> HERBERT *turns, calling 'Wheeler'. We see there is an arrow sticking in his back.* WHEELER *enters.*

WHEELER. I seen it –
MAURICE. You seen what?

> WHEELER *goes to* HERBERT *and pulls the arrow out, waving it. Then he stands looking from the arrow to* HERBERT *to* LEE.

WHEELER. I seen him shoot that. Into Shankers. (*Pause.*) It can't happen. No, for Chrissake! I seen him I did. (*He drops the arrow as if it were hot.*)

> ELEANOR *stands.*

ELEANOR. If we all just close our eyes –

> *They do so.* HERBERT *sings.*

HERBERT. The little duck, it is no swan
> It has no aspirations.
> Its universe is none the worse
> For being poor relations.

> Oh little duck, what can you do?
> Apart from shedding feathers –
> Your throaty quack will not bring back
> A lifetime's humble pleasures.

> *He opens his eyes.*

Anybody else got a song? A merry stanza? (*They open their eyes.*) You're a selfish lot.
WHEELER. Shankers – are you feeling well?
HERBERT. Perfectly, thank you.
WHEELER. No pains in the back?

HERBERT. Only the usual twinges.

WHEELER. I'm wrong then. Definitely wrong. I didn't mean to cause no trouble. Er . . . I've just remembered. Got to go. (*Pause.*) Got to get out of here. Got to try. Nothing to stop me. You walk in – you walk out. Easy. Just got to make your mind up.

MAURICE. Do try, Wheeler –

> WHEELER *makes a terrific sprint offstage. There is a crash and a yelp. He reappears, rubbing his knee.*

WHEELER. I made it! And fell flat on me face.

EDDIE. Where?

WHEELER. Me face.

HERBERT. I think the point is, Wheeler – where was your face? Where were you when you fell?

WHEELER. On the bloody landing. Where else? (*Pause.*) It's . . . er . . . it's great out there.

MAURICE. The man's demented.

WHEELER. No. I tell you. The last few times there was –

EDDIE. Who wants to know, Wheeler? Who cares? Who cares about *you?*

> Pause.

WHEELER. Nobody, I suppose –

EDDIE. Then bugger off.

> Pause.

WHEELER. I wish I could've –

ELEANOR. Yes?

WHEELER. I wish my life had been different. Wish I'd gone straight. Gone to church. Said me prayers. What's it say in the bible? Three score an' ten? Yes. Well. I haven't got long to go – have I? (*Pause.*) It's been a desert. (*Turning to go.*) An absolute bleeding desert from start to finish. (*Exits.*)

EDDIE. That's it, then. Wheeler made it. Poor bastard. Gives

you a bad conscience. Still. He was an unattractive little sod.
No talent for life and ugly with it. Won't change. Won't pull
himself together. He'll go out screaming, that one. When his
time comes. (*Pause.*) I think he'd have liked to rob the Bank
of England – you know? A job with a bit of ambition. Style.
(*Pause.*) What a hope!

> JANE *grabs his arm.*

JANE. I'm terrified.

EDDIE. You're just fine, you are. You've got real poise. Cool.
Bright. Won't take any bullshit from anybody.

JANE. I'm terrified.

EDDIE. You've got the best qualifications *I* ever came across –

JANE. For terror?

EDDIE. Come off it! Medical degrees and all that. Training.

JANE. I want to get married. I want an actual certificate of
marriage. I want a house. I want children. I want to give and
enjoy it. Be loved. Love. Rock the cradle. Stir the soup.
Attractive clothes. Keep my looks. Exist for you. Believe what
you believe. Accept what you accept. (*Pause.*) I've denied
myself. I want to be the most traditional sort of woman
imaginable. I want to be protected . . . and indulged . . . and
cossetted (*Pause*) In some remote place. Yes. An island. A
mountain. A beach. (*Pause.*) These longings!

> *Pause.*

MAURICE. A large canvas. Colour. Form. (*Pause.*) A stupendously
great idea!

> *Pause.*

LEE. Repossession. Dignity.

> *Pause.*

HERBERT. Gelignite!

EDDIE (*to* JANE.) You.

Pause.

ELEANOR. Just a few precious moments alone.

She moves downstage. The lights dim. A spot on her.

My own mother used to say: use your will power, Eleanor. But I don't know what is willed and what is not. Things just happen. Desire is not will. Action is not will. (*Pause.*) I became cunning, in the nursing home. (*Pause.*) That was before Vermont. (*Pause.*) I pretended to have stopped thinking the world a ruthless and violent plot against me. (*Pause.*) It's curious. They didn't mind my believing in God. But they *did* object – or at least they became patronizing and dissuasive – when I spoke of The Manipulator.

MAURICE. To create a sense of mass, on a two-dimensional surface –

LEE. The graves of my people –

ELEANOR. So I smiled, and said no more about it.

MAURICE. One beautiful . . . glowing . . . still . . . awe-inspiring picture. Only one –

JANE. The ache. The exhaustion. The impossibility, of going on with things as they are. (*Pause.*) Too much.

HERBERT. A little song? Something plaintive . . . and touching?

EDDIE. Do you like this garden?

ELEANOR. You should have heard some of their clichés. There's so much good in the world, Eleanor. So much beauty and kindness and . . . you name it, they said it. The meaning of life is life itself, Eleanor. You're still young, Eleanor. There's so much to live for. (*Pause.*) It would seem that a sense of evil denotes either a religious temperament or a disturbed mind. Neither of these explanations appealed to me. If The Manipulator has us locked in some incomprehensible, terminal struggle . . . that does not mean I ascribe to him the function of a disease. Why should I? Nor do I worry about who manipulates The Manipulator. (*Pause: she smiles.*) I am content with mystery.

The rest is not what we make it but what I would call the mundane poetry of what is going on.

A rising cacophony of sound: a montage of voices, political speeches, fragments of national anthems. Cars. Hooters. Machine guns. Pneumatic drills. Screams. Bombing. Bursts of pop music. Winds. Howling.

During this: the actors begin to huddle in the centre. The set is flown or dismantled as much as is technically feasible.

MAURICE. The white canvas. The first brushstroke. The long, lovely sweep of colour –

WHEELER *enters, almost crying with frustration.*

WHEELER. I didn't make it. I never could. I never –
HERBERT. The watch towers . . . the lights . . . the dogs –
JANE. He beats me, she said. He beats me –
EDDIE. A good life, a sound life in Chiswick –
HERBERT. What we *need* –
ELEANOR. Grace. Quiet. Contemplation. Oh, the autumn in Vermont –
HERBERT. Teeth –
MAURICE. Lust . . . disgusting –
WHEELER. Money!
JANE. Touch me. Touch me –
EDDIE. Afraid of what? Who's afraid?
HERBERT. A bundle of rags. A few bones. A human being –
MAURICE. My life –
JANE. Wasted.
EDDIE. My life –
JANE. Would you like to sit? Or will you lie on the couch?
WHEELER. I could never make no sense of it all –
HERBERT. Walnuts? Anyone got any walnuts?
MAURICE. Put the clock back, d'you see – ?
LEE. You have become a great people –

ELEANOR. Vermont –

LEE. And we have scarcely a place left to spread our blankets –

MAURICE. The arrogance –

HERBERT. The humiliation –

WHEELER. Get out of it, will you?

JANE. Depressed? Depressed? Then tell me –

HERBERT. Wounds –

JANE. *My* life!

MAURICE. Escalation –

JANE. Hysteria –

WHEELER. My bloody old age, blast you –

ELEANOR. The gentle in heart –

LEE. Be no longer their dupes –

MAURICE. Our need –

JANE. Desire! Can't you admit to one single desire?

HERBERT. Emptiness –

MAURICE. Darkness –

LEE. Our good father at Washington –

JANE. I won't! I won't!

LEE. Our God. The Great Spirit, seems also to have forsaken us –

EDDIE (*shouting.*) Quiet –

They huddle together around the buffalo stick.

TOGETHER (*singing*).
  Swans sing before they die
          'twere no bad thing
  Did persons die before they sing.

There is a long silence. The cuckoo clock begins to sound off.

Curtain

The Arcata Promise

THE ARCATA PROMISE was first presented by Yorkshire Television on 22 September 1974, with the following cast:

GUNGE   Anthony Hopkins

LAURA   Kate Nelligan

TONY   John Fraser

Director: David Cunliffe
Executive Producer: Peter Willes

Act One

1. **Exterior. Basement area.** *Steps leading to a small, cluttered well in front of a barred window. A door to one side. There are overspilling dustbins, an old bedstead, a rusting bicycle, empty bottles, etc.*

THEODORE GUNGE - *A tall, thin man of around thirty-five - stands swaying at the top of the steps.*

We hear a voice over, which is that of GUNGE's *alter-ego, called 'VOICE'. As the camera takes in the basement area:*

VOICE. This is the basement entrance of Theodore Gunge's town hovel. (*Pause.*) Filthy!

As camera pans up to GUNGE:

VOICE. And that is Theodore Gunge himself. (*Pause.*) Filthy.

GUNGE. I wish you'd shut up.

VOICE. Yes. But after all, I'm you as well.

GUNGE *begins to descend the stairs. Cut to:*

2. **Interior. Studio.** GUNGE *is dressed to play Richard II:*

RICHARD. Down, down I come; like glistering Phaeton, Wanting the manage of unruly jades. In the base court? Base court where kings grow base.

3. **Interior. Basement.** *A squalid, dingy room. A table with piles of used dishes and the remains of several tinned meals. Beer bottles. Glasses. Newspapers. A double divan with a heap of rumpled blankets.*

GUNGE *enters, closing the door behind him. He grabs a bottle of beer and flops on the bed.*

VOICE. Are we drunk?

GUNGE. Shut up.

VOICE. I like going out. But I wish we could go somewhere else besides the pub.

GUNGE. Can't you get on with the auto-biography or something? Occupy yourself. Stop wittering on. (*He faces the wall.*) I'm afraid to go out. Afraid I shall kill her.

VOICE. Not that again. Please. We're incapable of murder. Well. You may be but I'm not. So it's not a combination that leads to decisive action.

Pause.

GUNGE. There she is sitting in that bloody great office doing nothing and getting paid for it. My God! Through friends of mine, she -

VOICE. *Ex*-friends.

GUNGE. *Ex* then. Gets herself a flat, a job. Invited everywhere. Sleeping around. Psychotherapy - and who pays for that nowadays I wonder? (*Pause.*) Whilst I rot. Mentally fractured, emotionally paralysed and physically doomed.

VOICE. Everybody's doomed in the end.

GUNGE. Not usually in their prime, they're not. Oh no. There's still plenty of them out there getting on with it at my age. (*Pause.*) The bitch. Imagine. She spends three years getting a degree in sociology at my expense, and what then? A job answering the telephone in the office of the slug who produced my last film. I wonder what else she does for old Jacky-boy. I daren't speculate.

VOICE. No. And what do you do? Laura leaves you and you give up acting and everything else. (*Pause: wistfully.*) We're rich and famous, Theo. Can't we go on being?

GUNGE. What a way to use a degree in sociology!

VOICE. Can't we go on being?

GUNGE. Why can't you take me seriously? I'm finished. I've lost my nerve, not to mention everything else she took with her.

VOICE. Your self-pity revolts me.

GUNGE. I've often wondered why people get so scathing about self-pity. Quite a lot of us *are* pitiable. Why not let yourself rip and contemplate it from time to time?

He gets a can of soup and begins to open it moodily at a can-opener fixed to the wall. Cut from can to:

4. Interior. Studio.

RICHARD. A king of beasts indeed; if aught but beasts, I had been still a happy king of men.

5. Interior. Basement. *Close-up of can.*

6. Interior. Studio.

RICHARD. Doubly divorc'd! Bad men, ye violate ! A two-fold marriage; twixt my crown and me, And then betwixt me and my married wife. Let me unkiss the oath twixt thee and me; And yet not so, for with a kiss twas made.

7. Interior. Basement. GUNGE *pours the soup into a pan. Sets it on the stove.*

VOICE. I wish you wouldn't harp on Richard the Second. (*Pause.*) Now when you were playing Hamlet, I -

GUNGE. When I was playing Hamlet I'd never heard your bloody whining voice.

Pause.

VOICE. Laura stuck you a long time, you know. Longer than your wife -

GUNGE. Stuck me? *Stuck* me?

VOICE. I wish we still lived in the house in Chelsea.

GUNGE. I swear I'll get rid of you. Even if it means a bloody lobotomy.

VOICE. House in Chelsea.

Close-up of GUNGE's face as he stirs the soup.

8. Interior. Chelsea house, sitting room. *The room is furnished simply but expensively. Easy chairs and sofa, soft rugs, Mexican tapestries and sculptures. Bar. High-fi equipment and shelves of discs.* GUNGE *is lounging on the sofa, in jeans and shirt, listening to Elizabethan music.*

VOICE. You looked in quite good shape in those days, don't you think? Yes I know. You couldn't hear me then. (*Pause.*) You and she had just come back from California. (LAURA *comes in and sits lazily beside* GUNGE. *She is a girl of around twenty, with a fine, characterful face rather than an attractive one. Short hair. Large clear eyes. Unaffected and gentle-seeming. They kiss and caress each other.*) Mind you I was here all the time, Theo. Watching. Listening. I accepted your proper name then. It was quite painful when she left and I had to start calling you Theodore Gunge. (*Pause.*) There you are. Fresh from a big success in New York. A bit on the sleek side. A bit used to money and prestige, but only by your own quite modest standards.

GUNGE. I still can't get over your going all the way from New York to California on a bus. And to Arcata! God it was a grim place. What a holiday! I wouldn't have gone near if it hadn't been for you.

LAURA. I shall always remember the fresias round the house. And those little birds. Like big feathery moths. (*Pause.*) The bus was great, anyway. I wanted the experience. And you rode. . . and swam. . . and boozed. Quite a bit of boozing with that visiting English playwright they had. (*Pause.*) Why do you have to?

GUNGE. I was in one of his plays a long time ago. And a film. (*Pause.*) His drinking makes me feel like a teetotaller. It's good for me. Eases the guilt. (*Pause.*) Have you unpacked yet? Do you like this house?

LAURA. Yes. But it's very posh.

GUNGE. I worked for it.

LAURA. It's a bit impersonal -

GUNGE. It needs you.

   Pause.

LAURA. My parents are still furious about my coming to live

with you in England. They think I'm too young and you're too old.

GUNGE. I get anxious about that myself. Why didn't you let me meet them when we were in America? Afraid I'd get rotten drunk and insult them?

LAURA. You might have. They embarrass me. Talk about middle America personified! We had such a bad row about you and me. I don't want to face them again for a long time. And after all, when my father's work finished here in London they were quite ready to leave me here in school. At sixteen.

GUNGE. It was asking for trouble. Still you hooked yourself a famous actor. I might have been a dropped-out junkie.

LAURA. Oh they're impressed by you as an actor alright. Enough to stop my allowance and smugly inform me that *you* can keep me. And mother was able to throw one of her three-day migraines. I cried. She said I was practically a slut.

GUNGE. Don't they know what kids get up to these days?

LAURA. I'm supposed to be an exception.

GUNGE. You *are* an exception. Anyone who keeps their virginity till they're eighteen these days is bloody unique. (*Pause.*) I used to get quite a perverse thrill, picking you up at school. All those white blouses and grey gym slips. I used to attract quite a lot of giggly attention sitting there in the Ferrari. Then you'd come out, looking shy -

LAURA. My mother said: give it a month or two and you'll be corrupted, discarded and generally unfit for decent life.

She laughs, and kisses him.

GUNGE. Are you sure about coming to me?

LAURA. Positive.

He goes for a drink and brings one for her.

GUNGE. Let's have a pact. You remember what I said in Arcata? The Arcata promise? What else could give that town a place in history -

LAURA. What then?

GUNGE. I shall love you. Look after you. You should always do exactly what you want. I hope we never split. I don't want to hurt you or oppress you, or deny you in any way. (*Pause.*)

It's very serious.

LAURA. I know it is.

He raises his glass.

GUNGE. The Arcata promise, then -

They touch glasses and kiss.

GUNGE. Is it possible to say 'cherish' any more? Whether or not - it's what I do. Cherish you. And if you leave me -

LAURA. Or you me -

GUNGE. Or I you - I shall always be around if you need anything. I'd still want to help you if I could. Anything at all.

LAURA. You so often sound a bit unrealistic.

GUNGE. Do you think I'm not bloody well aware. There's plenty of wreckage and ruin in my job. So? I want us to be committed. And declare it. And live it. We're not just embarking on some casual experiment.

LAURA. But most people are afraid of just that. I'm not surprised. I'm anxious too. Never been with anyone else. It's not a question of doubt. If the word cherish still has meaning, so does the word inexperience.

He puts his arms round her.

GUNGE. But you love me -

LAURA. Yes.

GUNGE. And I you.

LAURA. I believe it.

GUNGE. For as long as we do.

LAURA. I want it to be long.

GUNGE. Am I being realistic?

LAURA (*laughing*). Yes.

GUNGE. And that's the Arcata promise.

9. **Interior. Basement.** GUNGE *sits spooning soup.*

VOICE. Oh, Gunge!

GUNGE. Oh Voice! You know, you run that stuff through my

head like some bleeding film.

VOICE. What an innocent -

GUNGE. Me or her?

VOICE. Both.

GUNGE. Look. This very night. I shall go out and kill her.

VOICE. You'll either get drunk or you'll watch telly. (*Pause.*) Why do we live like this? You've still got plenty of money. Could still act if you wanted to.

GUNGE. I certainly wish you and I could split.

VOICE. Or maybe - unite?

GUNGE. No fear!

Pause.

VOICE. Curious name, Gunge. Dunno how it came to me. Awful. Mess. Rubbish. Stuff in drainpipes. Stuff in people's eyes. (*Pause.*) The Gunge principle.

GUNGE. And what might that be?

VOICE. Oh. . . anywhere where there's depression. . . defeat. . . self-destruction. . . unexplained dire events. . . there's a Gunge there somewhere. All the trouble and mess in the world - that's Gunge at work.

GUNGE. A portrait to the life!

VOICE. Well we have to identify each other somehow.

GUNGE. Chap in the pub round the corner has that problem with his dog. It speaks to him. One day his wife let the dog in and locked him out. (*Pause.*) He's in a mental hospital half the time. You never encounter him? O'Reilly. He's a broken man.

VOICE. Once or twice. I feel sorry for the dog. One of those big dumb furry victim types. Poor animal.

GUNGE. Why am I a festering hulk, if not because of that woman going? I mean. (*He waves his hand at the room.*) All this did start when she left -

VOICE. Why indeed? You gave her a bad enough time.

GUNGE. What was the exact nature of the crime? Travelling all over the world. Money. Premières. Press conferences. Meeting all kinds of people. The gifted. The famous. The both.

Everywhere from the Caribbean sun to the jolly old Polar
night. (*Pause.*) She never wanted for a thing, did she? Of
course that side of it's all shit and nonsense. But it was what
was there. A life she'd never have come anywhere near, if it
wasn't for me. Some people might have envied her.

VOICE. Would they have envied the drinking? The insults? The
nights you never came home because you were in a stupor
on somebody's floor? The way you always used your money
and prestige against her? The *violence* in you? (*Pause.*) Time
for another session, I think -

GUNGE. Now wait a minute -

VOICE. Why? Scared?

GUNGE. If I couldn't hear you when the things happened. . . at
the actual time. . . how come I hear you when they're
repeated?

VOICE. That's a mystery. Don't ask me. It's *your* head! First
they were there then. Then they are sometimes here now.
Both then and now at once. Only now you can hear me and
by god I shan't let up on you. Is that clear?

GUNGE. No. Clear as cardboard. Clear as gunge. We've got to
clear this thing up, old Voice. You want me to wind up like
O'Reilly?

VOICE. *No.* But I'm as helpless as you are. And do you ever
think what it's like to be stuck inside a Gunge? It's not the
sort of privilege people would compete for. They wouldn't
exactly give their eye teeth for it. They -

GUNGE. Enough, enough!

Pause.

VOICE. I've got vulnerable feelings too, you know. Forgive me
harping on. But do look at this room for once. The disgusting
muddle and dirt. The way you live. Well it's not living. It's
a sort of vengeful compromise with suicide. Why give in just
because Laura pulled out? Unless we *are* going to have a
suicide -

GUNGE. I told you before. I'm more frightened of death than
I'm incompetent at life. Can we. . . can we edge round that
subject?

He crosses to a mirror - dusty and cracked.

10. Interior. Studio.

KING RICHARD. Say that again. The shadow of my sorrow!
Ha! let's see: Tis very true, my grief lies all within; And these
external manners of laments are merely shadows to the
unseen grief that swells with silence in the tortured soul.

11. Interior. Basement. GUNGE *lies on the bed.*

GUNGE. I can't imagine going on stage again. My stomach churns
at the idea. I sweat and cringe. Palpitations. Dry mouth. Oh,
I know everybody experiences *that.* But since Laura, it
overwhelms me. Dominates me.

VOICE. Snivelling actors!

GUNGE. Yes? And voices in the head?

VOICE. Watch out -

12. Interior. Chelsea house. Sitting room. *The room is almost
dark. A single lamp by the sofa, where* LAURA *is reading.*
GUNGE *blunders in, wearing a sweater and slacks. He is quite
unsteady.*

GUNGE. Still up? Sharpening the wits? Getting ready to slice
things up? (*Pause.*) What have you done today? Nothing, I
should think. Nothing as usual. What *do* you do with yourself?
What use are you to the world? Christ how I hate your
generation. (*Pause.*) I dried four times tonight. And I *hadn't*
been drinking.

LAURA. I worry about you. Whether you'll fall. Hurt yourself.
Because you've certainly been at it since you came off!

GUNGE. You really mean hurt you!

LAURA. It's been known to happen.

He sits down opposite her.

GUNGE. I feel as if this year's been going on for ten.

VOICE. Don't start on her. Don't go for her. She's innocent.
What's she done? And she waits up for you knowing what
state you'll most likely be in. I wish you could hear me. I
wish *she* could hear me.

GUNGE. Don't tell me you never heard about my boozing. Don't tell me you didn't expect any problems.

LAURA. I knew alright. It's quite a topic with some people. Can you do it when you're on stage? I don't understand. I try to. (*Pause.*) Why are you such a damaged man? There are plenty of talented people who don't drink.

GUNGE. Not in my bloody profession there aren't. It seems to be an occupational hazard. (*Pause.*) Anyway, I drank before I became an actor. (*Pause.*) I could only afford beer then. Success brings that evil graduation from beer to stronger stuff. Why? Because you can afford it.

LAURA. A few years of it, you'll be really sick.

GUNGE. I do not do it on the stage. I don't know about other people but *I* can't. Thank God there's afterwards. (*Pause.*) I'd had a few at that party where we first met. Not far gone, you know. Enough to quiet those social fears. (*Pause.*) Grabbed a drink. Stood there teetering and no doubt casting beady glances at the humans. And there you were. More than human! In a lime green dress. You looked very self-contained. Not so much mature as . . . as cool in a gentle way. Reserved. Shy. (*Pause.*) D'you know I don't think that dress hemline came more than two inches below the crutch? And I thought you had the most beautiful legs I'd ever seen. You held your head in a certain way. Shyly. (*Pause.*) That short haircut. . . round your face. . . well your face. . . it isn't that you're beautiful. It's that one knows straight away. . . there's the loveliest woman. The most incredible woman - while seeming in many ways ordinary - that I'd ever met. (*Pause.*) The face itself, at this moment, is wearing what I'd call an expression divided between gratitude and anger.

LAURA. I haven't much to . . . defend myself with. And you have so much to attack with.

He gets a drink and sprawls on the rug.

GUNGE. But you won't go -

LAURA. Only to bed.

GUNGE. You'll get into the habit of evading rather than confronting. Is it a family characteristic? Is that what your mother's migraines are about - are you a replica? It's provocative, I will say.

LAURA. I don't know what else to do. I can't drink with you.
I can't bear it when you're aggressive. It's as if you go away.
It ignores me. I just get to be a character in whatever's
obsessing you. It's nothing about me. Maybe I'm never the
real target but it's I who hear the abuse.

GUNGE. Was I abusing just now?

LAURA. No. Not until the bit about the expression on my face.
Your sarcasm's so often the prelude to something worse. I
try hard to think: he doesn't mean me. He doesn't (*Pause.*)
But I stand or sit in front of you. The words hit *my* ears.
My feelings. The words hurt *me*. So then what am I to do
with this hurt me? It's an actual person getting hurt you
know. Do you think of that? Then when you're sober you're
facing something in me you can't even remember. (*Pause.*)
You're usually feeling guilty by then of course. Apologetic.
Tender. So I try to push that damaged creature in me away
and respond to you. I'm always betraying myself.

GUNGE. Do you expect to get through life without trouble?
Bother? Violence and aggression? Do you visualise everything
always cool and calm with no eruptions?

LAURA. No.

GUNGE. Well where *is* your aggression then? What do you do
with it? I tell you where it is - it's in your passivity. And
you have these depressions. Classical. You spend whole days
in bed crying. I ask: can I help? Can you talk about it? You
dumbly shake your head and pull the sheets over it. Your
family must have been a commando assassination unit! I
suppose when there was some crisis you all went to your
separate rooms. Never spoke. Never mentioned it. Then
afterwards the usual old pretence that nothing had happened.

LAURA. That's about it.

GUNGE. You'll find it damned hard to live with me like that.

Pause.

LAURA. I do.

GUNGE. Oh get off to bed. Go anywhere. Go out. You're
stupid. You and your mute suffering. What have you been
through that was really tough? Real hardship. You've never
been anywhere near poverty. Have you ever even *thought*
about money? Survival? Ever really worked at something

pointless and repetitive and ill-paid just to eat? You haven't
been exposed to a damn thing except the cunning mental
atrocities your parents inflicted on you by way of keeping a
false and ugly peace.

LAURA. Is that all my fault?

He holds out his glass and deliberately lets it drop.

GUNGE. Of course it isn't your bloody fault. That's the trouble
with you. There's nothing you can be justly accused of. No
time for selfishness or greed to get really going yet. No exotic
vices or even small mean ones. No blatant defects of character.
You simply haven't had time. It's your youth, eh? With a bit
of effort you could have managed it though. Could have
become detectably self-interested, blind to anything but
ceaseless gratification. Vindictive, exploiting, boisterously
indifferent to any pain but your own. Pain? You would
have been able to avoid it with casual expertise! You know,
you've been missing a lot.

He gets another glass and another drink.

LAURA. I can see how your wife and those other women got
worn out! Have you always been like this?

GUNGE. Them? I tell you. All four that I've lived with, I
couldn't find a single thing against them. They were like you.
Oh, I mean. Don't let's waste time railing at petty human
faults. They were irritatingly, agonisingly virtuous. Magnificent
specimens of the capacity of the human soul for goodness. I
began to think there must be something in the notion of a
struggle between good and evil. And I, with my luck, get
stuck with four bloody goodies in a row. Now five. No
blended mixture for *me*. No. Sheer out and out, consistent
immunity to criticism. Talk about never having a leg to stand
on! I've spent decades like a bloody moral flamingo. I've beat
myself nearly to death on the problem. I searched for a bit of
evil in those women. . . well can you imagine a half-crazed
monkey grooming away at its mates? Picking away - and never
a single flea. I can't even say that's what drove me to drink.
I mean I was drinking even when *I* was a virgin!

LAURA. Do you want me to work on it?

GUNGE. Do you want me to pick up that broken glass and cut
your ears off?

LAURA *goes to pour herself a drink. She sips it, shudders, and puts it down. Coming to stand over him:*

LAURA. Can you still see and hear?

GUNGE. A bit.

LAURA *(kneeling)*. When *you* came into that party I was day-dreaming. My sister knew one of the women who'd lived with you. An actress.

GUNGE. Which one?

LAURA. Come on. You've only lived with one -

GUNGE. Oh, her. *(Pause.) Her?* There you are, you see. *She* was implacably good, sod it. A monument of the stuff. A tower of it. Her goodness reached to the stars, you might say. I tell you. Inside her, the tiniest little bubble of wind would tiptoe all the way down yards of gut. . . and sort of. . . sort of breeeeathe itself into the outer atmosphere on gossamer legs. Ghost-like. And why? A desire not to offend others. Now if you imagine that faculty applied to the woman's entire moral being - you can imagine how good she was. I'll bet she never spoke a wrong word about me to your sister.

LAURA. She didn't, as a matter of fact. She told her she'd never met anybody so lonely.

GUNGE. See? Charitable with it all -

LAURA. Listen.

GUNGE. Now that's not like me - is it?

LAURA. *Listen -*

GUNGE. Are you impressed by loneliness? Have you noticed it going on at all? You listen. Besides being deprived of the right to prosecute these women, I'm deficient also in counsel for the defence.

LAURA. I'd seen your performance the night of the party -

GUNGE. That wasn't a performance. It was a crusade against the theatrical arrogance of the bloody awful playwright.

LAURA. John -

GUNGE. Please. I'm Theodore Gunge again tonight.

LAURA. I don't like that game.

GUNGE. What?

LAURA. The Gunge game.

GUNGE. Aaaaaaaaaaaaaaaaaah -

He rolls over and over across the room. As she kneels watching, he presses his face into the floor.

VOICE. I'm sorry. I'd give anything if you could hear. I wish I'd never called you that name. But you started it. And *I* love her. I can see her kneeling there, out of the corner of your eye. There's a fine strength in that girl. And a fine feeling for *you.* (*Pause.*) Don't lose her -

13. Interior. Basement. GUNGE *is sharpening a long kitchen knife on an oiled slate. A mirror is propped on the table in front of him.*

GUNGE. Give me the glass, and therein will I read. No deeper wrinkles yet? Hath sorrow struck So many blows upon this face of mine? And made no deeper wounds? O, flattering glass!

14. Interior. Studio. RICHARD *smashes a looking-glass to the ground.*

RICHARD. For there it is, crack'd in a hundred shivers. Mark, silent king, the moral of this sport, How soon my sorrow hath destroyed my face.

15. Interior. Basement.

VOICE. When you were in Hamlet -

GUNGE *concentrates on sharpening the knife. He sings to himself - i.e. to* 'VOICE'.

GUNGE.   Oh how I love my little Voice
I hear it in my head.
The kindly things it says to me
They make me laugh in bed.

It takes me here it takes me there
We roam about in time.
And when I say my prayers at night
I call it Mister Slime.

Oh how I love my little Voice
It makes me laugh in bed.
I only wish that it could know
I really want it dead.

VOICE. *Not* very funny.

GUNGE. She knows I'm alone. She knows I'm ill. She knows
that if I don't go to the pub I don't see anybody from one day
to the next. And then there's the impotence. Is that what it
is though? Where's desire? (*Pause.*) The desire is for her. If I
don't get the twitches and tremors down below - it's because
she's not with me. And never will be again. (*Pause.*) Since I
retired to this basement a year ago I've met two women. I
don't know whether they were attractive or not. Can't say.
They were equipped, that's all. Anatomically. But when Laura
went she took more than her clothes, her books, her bits and
pieces. She took my passion. Even my compulsion to work.
I can't whip up a bit of promiscuity. A case of gential
anaesthesia. Let nobody say if you don't want it you can't
miss it - because you have your memories. Eh? No? Naturally.
(*Pause.*) I can't exorcise the wretched woman.

VOICE. I - I can't believe we're ill.

GUNGE. What do you think I was doing in hospital last month?

VOICE. Only for two days. Only for tests.

GUNGE. Being frivolous, was I?

VOICE. Well. All the tests were negative, anyway.

GUNGE. They always miss something. Your true hypochondriac
knows that. (*Pause.*) It moves about, d'you see. It has to.
Because they're trying to prove you haven't got it. It's a kind
of guerilla war. They triumphantly demonstrate you don't
have that brain tumour, eh? Well. A small, highly trained
force then slips into position somewhere else. Never take on
the enemy in superior numbers. Never attempt anything
without the support of the local population. That's
where I've got them. I *am* my local population.

VOICE. When we actually were playing Richard the Second -

GUNGE throws the knife down and puts his head in his hands.

GUNGE. And these external manners of laments are merely shadows to the unseen grief That swells with silence in the tortured soul; There lies the substance: and I thank thee king, For thy great bounty, that not only giv'st Me cause to wail, but teaches me the way How to lament the case.

Pause.

VOICE. Mmmm. We weren't very good in that - were we?

GUNGE slumps onto the bed.

GUNGE. You sod!

Pause.

VOICE. Really. Shan't we act again? Ever? It seems a dreadful waste.

GUNGE (*springing up*). Where did I put the gun?

He starts a hurried search of the basement.

VOICE. A knife. A gun. Why hang about fantasising when you could be on the stage?

GUNGE. You've hidden it -

VOICE. I didn't hide the knife.

GUNGE. *I* hid it? You want to imply that?

VOICE. You're not the only one who has blackouts, you know. Sometimes I just have to go under. When I can't bear it all.

GUNGE finds the gun and brandishes it. He takes out the clip, examines it, then rams it back. Sitting at the table:

GUNGE. The knife - or a bullet?

16. Interior. Chelsea house. Sitting room. *As in scene 12.* GUNGE *lies sprawled on the floor.* LAURA *is still kneeling nearby. She gets up and crosses to him. Kneels again.*

LAURA. What it is. . . people know too much about you because you never hide anything. (*Pause.*) You tell all sorts of lies, and invent stories about yourself. . . and that's fine by them so long as you're coherent. (*Pause.*) Once you get lost. . . blurred. . . and mumble. . . they enjoy your loss of dignity. They find you tiresome. A nuisance. But that's their moment. Their reward. (*Pause.*) When you're not entertaining them, either at their expense or your own - you become what they need to see. Not the actor. Not the man. John? You become abject in their eyes. (*Pause.*) For anybody who cares about you to watch, it's horrible.

GUNGE. You can't take it?

LAURA. It's hard.

GUNGE. You think *I* can take it?

LAURA. No. But you go on.

GUNGE (*sitting up*). Don't I!

LAURA. Why? Do you know?

GUNGE. That's what they all ask.

LAURA. Well?

She gets up and goes to sit on the sofa.

GUNGE. Don't you ask?

LAURA. I live with you.

GUNGE. Martyred?

LAURA. Not yet.

GUNGE. I don't crave for booze. I can't remember ever having the compulsion.

LAURA. You only feel compelled once you've started? (*Pause.*) Is there a difference?

17. Interior. Basement. GUNGE *is lying on the bed, holding the knife and the gun.*

GUNGE. The classifications of addiction to drink. Let's see. He's a drinker. A hard drinker. A sporadic drinker. A pissed-all-the-time man. A depression drinker. A dipsomaniac? An alcoholic? (*Pause.*) Oh, he can leave it alone when he wants, you know. (*Pause.*) It seems a long time since anyone phoned. Are they respecting my solitude? My privacy? My self-imposed exile? No. They don't phone because I might just agree to go out somewhere. Ho ho! A dinner. A drink. A film. (*Pause.*) Not the theatre, for God's sake! (*Pause.*) But I gave off the stench of despair. Who can put up with that for long?

VOICE. It's a long time since *you* phoned anyone.

GUNGE. Brennan hates me. So does his wife. Isobel James hates me. So does her dog. Awesome little brute. It looks like a comb with broken teeth. (*Pause.*) My agent doesn't want to know. My mother's gaga. (*Pause.*) That bloody phone! I could wring its nasty little flex.

VOICE. Nobody hates you. You're liked. You're very well liked.

GUNGE. Oh?

VOICE. I'd say a lot of people are very fond of you.

GUNGE. *Oh?*

  Pause.

VOICE. When you're sober, that is.

GUNGE. I'm sober nearly all the time.

VOICE. But you have this tendency. . .when you go out. . . er. . . social situations, I'd say. A tendency to overdo the wine, the scotch.

GUNGE. Nerves.

VOICE. What a pathetic excuse!

GUNGE. It's nothing to do with excuses. I start shaking as soon as I enter a room where there are other people. You know that. My vocal cords seize up. Eyeballs rolling in desperation. Sweat. Palpitations. I start itching all over. (*Pause.*) Nothing to say. Strain to follow the conversation but I never can. The mind wanders. If I open my mouth - something fatuous bound to come out. That increases the tension. (*Pause.*) Now Laura. A mysterious smile. Fascinating. (*Pause.*) I expect that's the way to do it.

VOICE. You have an unfortunate longing to seem interesting to people, all the same.

GUNGE. When in fact I'm not, you mean.

VOICE. Touchy!

GUNGE. 'This shambling, idiosyncratic actor,' one critic said. 'Touched with genius.' My crooked feet are my best friends.

Who bequeathed me this disjointed skeleton? Of course the critics have fun comparing me with various animals. Ugly, skinny ones needless to say. A merry spectacle.

VOICE. People will forget you, you know. It won't be long. 'I wonder what became of him' they'll say.

GUNGE. How true. That neurotic, fragile talent - eh? What else?

VOICE. I wish you wouldn't brandish those weapons -

GUNGE throws the gun and knife onto the floor. The doorbell rings. GUNGE stares in the direction of the door without moving.

VOICE. Aren't you going to answer it?

GUNGE. It's never happened before.

VOICE. It has now.

GUNGE. They've got the wrong door. Nobody comes here.

VOICE. Why not see?

GUNGE. I'm frightened.

VOICE. Lazy.

GUNGE. No no. Fright. The real thing.

The doorbell rings again.

GUNGE. I'm a coward. I can't defend myself. I'm a pacifist. I wouldn't hit anybody. (*Pause.*) I'm so angry I could split somebody's head open. Too dangerous to open the door. I might do them bodily harm. (*Pause.*) I wish I was floating on the sea under a great big hot sun somewhere. (*Pause.*) No. Be quiet. I'll go.

He crosses to the door and opens it. In the doorway, a small neat man in a raincoat - TONY.

TONY. Good afternoon -

GUNGE. Er. . .?

TONY. It *is* a nice afternoon, actually.

GUNGE. Oh?

TONY. Yes. And such a pretty square you live in. Children playing and so forth. (*Pause.*) They have a large white ball with red spots on it. (*He executes a brief dancing, kicking movement.*) Goal!

GUNGE. Little bastards.

TONY. One of them did kick me rather hard as a matter of fact. (*Pause.*) I try to overlook it, with children.

GUNGE. Can I. . . er. . .?

TONY. Your advert.

GUNGE. My - advert?

TONY takes a scrap of newspaper from his pocket and holds it out. GUNGE examines it wonderingly.

GUNGE. *I* never advertised for a valet -

TONY. Mr Theodore Gunge, is it?

GUNGE. Yes.

TONY. It looks as if you did, then. Advertise. (*Pause.*) Shall I go away.

GUNGE hesitates a moment, then steps back.

GUNGE. No. Come in.

TONY (*entering*). Perhaps you were more hoping for - well for a. . . lady valet? Mmmm? If there are such creatures.

GUNGE. I don't know anything about it.

They are in the centre of the room. TONY looks round at the mess with distaste.

TONY. Are we letting ourselves go to seed then?

GUNGE (*thumping the table*). *He* dreamed this one up!

TONY. Who did, Mr Gunge?

GUNGE. Somebody I know. Name of 'Voice'.

Pause.

TONY. What an unusual name. (*Pause.*) Is he here. It doesn't say *two* gentlemen.

GUNGE. Oh, he's here alright.

TONY looks enquiringly round the basement.

GUNGE. He's. . . well frankly, he's invisible.

TONY. Ah!

GUNGE. Look. He takes things into his own hands from time to time. That advert for example -

TONY. A little joke? Nnnn?

GUNGE. So I think, if you understand me. You'll not be wanting to. I'm sorry you've wasted your time.

TONY. No point in being hasty. (*Pause.*) Things *are* in a mess, aren't they? (*Pause.*) I'm very efficient. But perhaps you can't really afford? On the other hand I sometimes take jobs just for room and board. If I like the person. (*Pause.*) I'm a bit of a fugitive from life myself. *You* are, I can see.

GUNGE *picks up the knife and gun - puts them on the table.* TONY *stares at them.*

GUNGE. Just a couple of little toys.

TONY. I see. They look awfully real.

GUNGE. I didn't say they weren't real -

TONY. Dangerous, I'd say.

Pause.

GUNGE. Voice -

VOICE. Yes?

GUNGE. What bloody nonsense have you been up to now?

TONY. I beg your pardon?

VOICE. I thought we. . . I thought we needed looking after. You know? The odd hot meal. The laundry. The shopping. (*Pause.*) Get the place cleaned up.

GUNGE. You stupid, pusillanimous, interfering idiot!

TONY. I beg your pardon?

GUNGE. Not you. I was talking to *him*. The bloody voice.

TONY (*reflecting*). I see.

GUNGE. No you don't. You think I'm deranged.

TONY. Nothing so hasty. I wouldn't presume. Of course it's not usual. Not exactly common.

GUNGE. No? Do you live alone?

TONY. 'Fraid so. At the moment. I take your point. Well, I talk to myself. So many people do in our predicament. But no one answers. There is no friendly voice to answer me -

GUNGE. Friendly! Huh!

TONY. So it was mischevious Mr Voice who put the advert in? And you didn't know about it?

GUNGE. He sometimes takes the body out when I'm asleep. Or daydreaming.

TONY. Yeeees -

GUNGE. So you'll definitely not be wanting to - eh?

TONY. May I sit down?

> GUNGE *points at a chair.* TONY *examines it and sits down fastidiously.* GUNGE *sits on the bed.*

GUNGE. There's really no point in -

TONY. I never have trouble finding work, you know. I'd be offended if you thought I was. . . pushing. No. There are several possibilities at the moment.

GUNGE. Hardly much point here, is there? One room. No visitors. Subsistence meals. Nothing to do. I manage, you know.

TONY. I saw you in Richard the Second.

GUNGE. I've given up the stage.

TONY. I heard rumours. A couple of friends of mine are dressers. People talk as if you simply disappeared off the face of the earth. These gossips. (*Pause.*) What I mean is, when you opened the door I recognised you at once. Your real name came to me, straight away. Or is Gunge your real name and the other -

GUNGE. We're definitely wasting your time, er -

TONY. Tony. Tony Greeves. *Does* Tony grieve? they used to twit me at school. I was a skinny spineless butt. A born victim. Obsequious through fear. It was all blows and insults. But I've been more fortunate since. I've looked after some delightful people. I'm a genuine all-rounder, Mr Gunge. Cleaning, cooking, ironing. I could answer your letters. I can drive. (*Pause.*) I *devote* myself to a person:

GUNGE. I don't write letters. Or get them. I haven't got a car. I don't go anywhere. You'd be wasted on me. You'd be dissipating your talents. Doing yourself an injustice. (*He sits up glaring at* TONY.) And I'm planning a murder.

Pause.

TONY. You won't be the first.

GUNGE *turns away, hunching himself up against the wall, his arms round his knees.*

GUNGE. Is that all you can say?

TONY. I'd have to know more about it.

GUNGE. You don't reject the idea out of hand? In principle? You aren't shocked? Disturbed?

TONY. I try to judge things on their merits. I can tell straight away you're not just flying a kite, as they say. Not just having a little vulgar fun. Why shouldn't you fritter your life away down here and enjoy a few dark thoughts.

VOICE. Send him away. He's dangerous. You're too impressionable. God, the last thing we want round here is an accomplice for you!

GUNGE. Who advertised? *Who?* (*To* TONY.) I'm talking to him, not you -

TONY. We could make some kind of arrangement.

GUNGE. About what?

TONY. Well. Let's say. . . when you're talking to your Voice, you could wag your finger or something. Some kind of little signal. Then there'd be no confusion.

GUNGE. I'm not taking you on, you know.

TONY. You could do with a bit of help, all the same. Give me an hour to go back and collect a few things. Jot down a shopping list, if you need some odds and ends.

GUNGE. What are you up to? What's your game?

TONY. I took to you straight away. No ulterior motives. An honest job. I promise you, you won't have to lift a finger. This is no sort of existence for you, now is it? (*He crosses to a door and opens it.*) There *is* a spare room. I can soon clear the junk out. (*He closes the door.*) Can you really go on the way things are? I'm self-effacing. I get to know people's moods very quickly. (*Pause. Taps the door.*) I'd be quite snug in there. You can banish me whenever you feel like it.

VOICE. Don't listen to him -

GUNGE wags his finger. TONY *smiles.*

TONY. That's the idea -

GUNGE. I might try it out -

TONY. Yes. Why not give it a chance?

GUNGE. We seem to have got off the subject of homicide -

TONY. For the time being.

GUNGE. You're a cool one!

TONY. I've learned a thing or two Mr Gunge. I had a harrowing
childhood but it hasn't warped me. We can't blame everything
on our childhood, can we? Can't go through life like that.
Your situation - it's a challenge. Take your disembodied Voice.
I shall have to get used to that. It won't be easy. I'm not
surprised you're feeling morbid.

GUNGE. I don't like being humoured. The Voice tries it, when
he's not being censorious. You should hear it. He goes into
a smug whine, he's a bloody athlete of self-righteousness.

TONY. You don't look at all well. It's this tinned food I should
think. And no exercise?

GUNGE. As far as the pub.

TONY. Beer or spirits?

GUNGE. Both.

TONY. I had a walk in Regent's Park this morning. The ducks
were looking very amiable. Then I took a boat out and rowed
for an hour. Ducks everywhere. I wouldn't dispute - life's a
sad business. I put up the oars and sat there, out in the lake
for ten minutes. What about throwing yourself in, Tony, I
said to myself. But I'd no inclination. And then when I
opened the paper to jobs vacant I had a *feeling* about your
advert -

GUNGE. *His.*

TONY. Yes his. I had this odd feeling. You get them sometimes.
You somehow *know.*

GUNGE. Absolute bloody rubbish!

TONY. Say what you like - that's what brought me here. And
fancy. It wasn't you at all! It was your other half. Your. . .

what shall we say?. : . alter ego? I like an unconventional situation. I've had one or two quite boring ones. You know the sort of thing. When they expect you to walk their dogs - it can lead to misunderstandings on the street.

GUNGE. What if I'm sick?

TONY. I've nursed more than one employer through thick and thin. One pleurisy. One glandular fever. Two with broken limbs, St Moritz and the Edgware Road respectively. One with severe chronic migraines, one -

GUNGE. I mean: mentally sick.

TONY. Mr Gunge, I have no idea what constitutes sanity. Are you violent, aggressive, subject to hallucinations? Paranoid, anxious, compulsive? Withdrawn certainly, I can see that. I can't bring myself to judge another person in the matter. So long as the community has no need of protection from you, what have we to go on? Have you taken an opinion?

GUNGE. No.

TONY. It's usually unwise. Shall we discuss it later? Kick it around a bit.

Pause.

GUNGE. You can come for a week. Understood? We reconsider after a week.

TONY. I think you've made the right decision.

He stands smiling a moment, then lets himself out.

VOICE. I can't say I don't feel guilty.

GUNGE. I should think so!

VOICE. It *was* one of your bad days when I rang the newspaper office.

GUNGE. He's a desperate little sod, I'd say.

VOICE. We don't know anything about him -

GUNGE (*shouting*). It's all your fault!

VOICE. I'm going to keep a strict eye on *both* of you.

GUNGE (*standing*). I wasted time, and now doth time waste me -

18. Interior. Studio.

RICHARD. For now hath time made me his numbering clock:
My thoughts are minutes, and with sighs they jar Their
watches on unto mine eyes, the outward watch, Whereto my
finger, like a dial's point, Is pointing still, in cleansing them
from tears.

19. Interior. Basement. GUNGE *takes the knife and jabs it into
the table. He picks up the gun and fires it into the ceiling.*

Act Two

1. **Interior. Basement** *The place is noticeably cleaned and cleared up.* GUNGE *is finishing a meal at the table.* TONY, *in shirtsleeves, is ironing.*

TONY. Did you like that?

GUNGE. Not bad.

TONY. Was the retsina nice and cool?

GUNGE. Just about.

TONY. You can't have your moussaka without retsina.

GUNGE. I don't give a damn.

TONY. Was your lady a good cook?

GUNGE. My *what?*

TONY. What did you say her name was? Laura?

GUNGE. Brilliant. She was brilliant. And shopping? A wizard in the supermarket. Took her time. Economical. She really took advantage of those supermarkets. (*Pause.*) I put her in my will. I shall have to change that will. (*Pause: declaiming.*) Let's talk of graves, of worms and epitaphs; Make dust our paper, and with rainy eyes Write sorrow on the bosom of the earth; Let's choose executors and talk of wills.

TONY. I love Dicky Two. (*Declaiming.*) All murdered: for within the hollow crown That rounds the mortal temples of a king Keeps Death his court, and there the antick sits -

GUNGE. Ugh! Stop it.

TONY. Sorry Theo -

GUNGE. And now he calls me Theo!

TONY. Do you mind? I thought things were getting nice and

friendly. You've only spoken to Voice three times today. Isn't that a good sign?

VOICE. He's undermining you. Taking advantage of you. Can't you see it - how insinuating he is? You shouldn't talk to him about Laura -

GUNGE. She's a hustling, cheating, calculating whore.

He raises his right forefinger. TONY *notices, and pauses in his ironing.*

VOICE. No she isn't.

GUNGE. I'd like to feed her into a concrete mixer. Limb by limb.

TONY *hurriedly resumes his ironing.*

VOICE. I shan't let you do anything violent. (*Pause.*) She's only trying to lead her own life. Find herself.

GUNGE. Don't give me that 'identity crisis' bullshit!

VOICE. People do have them. And a girl of twenty-three isn't exactly the same as she was at eighteen. (*Pause.*) I mean. Really still a schoolgirl when you met her. So fragile

GUNGE. About as fragile as a steel girder.

VOICE. She did right to leave you.

GUNGE. *What?*

VOICE. You're intolerable to live with. *He's* just deceiving you -

GUNGE *blunders away from the table to the bed and sits with his head in his hands.*

TONY. Is he getting at you Theo?

GUNGE. Shut up.

TONY. Me. . . er. . . or him?

GUNGE. *You.*

VOICE. Everybody liked her.

GUNGE. And didn't she just like them!

VOICE. Well why not? Before she met you they were all just names in the papers. Film credits. Theatre programmes. Reviews. It isn't a crime to be impressionable, especially at that age.

GUNGE. She exploited me.

VOICE. She loved you.

GUNGE. I suppose that's why she left?

VOICE. She left because you were a threat to her sense of security. She left because you were always telling her to go. She left because you said hideous things to her. Because she was ashamed of you in public and afraid of you in private.

GUNGE. What a monster!

VOICE. You *were* a monster -

GUNGE. All the time?

VOICE. *Often.*

Pause.

GUNGE. I wish I could burn you out of my mind.

VOICE. Of course you do. Naturally. You treat the girl despicably - then you can't forgive her for getting out. Well *I* don't blame her.

TONY *goes to sit beside him on the bed.*

TONY. Theo -

GUNGE. What?

TONY. It upsets me when you two wrangle and bicker. (*Pause: in a steely tone.*) Why don't you try and forget that little bitch Laura?

GUNGE. If I could, I wouldn't be planning to liquidate her. And you keep out of it -

TONY. Sorry I'm sure!

He returns to the ironing, very piqued.

GUNGE (*softly*). Laura -

2. Interior. Studio.

RICHARD. I have been studying how I may compare this prison where I live to the world; And for because the world is populous And here is not a creature but myself, I cannot do it; Yet I'll hammer it out.

3. Interior. Basement.

GUNGE. Laura -

4. Interior. Chelsea house. Bedroom. *Modern, austerly furnished, quietly luxurious. Double bed - tables with lamps on either side. One lamp is lit - on* GUNGE's *side. He sits up in bed, smoking.* LAURA *lies with her back to him, her eyes closed.*

GUNGE. I wish you'd bloody well open your eyes. You're not asleep.

LAURA. I've taken two sleeping pills. I waited till nearly three a.m. for you. Then I took them. (*Pause.*) Drunk again?

GUNGE. There isn't a damn thing in this house. . . or in your possession. . . that hasn't been paid for by my *sober* labour.

LAURA. Please don't start that.

GUNGE. True, or not true?

LAURA. Oh, true.

GUNGE. What do you think it's like, going onstage night after night? Week after week? Spewing out those interminable lines.

Pause.

LAURA. I do know. But it's what you want to do. How many people have that chance.

GUNGE. And what do you do? *Nothing* I mean - what *do* you do with yourself?

LAURA. Nothing.

GUNGE. Right!

LAURA. Right.

GUNGE. Four pretty easy years you've had -

LAURA. Oh yes. Easy. (*Pause.*) And I'm exhausted. (*Pause.*) George Brennan's wife rang this evening. To ask us to supper after your show tomorrow. (*Pause.*) She said: Is John drinking? (*Pause.*) People have been asking that ever since they thought they knew me well enough. How do you think *I* feel?

GUNGE. Self-righteous?

LAURA. They can't take it, you know -

GUNGE. I'd like to ram this cigarette into your face -

LAURA (*sitting up*). I think you would.

GUNGE. Yes I would!

LAURA (*getting out of bed*). I'm going.

GUNGE. Again?

LAURA. I can't stay here when you -

He leaps out of bed, and taking her roughly by the arms, throws her on the bed.

GUNGE. You're staying.

She doesn't move. He gets back into bed. She is trying to stifle tears.

LAURA. Do you enjoy my living in fear of you.

GUNGE. Why can't you fight back for God's sake?

LAURA. *I can't -*
Pause.

GUNGE. Bloody masochist!

LAURA. Bloody sadist!

Pause.

GUNGE. I drink out of self-hatred.

LAURA. Then it's yourself you can destroy. And I don't want to watch. (*Pause.*) I feel so precarious. Can't you understand it makes me want to run away?

GUNGE. You understand nothing *but* running away. And what to? What have you got? Talent? Interests? Ambition? (*Pause.*) Will you ever do anything? You say you want something besides just being with me. Something of your own. Like what? You just aren't interested in the actual world. It *is* there, you know. And it's not just for shopping in. Strife. Turmoil. Conflict. Torture. Oh it's all going on. But you, you're useless. No good to anybody or for anything. I hate the sight of you. What are you doing here breathing good air somebody else could use?

Pause.

LAURA. I hate you too.

GUNGE. Well that's it, then. Don't forget to leave your keys.
House. Car. And don't take anything. Not one thing. See
what's it's like, out there.

*She gets out of bed and takes her clothes from a chair, her
handbag from the dressing table. She throws down two key
rings and goes out, slamming the door. GUNGE dials the
phone beside the bed.*

GUNGE. George? (*Pause.*) Yes. John. Tell Anna Laura's left
again. She'll be coming your way no doubt. And if you take
her in, I'll kill you both.

He slams the phone down.

5. Interior. Basement. GUNGE *lies on the bed singing.*

GUNGE.   Do you hear my little Voice?
Do you hear my head?
Those tales of love and murder,
They haunt my lonely bed.

TONY *is draping ironed clothes on a rack, neatly.*

TONY. Don't you think we should take a holiday? Somewhere
in the sun. Wouldn't it be good for you?

GUNGE. Face up to it. Sooner or later I shall bully you into
phoning Laura and telling her I've taken an overdose.

TONY. Ibiza? Majorca? One of those lovely Greek islands?

GUNGE. Voice once made the mistake of ringing somebody. I
was out on the roof somewhere. Rang a friend, he did. John,
says he - John is about to commit suicide. He's out on the
roof now. What did this friend say? 'Oh God, and I've got
people here for dinner.' Sent the police, firebrigade and the
ambulance. I was inside by the time they arrived. Gave them
a drink and a lecture on the evils of drug taking.

TONY. I don't think the Costa Brava. No. It's ruined. Absolutely
ruined. (*Pause.*) Maybe - somewhere a little more exotic?

GUNGE. She won't come round unless she thinks I'm dead or
dying. There's an appalling amount of indifference in that
woman. She genuinely doesn't mind if I get maimed, crippled,
dead. She -

VOICE. She's protecting herself.

GUNGE. Is my destruction worth her preservation?

VOICE. She's not responsible for it -

GUNGE. No? She's only the cause, eh?

VOICE. What you're doing is *your* responsibility.

GUNGE. I see. And we just ignore that it dates from her leaving? Pure coincidence is it?

VOICE. Nothing and no one made you give in. Shut yourself alone. You've managed it all quite unaided. It's your own choice.

GUNGE. I wouldn't be like I am if she'd stayed. Can you deny that?

VOICE. No.

GUNGE. Then bloody leave me alone.

VOICE. It's she who'd have suffered if she had stayed.

GUNGE (*shouting*). Bloody leave me alone!

TONY *clears* GUNGE's *plate from the table and sits down. He regards* GUNGE *with sympathy.*

TONY. It really is too much. An affliction.

GUNGE. Tony Greeves. Where did you come from? What are you doing here? Pass me the scotch.

TONY *finds the scotch and hands it over with a glass, resuming his seat. He watches* GUNGE *pour a very large drink.*

TONY. Have you thought of - suicide?

GUNGE. Who hasn't?

Pause.

TONY. The last person I worked for used to hit me. He did really. I had to wear dark glasses when I went out. (*Pause.*) I'd sit in my room and swear to leave. One night I took an overdose. He drove me to the hospital and had me pumped out. When I came to, there he was crying at the bedside. It was lovely for two weeks then we quarrelled and he hit me again. Up and down the stairs, all over the place. So I took an overdose again. He came into my room just as I was fading

away - and he laughed. 'Get on with it,' he said. And walked
out. (*Pause.*) The next thing I knew I was retching it up in the
bathroom. It was his saying get on with it, you see. Oh, the
body knows. It has its way of dealing with things. 'Don't kill
yourself for him,' it was saying. 'He's not worth it.' (*Pause.*)
I feel safe here, Theo. Peaceful. (*Pause.*) I just wondered if
you'd ever been tempted. One gets to the point so easily.
It's almost like being hypnotised. All you want is to quietly
slip away. No fuss. No dramas. Just a weary admission that
you've had enough.

VOICE. We can't listen to this! Gunge. Do you hear me? Do you
see what he's at?

Pause.

GUNGE. Voice thinks you're trying to *recommend* suicide. To
influence me.

TONY. Then you can tell your mean and spiteful Voice that
he's mistaken. What a thing to say!

Pause.

GUNGE. I've thought of suicide -

TONY. Can you be sure anybody'd mind so much? Mind for
long? (*Pause.*) Have you thought of any particular way?

GUNGE. Nothing original.

TONY. What was your childhood like?

GUNGE. Unremarkable.

TONY. Lonely?

GUNGE. Maybe a bit lonely.

TONY. Not a good mixer -

GUNGE. Definitely not that.

TONY. A bit shunned by the others?

GUNGE. Kids tended to leave me alone.

TONY. No special reason?

GUNGE. None I can think of.

TONY. Lonely?

Pause.

GUNGE. Why ask me again?

TONY. I meant - now?

GUNGE. At this minute?

TONY. Lately -

GUNGE. Since you came?

TONY. Not necessarily.

GUNGE. A happy childhood really. Fed. Cared for. Told what to do and what not. Obedient. (*Pause.*) Ignorant. (*Pause.*) Not at all clever. No. At school there was no question of ambition. Brains like jelly. Just couldn't take anything in. Physically rather weak, too. No sports. (*Pause.*) Not really at home in the world. Looking back I can see that. Couldn't at the time. But no problems.

TONY. Mmmm. It certainly doesn't sound too bad, does it?

GUNGE. Destined for a pretty flat sort of life, I'd say. Unexceptional.

TONY. Not a murderer's sort of childhood -

GUNGE. Is there such a thing?

TONY. People speculate, don't they? Early environment. Family relations and so on. (*Pause.*) Traumas.

GUNGE. Nothing to get a firm grip on there.

TONY. Nothing to get hold of, eh?

GUNGE. What a sympathetic kind of chap you are! But I'm sorry. There aren't any clues, you see. (*Pause.*) I once blew up an anthill. Terrible destruction, there was. (*Pause.*) How does it rate by way of early violence? A few ants. Not much. I lit a squib. Poked it in the anthill. Bang! I don't think there's any significance there. (*Pause.*) What about you?

TONY. Timid as could be.

GUNGE. Timid now, are you?

TONY. I couldn't harm a thing. Oh no.

GUNGE. No dark thoughts about it?

TONY. I feel sad and peevish when *I* get hurt. But I never want to retaliate.

GUNGE *reaches into his pocket for his wallet. Takes out a five pound note and hands it to* TONY.

GUNGE. Go and fetch another bottle of scotch, will you?

Taking the note, TONY *looks at him a moment. As* TONY *makes for the door.*

GUNGE. I'll find some violence in you. I'll find some hatred in you. And then we'll see what timid means -

TONY *exits.*

6. Interior. Studio.

RICHARD. Cover you heads and mock not flesh and blood with solemn reverence: throw away respect, Tradition, form, and ceremonious duty, For you have but mistook me all this while: I live with bread like you, feel want, Taste grief, need friends: subjected thus, How can you say to me I am a king?

7. Interior. Basement.

GUNGE. Voice? (*Pause.*) Voice?

He strides up and down - bangs the table with his fist.

GUNGE. *Voice?*

VOICE. I can hardly hear you -

GUNGE. What's happened then?

VOICE. I am weak.

GUNGE. Oh yes? You need me to be alone - don't you?

VOICE. Don't persuade him to get Laura here. Don't harm her. Tell him how much you love her -

GUNGE *takes a blanket from the bed and swathes it round him.*

GUNGE. I shall tell them all in court! Good my lords! Oh you merry-wigs - who stands before you? (*Pause.*) I used to wake in the mornings. . . look at her beside me. . . touch her hair. . .

kiss her shoulder. Delighted, I was. That she existed. (*Pause.*)
She would sleep so quietly. (*Pause.*) But then too, we often
made love in the mornings. (*Pause.*) We made love all over the
world. We were inseperable. We breathed each other. (*Pause.*)
How can an otherwise unremarkable woman seem so unique?
What extraordinary qualities does it take to provoke such
feeling? (*Pause.*) Well, one doesn't choose to love - or whom.
And I a king? Well, I have played many kings. The occasional
fool. Once a lecher. Many times a creature thwarted in one
way or another. (*Pause.*) But that was on the stage. And before
I consigned her to the mortuary sirs, that woman actually
made *me* feel real. For bonus, dear coz - she was real to me.
Because I must confess that life outside the theatre. . . well
of course they talk a great deal of rubbish on this subject. . .
but I can assure you that things outside had always been
insubstantial. Solid brick and stone seemed like water. I
didn't so much move about the world as *swim*. And by way
of paradox, I would say I tried to solidify the state of affairs
by drinking. (*Pause.*) That murdered girl, your honour, had
the edge on vodka, or scotch - or whatever your favourite
brew might be. Yes. In her presence, the watery scheme of
things grew solid - and took on their proper shapes. Cities
grew out of my ocean. Ghosts became people of flesh and
bone. Chaotic sounds became voices. (*Pause.*) No doubt you
think I exaggerate. This is not an age when people speak so
extravagantly of loving! Poets have a tough time of it, you
might say. Indeed they have. I wouldn't be a poet at this
time, not for anything. And as for a non-poet like me - well
it's only idealisation of the woman, isn't it? A damaged
circuit in the mind? The idiot gibberings of remorse and grief
let loose on your prosaic ears!

GUNGE *pours the last of the scotch, and sits cross-legged on
the bed, his back to the wall, the blanket pulled round him.*

VOICE. I think you'll not hear me again -

GUNGE (*declaiming*). We are amaz'd; and thus long have we
   stood to watch the fearful bending of thy knee, Because we
   thought ourself thy lawful king.

He raises the glass, hesitates, then drinks.

8. Interior. Studio.

RICHARD. For well we know, no hand of blood and bone Can gripe the sacred handle of our sceptre, Unless he do profane, steal, or usurp. And though you think that all, as you have done, Have torn their souls by turning them from us, And we are barren and bereft of friends; yet know, my master, God omnipotent, Is mustering in his clouds on our behalf Armies of pestilence -

9. Interior. Basement.

GUNGE. - and they shall strike Your children yet unborn and unbegot, That lift your vassal hands against my head And threat the glory of my precious crown.

He pulls the blanket off and throws it to one side. Finishes the scotch.

GUNGE. I wouldn't be a poet at this time, not for anything. (*Curling up, foetus-like.*) Voice? (*Pause.*) Voice?

10. Interior. Chelsea house. Bedroom. Morning. GUNGE *lies in bed watching* LAURA *as she finishes packing a suitcase and closes it. He is drinking.*

GUNGE. Don't go -

LAURA. I have to.

GUNGE. I love you -

Pause.

LAURA. How many times have I left this house the way I did last night? How many times have you told me to get out? Asked for the car keys - the house keys. Even my purse, more than once. (*Pause: she sits on the end of the bed.*) I'd never done anything to make you angry. . . make you attack me. (*Pause.*) Have I?

GUNGE. No. Bloody hell no. I don't know how you put up with me. Or why? Why did you, if I've been so bloody awful? I mean, there's nothing mercenary about you - is there? You weren't exploiting me or anything - were you? (*Pause.*) Oh no. It's not in you. You've just been badly *gunged* - eh?

LAURA. Your idea of loving doesn't seen to involve concern for the actual person. Wouldn't anybody do? So long as your house is kept, your meals appear, your laundry gets done.

GUNGE. Don't be funny. I can *pay* somebody to do all that.

LAURA. It's not really what I'm talking about.

GUNGE. If you love me - you won't leave.

LAURA. I *can't* live under the constant threat of you getting drunk and abusing me!

GUNGE. And what about the constant fact of my being *sober* most of the time?

LAURA. It's the anxiety -

GUNGE. And that's a reason for going!

LAURA. You don't understand, do you? Drunk - sober, it's two completely separate things for you. But *I'm* there all the time, (*Pause.*) The years I've been with you and nothing changes!

GUNGE. That's the sad fate of the reforming spirit!

LAURA. *I* didn't want to change you. I thought you'd want to change yourself.

GUNGE. For you.

LAURA. No. For you.

GUNGE. You can't leave me.

LAURA. I can.

GUNGE. You don't really want to -

LAURA. Now - I do.

GUNGE. And what about love?

LAURA. What about self-preservation?

GUNGE. If you go - it'll finish me off, Laura. Nothing dramatic. Nothing to do with booze, even. Just a steady, remorseless decline into apathy.

LAURA. Blackmail.

GUNGE. No. Prediction.

LAURA. And your work?

GUNGE. Why do people always think achievement is some huge consolation in life? Why do they think being successful can compensate for just about everything? More often than not, success is meaningless to the person who has it. *They* can't experience it. (*Pause.*) At first it's exhilerating - then it becomes irrelevant.

LAURA. What's relevant then?

GUNGE. Look - you're not interviewing me you know. You're in the process of *leaving* me. (*Pause.*) And I'm. . . begging you. . . not to.

LAURA (*standing*). I've loved you. I believe you love me. But you've lived and behaved exactly as you wanted - with me like some kind of appendage. (*Pause.*) Where have I been? Who did anybody ever think I was? Some of your friends still can't even remember my surname! Others pity me. I can count on one hand the number of times I've ever been asked a question about myself. I imagine people find me dull and boring. You drink. You talk. You dominate. *I'm* the one who drives you home. You rant. You rave. You're the evening's entertainment. I'm the one you turn on when we get home. I should think I'm despised. Not because anyone's taken the trouble to find out what I'm like. No. But because I must seem like your bloody shadow. (*Pause.*) I'm not envious. I admire your acting and respect it as much as anybody else does. But I'm not just a servicing arrangement to your needs. I'm *something* else. (*Pause.*) And I'm going to find out what that is.

Pause.

GUNGE. You *can* leave?

He reaches out his hand. She sits beside him on the bed and takes it. He burries his face in the pillow.

11. Interior. Basement. GUNGE *is lying curled up, asleep on the bed.* TONY *enters with a bottle of whisky. He tiptoes to the bed and stands looking down at* GUNGE. *Looking round, he finds* GUNGE's *jacket and begins to go through the pocket. He finds a small address book and begins to turn the pages. After a moment, he goes to the telephone and dials.*

12. Interior. Chelsea house. Bedroom. *As at the end of Scene 10.*

LAURA. Do you remember the Arcata promise?

Pause.

GUNGE. Yes.

LAURA. Well you needn't keep it. (*Pause.*) I shouldn't think you'll want to - after all.

Pause.

GUNGE. Pass my cheque book. It's over there in my coat. And a pen.

She hesitates, then goes to his coat which is lying on a chair. She gets the cheque book and a pen – brings them to him. He starts to write a cheque. She sits watching him.

LAURA. I didn't mean money. (*Pause.*) Why do you think of money straight away? (*Pause.*) Do you know you've never actually bought me anything? A hug and a cheque when it was time for a present. (*Pause.*) I used to spend hours, sometimes, looking for exactly the right thing to buy you.

GUNGE finishes writing the cheque and waves it around to dry it. He reaches to the floor for his glass and drinks - drains it.

GUNGE. You'll not be wanting this then?

LAURA. I didn't ask for it. (*Pause.*) I've got my student grant.

GUNGE. Oh yes. What is it? About nine pounds fifty a week? After the kind of life you've had these years? A bit of a jolt - eh?

LAURA. Everybody else has to manage. So shall I.

GUNGE. No. Take it.

He holds out the cheque. After a moment she takes it.

LAURA. Thank you.

GUNGE. I knew you would. A practical girl.

LAURA. We've had plenty of rows over money and the fact that you're the one who makes it. I don't really own *anything* - do I? My clothes, my shoes - there's not a thing of *mine* in this house. Is there? (*Pause.*) You either want me to have this or you don't.

GUNGE. But if I do - you'll take it?

LAURA. Yes. I will.

There is a bottle of scotch, half empty, beside the bed. He pours a drink. She watches this impassively.

GUNGE. Funny time of the day to be drinking.

LAURA. Don't -

GUNGE. I've never had booze for breakfast in my life.

Pause.

LAURA. So when I've left and you drink - you can blame me!

GUNGE. Gentle, passive, loving Laura! And what besides? When it comes to it, you're absolutely for you. Aren't you?

Pause.

LAURA. In these circumstances. . . if I'm not. . . I shall regret it.

GUNGE. Convenient time to go - just when your finals are coming up. Oh, you'll get your degree, there's no doubt. Then you'll be qualified for something. What *does* sociology qualify people for? (*Pause.*) At any rate, it's perfect timing.

LAURA. You think I'm so calculating?

GUNGE. You're capable of it.

LAURA. I'm capable of leaving you because I *have* to. And yes it's for me. For my own sake. I want to be independent of you -

GUNGE. On *my* money?

LAURA. Emotionally independent.

GUNGE. It's much easier, of course, with a few quid in the bank.

LAURA. You can have the cheque back -

GUNGE. Don't let's haggle over a cheque. Let's haggle over your opportunism.

LAURA. I'm going.

She takes her case and goes to the door. Puts it down as she opens the door. Turning to GUNGE:

LAURA. I came to live with you because I loved you. I stayed

with you because I loved you. (*Pause.*) I endured you because
I couldn't imagine life without you. (*Pause.*) I feel *battered.*
Ignored. Belittled. (*Pause.*) I didn't care for you because
you're a famous actor. You remember talking about that
party where we met? Well when *you* came over and talked to
me - I thought I'd never seen a man so haunted. So defensive
and uptight. (*Pause.*) I never thought you'd find me attractive.
I never thought you'd see me again. (*Pause.*) When you asked
me to, I said yes for *you.* Not because I was impressed, or
flattered, or anything like that. I almost didn't *dare* to think
you'd have any serious interest in me. (*Pause.*) But you did.
(*Pause.*) Girls at school used to laugh at me because I said
I wouldn't go to bed until it was somebody I loved. *Very*
old-fashioned, or whatever. At my school you were considered
freaky if you were still a virgin after sixteen. (*Pause.*) And
because of you - I was *glad.* I was happy I'd never been with
anyone else. (*Pause.*) I've been happy with you - but too sad
as well. Too humiliated. (*Pause.*) Too hurt. (*Pause.*) I never
thought it mattered at all your being so much older. Now I
can see it does. Not the years. Not the difference in experience.
(*Pause.*) It's that you'll go on being exactly the same. (*Her
voice rising.*) And I'm *changing* -

She goes out, closing the door quietly behind her. GUNGE
pours more whisky into his glass, and lies staring at the door.

13. Interior. Basement. *As in Scene 11 - but* TONY *sits primly
on an upright chair near the bed.* TONY *looks at his watch.*
GUNGE *is moving about restlessly, and suddenly wakes up;*
TONY *goes to pour whisky from the fresh bottle and takes the
glass to* GUNGE. *Sits down again.*

TONY. I made a little phone call -

GUNGE. You - did what?

TONY. Yes. To Laura.

GUNGE. Damn and blast you!

TONY. Very skeptical, she was.

GUNGE. And how did you find the number?

TONY. In your address book.

GUNGE. You went through my pockets?

TONY. Didn't you want me to call her?

He crosses the room, and from a drawer takes the knife and gun. Puts them on the table.

TONY. You weren't serious?

GUNGE. Well, I -

TONY. You were dreaming, just now?

GUNGE. Remembering.

TONY. Remembering in your sleep -

GUNGE. What did you tell her?

TONY. That you were very ill. Seriously. In delirium, I think I said. And that you were asking for her. (*Pause.*) Very skeptical she was.

GUNGE. What did she say?

TONY. She said: What did the doctor say? Have you called one in, she asked. I told her yes. I told her you might have taken pills. Pills and whisky, it can be lethal.

GUNGE *props himself up on one elbow, looking past* TONY *to the weapons on the table.*

GUNGE. And who did you say *you* were?

TONY. A friend.

GUNGE. I'll bet she was skeptical about that, as well.

TONY. When I went into the pub for the whisky, I had an idea. (*Pause.*) He can't spend the rest of his life in that basement, I thought. What a loss to the stage, the screen. Such a waste of talent. (*Pause.*) How shall we get him up? Get him out and about? (*Pause.*) What shall we do about that nagging voice of his?

GUNGE (*fiercely*). Is she *coming?*

TONY. Take him at his word, I thought. Ring her up. Tell her some story. You won't sound plausible, but she can take the risk? (*Pause.*) She asked me if you'd been drinking. He looks, I said - he looks as if he's never stopped since you left him.

Pause.

GUNGE. *And?*

TONY. I'm not coming then, she said. What if he dies, I said. (*Pause.*) He won't, she said. And in any case, why isn't he in hospital if he's so ill? (*Pause.*) Rather a callous tone of voice, I thought. You're a hard one, miss. (*Pause.*) But I expect she thought it was some kind of ruse on your part. (*Pause.*) What does Voice have to say about it?

GUNGE. Not a word. He's stopped. Whilst you were out.

TONY. Now isn't that peculiar? Wouldn't it be marvellous if he kept his trap shut for good?

GUNGE. You've taken a lot on yourself, haven't you. (*Pause.*) You've taken a pretty drastic step!

TONY. You can't spend your life in this basement. It's all very well to hang about telling me to phone her, then get cross when I do. (*Pause.*) I mean, has it occurred to you that you actually *can* kill her? If you want to.

GUNGE. You're mad!

TONY. I thought it was *you* we were supposed to be worried about - madnesswise.

GUNGE (*moves to sit on the edge of the bed*). Pack your gear, and get out.

TONY. I'd say from the tone of her voice - she won't come. Didn't believe a word of it. I imagine you've pulled one or two tricks on her before.

GUNGE. *Out -*

TONY. Don't turn on *me*, Theo -

Pause.

GUNGE. Why did you leave your last job?

Pause.

TONY. He died.

GUNGE. From natural causes, I hope!

TONY. Coronary. (*Pause.*) He left me a bit of money, as a matter of fact. Not much. Enough to allow me to be choosy for a couple of years. (*Pause.*) He loved me. Wouldn't do anything or go anywhere without me.

GUNGE. Who was it?

TONY. Billy Raynor. D'you remember Billy Raynor? He was one
of your teachers at drama school. (*Pause.*) Fencing, wasn't it?

Pause.

GUNGE. Fencing -

TONY. He had private means. We lived in style. We had two
Persian cats. Lovely creatures. (*Pause.*) Isn't it a coincidence?
The first day I came here and you opened the door, I was
flabbergasted. (*Looking round.*) I think I've transformed this
place. And now you want me to go!

GUNGE. *I* think - *I* think. . . you're an evil little bastard.

TONY. You're the one with the homicidal compulsion.

GUNGE. *Out* -

TONY *gets up and puts on his outdoor coat. He stands looking
at the weapons.*

TONY. You weren't very nice to Billy - were you? (*Pause.*) It's
fate, I thought. Fate, my reading the ad in that newspaper.
(*Looking at* GUNGE.) You've been rotten to a lot of people.
Everything gets about, doesn't it? (*Pause.*) Now look at you.
The state you're in. Decrepit. Hearing voices. Moral and
physical deterioration. (*Pause.*) You've brought it on yourself,
haven't you? (*Pointing.*) I stood in that doorway and I thought:
He's really had it! *He* won't last. (*Pause.*) What was the last
thing I saw you in? Strindberg was it? Magnificent! He's the
best of his generation, Billy said. Drinks too much, but then
a lot of them do. What an actor! The control. . . the timing. . .
he has the sort of discerning humility that the best of them
have. See what a grip he has on the audience? (*Pause.*) I'll
come for my things tomorrow. (*Pause.*) I should have known
that taking you at your word was bound to confuse you.
(*Pause.*) Nice voice, Laura has. Pleasant. (*Pause.*) I'd bet on
her not coming. (*Pause.*) There was a touch of anxiety. Just
a touch. (*Pause.*) But you're not one for suicide, are you
Theo? (*Pause.*) Not to worry.

He goes out. GUNGE *refills his glass - sits at the table staring
at the weapons, touching them hesitantly.*

14. Interior. Studio.

RICHARD. Thus play I in one person many people and none
contented; sometimes I am king; Then treason makes me wish
myself a beggar, And so I am: then crushing penury Persuades
me I was better when a king -

15. Interior. Basement *As at the end of Scene 13.*

VOICE. I'm still here -

GUNGE. I thought you might be.

VOICE. I didn't expect him to go so easily.

GUNGE. Was he really here?

VOICE. He was. And he *did* telephone Laura. (*Pause.*) D'you
think she'll come?

GUNGE. No. (*Pause.*) There'll just be you and me. (*Pause.*)
I quite liked him, in a way. He still had a bit of spite. A bit
of malice.

VOICE. I warned you -

GUNGE. We know about your warnings. They didn't start till
she'd gone - did they?

The doorbell rings. GUNGE *stands up, looking at the door.*

VOICE. You'd better answer. (*Pause.*) *I* won't interfere any more.
(*Pause.*) Depression and apathy like yours - no one can help
you. It's almost obscene, the amount of grief and mourning
you've gone in for. There's something dogged and blind about
it. Not even a touch of the heroic. . . just seedy and sad. The
only ambition you have left is to demonstrate your own
misery. (*Pause.*) What does it matter who's ringing the
doorbell?

The bell rings again. GUNGE *goes to the door - opens it.*
LAURA. *They stare at each other numbly for a moment. He
gestures her into the room. She takes a few steps in. He closes
the door - goes to sit on the bed.*

LAURA. Who was the man who phoned?

GUNGE. I don't really know him.

Pause.

LAURA. And needless to say - you're alright!

GUNGE. Obviously I'm neither dead nor dying - am I?

LAURA. I didn't expect you to be. (*Pause.*) So now I can go
away again. If it happens again, I shall ignore it.

Pause.

GUNGE. How are you?

LAURA. I'm fine.

GUNGE. I'm sorry about this. I kept asking him to ring you. Tell
you some story. I don't think it ever occurred to me that he
might.

LAURA. Just like you thought I might never leave you!

GUNGE. I was always afraid of it.

LAURA *sits by the table and points at the weapons.*

LAURA. What's this about?

GUNGE. I have this fantasy of killing you. I had quite a lot
of trouble getting that gun.

LAURA. And when you've killed me?

GUNGE. I don't know. It never gets further than the gun going
off. You falling. (*Pause.*) Unreal. (*Pause.*) I sit here most of
the day and talk to myself. There was a short interlude.
Somebody stayed for a bit. It didn't work out. I don't ever
actually *do* anything at all. There's a dread of going anywhere.
I start shaking and sweating as soon as I get on the street.
Never seem to care what time of day it is. What season. (*Pause.*)
The sun rises and sets. Sometimes it's warm - sometimes cold.
I go days - I think it's days - without bathing or changing.
Without a shave. Till the stink and the shame of it nudge me
to clean up. (*Pause.*) I miss you dreadfully. How long is it
now? A year? Surely after a year -

LAURA. It's you you're killing - not me.

GUNGE. If you're right, I've picked a laborious method.

LAURA. Nothing can get me back, John.

GUNGE. How *is* it out there? What are they all doing out there? Working. Eating. Screwing. Going out and about, are they? (*Pause.*) I have occasional stabs of nostalgia. Trite yearnings for normality. (*Pause.*) What are *you* doing?

LAURA. I go to the office. I see films and plays. I stay in my flat quite a lot. Reading. Music. I don't mind being alone. It's all a bit reassuring, after being with you. It's quiet. No threats. None of that endless anxiety.

He darts across to the table, takes the gun and the knife back to the bed.

LAURA. Don't be stupid -

GUNGE. Which would you prefer?

LAURA. Am I worth life imprisonment?

GUNGE. That's what I've already got, anyway -

LAURA. I'm going now.

GUNGE. Don't you bloody well move!

LAURA. It looks as if you haven't *entirely* given up acting!

GUNGE. I'm warning you -

LAURA. You look absurd, sitting there like that.

GUNGE. The whole thing's inconceivable isn't it?

LAURA. *Yes!*

GUNGE. But - you're not entirely sure.

LAURA. I know I can simply get up and walk out.

GUNGE. You're certain?

LAURA. Of course I am.

Pause.

GUNGE. Come back to me -

LAURA. You know I can't.

GUNGE. Won't.

LAURA. I don't want to.

GUNGE. All I have to do is pull the trigger -

LAURA. It's ludicrous.

GUNGE. People don't do it this way, that's the safe assumption.
The reasonable one. A clear question of motive, or at least
something passionate - maybe random. Spur of the moment,
sometimes? Where's the greed, the hatred, the vengeance?
(*Pause.*) I *have* no motive!

LAURA (*shouting*). Stop rambling then!

Pause.

GUNGE (*quietly*). No cause. No reason. What's required then?
What's needed? What sort of crime would it be? A crime *at
all*? (*Pause.*) I lead a bare and abject life. Prison could be no
worse. (*Pause.*) I flirt with these thoughts - these melodramas.
Then sometimes they make me laugh. I sit here crooning with
glee and then shake myself and make a solemn face. I'm
rational. My judgement is unimpaired. It wouldn't even satisfy
me in any way to kill you. (*Pause.*) But aren't you a *little*
afraid?

LAURA (*standing*). More than a little. Now.

GUNGE. I'll tell you why. Because to any right-minded person. . .
if I do it. . . it has to be a disturbance, an aberration. And if
I'm mentally disturbed. . . it follows the act is possible. The
one depends on the other. You'll only know when you walk
out unharmed, or when the bullet smashes into you. (*Pause.*)
No one will think me mad, *unless* I do it. (*Pause.*) I've been
harmless. Broken no laws. Offended no one. Displayed no
quirks or peculiarities outside this room. I don't want my name
in the papers. Public attention I've already had. Night after night
I've been looked at. Applauded. Naturally I've had some bad
notices in my time. But more good ones. Even raves. (*Pause.*)
So I don't need any of that. (*Pause.*) I'm rich enough to live
for years without working. (*He waves at the room.*) Especially
like this. (*Pause.*) And violence itself repels me. I don't want
power of life or death over anyone. Not you. Not anyone.
Murder has no perverse attraction for me. I haven't the *impulse*
to it, either. If you manage to walk out without my pulling
the trigger, then we shall know whether I must or needn't.
That's the only way. I've nothing else to add. I feel nothing
at all - one way or the other. Perhaps a mild curiosity. Nothing
more.

LAURA *moves a few steps towards the door, then turns to him.*

LAURA. You. . . only want to see if you'll do it?

GUNGE. Quite.

LAURA. That *is* insane!

16. Interior. Studio.

RICHARD (*with a sword*). Go thou and fill another room in hell -

17. Interior. Basement.

GUNGE. Go thou and fill another room in hell! (*Pause.*)
  We weren't very good in Richard the Second - were we?
  (*Pause.*) There. That sounds dotty enough. Oh, I could
  resume the same old life tomorrow you know. If I wanted to.
  But I haven't wanted to - since you left me. I'm hardly more
  than a marginally animated corpse. (*Pause.*) Are you going?

  Pause.

LAURA. And - love?

GUNGE. Two nights before you walked out of the Chelsea
  house, you lay beside me and said: I love you. You didn't
  talk about my drinking, my cruelty, my selfishness - no. I
  had my arms round you and you talked of loving. (*Pause.*)
  What changed in two days?

LAURA. What if I'd never come here?

GUNGE. I can't speculate. I only know that in effect - *you*
  murdered *me.*

  Pause.

LAURA. Put the gun down, John -

GUNGE. Name of Gunge. Theodore Gunge. (*Pause.*) Quaint.

  Pause.

  LAURA *sits down by the table again.*

LAURA. Then I shall wait until you do.

There is a long silence. He is looking round the room, at her, at the gun. Slowly he lifts it and points it at her.

GUNGE. Murder for grief and loss of the loved person? It's inconceivable!

He shoots - LAURA falls sideways to the floor. He walks round and looks down at her for a moment.

GUNGE. Now who did that? (*Pause.*) And why?

He sits on the bed once more. Sits with his arms hanging loosely between his legs.

18. Exterior. Basement door. TONY *stands with his finger on the bell for a second. Steps back and waits. Rings again. There is the loud sound of a shot inside. TONY exits frame.*

Find Me

FIND ME was first presented by BBC Television in December 1974 with the following cast:

MAREK	Anthony Hopkins
OLIVIA	Sheila Allen
STANTON	David Collings
CATHERINE RAYNOR	Charlotte Cornwell

Designed by Judy Steele
Directed by Don Taylor
Produced by Mike Wooller

Scene One. *Interior. Prison cell: dawn.*

The cell is dark, except for the square of light from a small window. A MAN's *head moves into position in front of the window. His name is* MAREK. *We see him from the back.*

Scene Two. *Exterior. Prison yard: dawn.*

We see MAREK's *face looking down into the yard. Against a wall at right-angles to his block, a* PRISONER *stands waiting to be executed. A* FIRING SQUAD *is at the ready. An* OFFICER *gives the order to fire, and the* PRISONER *slumps dead. Close-up* MAREK's *face at the window.*

Scene Three. *Interior. First-floor London sitting-room: morning.*

The room of a writer. Books, desk, typewriter, anglepoise lamp, a wall-board with various photographs, cards and pieces of paper pinned on it. One large easy leather chair. By one wall a long comfortable couch in dark corduroy. Also a long trestle table with wire trays, a small desk filing cabinet, rows of manuscript neatly laid down.
A WOMAN *stands at the high window, looking into the street. She is smoking and looking down. Her name is* OLIVIA.

Scene Four. *Exterior. London street: morning.*

Close-up OLIVIA *at her window. In the street,* MAREK *stands searching wildly in his pockets. As he does so, he turns slowly on his feet. He pulls from his pockets bits of paper and thrusts them back. Obviously he can't find what he is looking for. He suddenly goes still, looking vacantly in front of him.*

Scene Five. *Interior. First-floor London sitting-room: morning.*

OLIVIA *sits at her desk, stubs out her cigarette and picks up the microphone of a tape-recorder.*

OLIVIA. Certainly Marek hasn't changed much. There he stands in the street, confused . . . absent-minded . . . short-sighted . . . going through his pockets. (*Pause.*) I wonder what he's lost this time? His passport? The address he was heading for? Matches? Cigarettes? (*Pause.*) Perhaps nothing at all, really. I've seen him do that before when he was gaining time after some dread or fear or memory had crossed his mind.

Scene Six. *Exterior. London street: morning.*

We see MAREK *thrust his hands into his pockets and walk away up the street. A jet plane thunders overhead and he pauses to look up at it.*

Scene Seven. *Stock shots.*

German planes are strafing long lines of refugees. Bullets are whining and there are puffs of earth where bombs are exploding.

Scene Eight. *Exterior. Roof: morning.*

MAREK, *in some drab and ragged uniform, is wildly firing a machine-gun into the sky.*

Scene Nine. *Interior. Conference room: afternoon.*

We do not see the audience. On the stage, a row of chairs with perhaps a dozen people sitting there, including OLIVIA. *At a microphone in front of the chairs,* MAREK *is reading from notes. His English is faultless, with only the slightest trace of an accent.*

MAREK. I should say the questions of literature being discussed at this conference seem remote to me. (*Pause.*) I have heard much said. I am grateful to be your guest. Yet my mind is a silence. My head is . . . how would you say? A void.

Scene Ten. *Exterior. Woods: morning.*

MAREK *and another man, an Englishman –* STANTON *– are sitting with their backs to a tree.* MAREK *wears a long, tattered overcoat and has an automatic rifle across his knees.* STANTON *is dressed in rough, nondescript clothes.* MAREK *drinks from a small flask and passes it to* STANTON.

MAREK. I could certainly have done without you, Mr Stanton.

STANTON (*drinking*). I'm sure you could. It was most inconvenient of our people to parachute me into the wrong place.

STANTON *hands back the flask and gives a cigarette to* MAREK, *taking one himself. They light up.*

MAREK. Since when did the English start bringing philosophers into the coat and dagger business?

Pause.

STANTON. Cloak and dagger.

MAREK. Excuse me!

STANTON. I have this habit of pedantry. I have a Jewish friend who calls it 'shmatters and dagger'. (*Pause.*) The buggers quite often drop us in the wrong place, you know –

MAREK *turns and looks at him for a long time, almost sadly. Then he turns away.*

MAREK. This time no accident. The Germans caught one of your wireless operators about ten miles away. They got the code . . . everything. (*Pause.*) You were meant to be a guest of the Gestapo, Mr Stanton.

STANTON. I wish you wouldn't call me 'Stanton' –

MAREK. What should I call you?

Pause.

STANTON. Regrettably, I'm known to some of my waggish intellectual colleagues as 'Dodo'.

Pause.

MAREK. The bird?

STANTON (*sighing*). That's right. The bird.

Pause.

MAREK. It is extinct.

STANTON. Quite. So Dodo is regarded by many as an apt nickname for a philosopher. (*Pause.*) How long do we have to wait here?

MAREK. Are you married?

STANTON. I married one of my students last year. Eighteen years old. (*Pause.*) Twenty years younger than me.

MAREK. Very nice! And what is *she* called?

STANTON. Olivia. (*Pause.*) I spent several ineffectual months bashing her with Wittgenstein. Then she informed me she intended to be a poet. I think I married her in a state of numbed relief.

MAREK *takes up a pair of binoculars and sweeps the landscape.*

MAREK. And here you are, wandering around Poland, Dodo!

STANTON. Olivia thinks I'm sitting behind a desk somewhere in Buckinghamshire. (*Pause.*) Christ! Whoever thought up 'cloak and dagger'? It should be nappy and hat-pin –

MAREK (*still looking out*). Do you know what you are doing?

STANTON. I *thought* I did. Until your lot picked me up. (*Pause.*) And where *were* the Gestapo after all that efficiency?

MAREK. That's what I would like to know.

He puts down the binoculars. They both take another drink from the flask.

MAREK. Well, Dodo. I was a philosophy student myself until the war. (*Pause.*) But if we win . . . if I survive I shall try to be a novelist.

> *Gazing into the distance, he notices something. Takes up the binoculars again. He stiffens. One hand presses* STANTON's *shoulder.*

STANTON. What is it?

MAREK. A German patrol. Two and a dog. (*Pause.*) Two nice-looking young boys. Round faces. I think one of them is eating a sausage –

> *Pause.*

STANTON. *Well?*

> MAREK *smiles at him.*

MAREK. If they don't miss us – we kill them.

STANTON. Oh Christ! I think I've got diarrhoea.

MAREK. Don't worry, Dodo. If it comes to it – I will take the boys and you can take the dog.

> *Close-up* STANTON.

STANTON. You needn't be such a superior bastard!

> *Close-up the two* GERMAN SOLDIERS *meandering through a field beyond the woods. They look absolutely harmless.*

Scene Eleven. *Interior. Conference room: afternoon.*

We see the empty stage – the session is over.

Scene Twelve. *Interior. Conference: tea room.*

There are small tables and easy chairs. A mess of tea-cups, plates, overflowing ashtrays, crumpled sheets of paper. Only OLIVIA *and* MAREK *are in the room, both smoking.*

OLIVIA. What's it like to be a legend?

> *Pause.*

MAREK. Is that what I'm supposed to be?

>OLIVIA *itemizes on her fingers.*

OLIVIA. Well. You're a fine novelist. You were a partisan during the war. A maverick communist imprisoned by the communists. Etcetera –

MAREK (*drily*). Impeccable qualifications!

OLIVIA (*rapidly going on*). Some of your drinking adventures have been spectacular –

MAREK. Merely childish.

OLIVIA. Not in *our* newspapers. At any rate, not *only* childish.

MAREK. What? Because I once held up a diplomat by his ears in Amsterdam?

>*Pause.*

OLIVIA. And then –

MAREK. Don't tell me. The women?

OLIVIA. Not to mention the rumours of possible defection. Of obsession with suicide, of –

MAREK (*sarcastically*). Of heroic dissent?

OLIVIA. And so on and so on.

>*Pause.*

MAREK. What dreary fools you all are!

OLIVIA. Why should you include me?

MAREK. You raised the subject, didn't you?

>OLIVIA *stands up, gathering together her cigarettes, lighter, a notebook and pen, cramming them into her large handbag.*

OLIVIA. I didn't mean to provoke you. But I *am* curious. After all, you were there when my husband was killed during the war – weren't you?

>*And she unhurriedly leaves the room.* MAREK *watches her thoughtfully, stubbing out his cigarette. After a moment he gets up and hurries after her.*

Scene Thirteen. *Interior. First-floor London sitting-room: evening.*

As in Scene Five, OLIVIA *sits at her desk with the tape-recorder. There is a tray beside her with a coffee pot and a mug. Into the microphone.*

OLIVIA. Five years since that bloody awful conference! And now he's staying here –

> *She pours some coffee and drinks it. There is a glossy new book on the desk. She pulls it towards her, into the circle of light from the anglepoise lamp:* THE FINAL GRACE, poems by Olivia Stanton.

Scene Fourteen. *Exterior. Country road: afternoon.*

OLIVIA *(at eighteen) and* STANTON *are driving very fast, with* OLIVIA *at the wheel. We see the hedges and trees flashing past for several seconds, then suddenly the engine begins to fade. The car gradually slows down and* OLIVIA *pulls it in to the side of the road. She turns to* STANTON, *laughing.*

STANTON. You silly bitch, Olivia! I told you we were nearly out of petrol. And that was my last three gallons –

> *She still laughs into his face, and kisses him. She points beyond the roadside hedge.*

OLIVIA. Let's go and make love in that field –

> *She springs out of the car and stands making a face at him. Close-up* STANTON's *face: from his point of view, a big cornfield with thick hedges and a copse of trees at the far end.*

OLIVIA. *Come on* –

> *He seems sad. Then he smiles and gets out of the car. She takes his hand, and they go off into the field.*

OLIVIA. A Dodo crept into the field to see
  How the little field-mice pee –

Scene Fifteen. *Interior. Bedroom, London: dawn.*

OLIVIA *is in bed asleep. The phone rings. After a moment she blearily answers.*

OLIVIA. Hello –

  Pause.

  Marek? (*Pause.*) I see –

  Pause.

  Find you? Find you where? (*Pause.*) Wait a minute –

  She switches on the bedside lamp and fumbles for a pen and pad.

  Right. Go on –

  She writes an address. Pause.

  All right. I'll come now.

  She gets out of bed and starts dressing.

Scene Sixteen. *Exterior. London streets: dawn.*

OLIVIA *driving her car. It pulls into a drab street and stops. She gets out, looking at the house numbers. Two or three houses farther along she finds the one she is looking for and goes down some steps to a basement door. There is no bell. She knocks gently. A rather haggard-looking young* WOMAN *comes to the door in a dressing-gown. She says nothing – simply stares at* OLIVIA. OLIVIA *is confused and says nothing either. The* WOMAN *steps back a little and gestures* OLIVIA *past her. The door closes behind them.*

Scene Seventeen. *Interior. Woman's room. London: dawn.*

A dingy basement room. A rumpled bed, two chairs, a table, a dressing-table. Sitting on the bed, his head in his hands – MAREK. OLIVIA *enters, followed by the* WOMAN, *who goes to sit at the dressing-table with her back to them.* MAREK *looks up at* OLIVIA, *spreads his hands in a helpless shrug.*

MAREK. I'd no money to get back. *She* speaks no English. At least what she has is unintelligible –

WOMAN (*turning*). He was shock to me.

>   *Pause.*

OLIVIA (*bewildered*). *Chic?* Chic French?

MAREK. I think she means sick. And not to her. *On* her.

>   *Pause.*

OLIVIA. Come on. We'd better leave –

MAREK. I haven't been sick for years. Didn't expect it. Then – whoosh!

OLIVIA. Are you coming?

MAREK. How to apologize? She has neither English nor French. Russian nor Polish. (*Pause.*) I think she is some sort of house-keeper for the people who own this house –

OLIVIA. Where did you find her?

MAREK. I don't remember.

OLIVIA. It's time you went back to Warsaw.

MAREK. I'm just the same in Warsaw, except, I must say, for the being sick.

>   *He crosses to the* WOMAN *and put his hand on her shoulder. She knocks it away.*

MAREK. Sad thing. You don't need common language for them coming to bed. Escape is another problem – without words, it lacks the human dimension.

OLIVIA. *Is* there one?
MAREK. *Now, Olivia!*
OLIVIA. I'm bloody annoyed with you!

> *She goes out, leaving the door open. After a brief glance at the* WOMAN, MAREK *follows her.*

Scene Eighteen. *Exterior. Field: day.*

As from Scene Fourteen. OLIVIA *and* STANTON *lie in a post-coital languor. He is smoking. She is twisting cornstalks together.*

STANTON. That poem you showed me yesterday –
OLIVIA. Yes?

> *Pause.*

STANTON. It's about suicide, really –
OLIVIA. I suppose it is.

> *He turns on one elbow to face her.*

STANTON. I think of death. But not suicide. Never.
OLIVIA. Oh dear. And you a philosopher!
STANTON. I'm a soldier, at the moment.
OLIVIA. Yes. From behind a desk –

> *Close-up* STANTON's *face.*

Scene Nineteen. *Exterior. Another field: day.*

As from Scene Ten. The two GERMAN SOLDIERS *and the* DOG *lie dead.* MAREK *stands looking down at them, his gun crooked in his arm.* STANTON *is retching in the grass a short distance away.*

MAREK. You didn't even take the dog, Dodo!

> STANTON *gets up, wiping his mouth.*

STANTON. You *deliberately* drew their attention –
MAREK. That would have been stupid.

STANTON. I couldn't agree more. Except you *wanted* to kill them.

Pause.

MAREK. They turned our way – and they had the dog. Come. I must get you to our people. Have you finished to be sick? Or, since you are philosopher do we sit down and have some ethical debate about this?

STANTON. And balls to you too! Anyhow, I'm weak on ethics.

MAREK. And so is your stomach?

STANTON. I haven't any illusions about what's *necessary*.

MAREK. But you don't think this was necessary? You find me . . . how is it? Degraded?

Pause.

STANTON. Look. If you're going to save my skin – save it. Let's move on –

MAREK. Yes. I am taking you to an interesting place.

STANTON. Which is?

MAREK. A pig farm.

Scene Twenty. *Interior. Olivia's bathroom.*

A spacious, comfortable bathroom. MAREK *lies in a foamy bath, his head resting on the edge, his eyes closed.* OLIVIA *sits on a stool smoking. She is irritable.*

MAREK. It's true, Olivia. Your husband was killed by a pig.

Pause.

OLIVIA. Not funny, Marek.

MAREK. But a fact.

OLIVIA. And I've known you on and off since that literary conference . . . and you never felt the urge to mention it! O.K. So how does a man get killed by a pig?

MAREK. It fell on him.

Pause.

OLIVIA. I see. It was a *flying* pig! Somebody shot it down and poor old Dodo was underneath when it crashed!

MAREK *opens his eyes and smiles at her.*

MAREK. How did they tell you he died?

Pause.

OLIVIA. They said: in action, somewhere. Which was peculiar because I always thought he was what used to be coyly known as 'something at the War Office'. One of its evacuated or hush-hush departments in the country. (*Pause.*) Nothing about pigs. Were pigs hush-hush?

Pause.

MAREK (*musing*). Olivia. You had twenty-seven years to digest his death. How do you feel about it?

OLIVIA. This minute, I feel like stubbing my cigarette out on your bloody stomach!

MAREK. On account of Dodo?

OLIVIA. On account of you lie in *my* bath talking about pigs.

Pause.

MAREK. I have forgotten what it means, 'hush-hush'.

OLIVIA. Clandestine operations.

MAREK. That's a mouthful. (*Pause.*) What Dodo used to call, via the Jewish vernacular: Shmatters and dagger?

She flings her cigarette into the bath, where it sizzles out somewhere in the foam above MAREK's genitals.

OLIVIA. He *did die!*

Pause.

MAREK. Beneath a pig.

OLIVIA. How many more times is the phone going to ring at dawn with you at the other end saying 'find me'? I wish you'd never come to that bloody conference. You didn't have anything to say, anyway. All you did was eat, booze and screw, in various permutations of that order, then skulk back to Poland.

MAREK (*laughing*). Didn't everyone?

OLIVIA. Shall we say *your* performance was superlative!

MAREK. We were truly a crowd – swarm, is it? – of locusts. Such hospitality we were given!

OLIVIA. Yes – and didn't you all abuse it!

MAREK. If people *will* throw their homes open to an international gang of writers –

OLIVIA. There were precious few lean and hungry ones! God! Some of those flats and houses after you lot had drunk and chewed your way through them! It was one shambles after another –

Pause.

MAREK. And yet – there it was that you and I met –

Pause.

OLIVIA. I don't regret *that!*

Pause.

MAREK. But . . . you still don't live with someone?

OLIVIA. Anybody who's lost their first husband then eventually married and divorced their publisher . . . well, you know what I mean? Women tend to suffer pretty early on from the law of diminishing returns.

MAREK. Ah yes. Your publisher –

OLIVIA. Well, at least he was the first person to print *your stuff* in this country. *And* invited you to that conference!

MAREK. And since I went back to Warsaw?

OLIVIA. Are you going to lie in that bath all day?

MAREK. Are you going to sit and watch me all day?

Pause.

OLIVIA. How *did* he die, Marek?

Pause.

MAREK. I told you.

She stands up and angrily throws a towel at him.

OLIVIA. I wish you'd damn well die in that bath!

And she goes out.

Scene Twenty-one. *Exterior. Pig-sty. Country: night.*

MAREK *and* STANTON *crouch in the midst of a throng of squealing pigs. An Allied bombing raid is taking place. There are flashes and explosions, the drone of aircraft.*

STANTON. A fine place to hide!

MAREK. It's not so incongruous, Dodo. The Germans occupied our country. Our Allies are bombing it. One English academic and one Polish partisan on the run. Where's your sense of humour?

There is a loud explosion and they both flatten themselves into the straw and dung. The pigs jostle around them, and STANTON *inefectually pushes at a huge sow.*

STANTON. Oh yes! It's bloody funny all right. I can imagine the briefing: There it is, chaps – you've got your target. A pig-sty in Poland. That's all, and jolly good luck!

A deafening explosion, a flash and thunder of flying earth near-by. The pigs go berserk. Silence gradually comes and we see MAREK *pushing his way through the grunting animals to where the sow lies dead. On top of* STANTON. *With an effort,* MAREK *lugs the sow to one side. He stares down in disbelief.* STANTON *is dead – his neck broken.* MAREK *lifts him gently.* STANTON's *head dangles horrifically to one side. His eyes are open.*

Scene Twenty-two. *Interior. Olivia's living-room.*

She is speaking into the microphone.

OLIVIA (*drily*). Since this is supposed to be one of those serious, truthful articles . . . one might as well say it. Our Polish friend has developed over the years a nauseating streak of frivolity.

> MAREK *enters in a towelling bathrobe, rubbing at his hair with a towel.* OLIVIA *ignores him but puts the microphone down and pulls her typewriter towards her. As she fits in a sheet of paper, he wanders over to the desk and picks up the book of poems,* THE FINAL GRACE.

MAREK. New poems?
OLIVIA. No. A new anthology of old ones.
MAREK. What are you writing *now?*

> *Pause.*

OLIVIA. One of those articles about WRITER X: THE MAN, THE WORK AND THE LEGEND.
MAREK. A magazine?
OLIVIA. Yes. One of those glossies for 'the intelligent woman'. About as relevant to intelligent women as the profit motive is to a Bolivian tin miner.

> *Pause.*

MAREK. And . . . who is X?
OLIVIA. That's a secret.

> *He turns back to the front dust-cover.*

MAREK. 'The Final Grace' – what does this title mean?

> *Pause.*

OLIVIA. Well. Some time before Dodo was hurled into oblivion by that alleged pig . . . he told me one of my obsessive themes in poetry was suicide. And brooding on that, the phrase 'The Final Grace' popped into my mind.

MAREK. Which is the final grace? Death itself – or suicide?

OLIVIA. What do you think?

Pause.

MAREK. The profit motive *is* relevant to a Bolivian tin miner.

OLIVIA. I didn't mean it that way. I just meant these clever glossies for women are just as corrupt in their own way as the image and lie-spinning ones.

MAREK *puts the book back on the desk and wraps his towel round his neck.*

MAREK. All too complicated for me!

OLIVIA. I must admit, you don't have a complicated attitude to women.

MAREK. Oh well. It's you who is writing for this magazine –

OLIVIA. And what are *you* writing these days?

Pause.

MAREK. I haven't written for months –

He throws the towel on the floor and walks out.

Scene Twenty-three. *Interior. Interrogation room: day.*

A British army intelligence OFFICER *sits behind a desk in a bare room.* MAREK *sits in front of him, dressed in army-issue khaki shirt and trousers.*

OFFICER. And you say Stanton was a British agent, and that you were helping him to escape the Germans – ?

MAREK. That is true.

OFFICER. Yet Stanton disappeared, and we find you in a concentration camp in Germany!

MAREK. So?

OFFICER. One wonders how you managed to survive the Gestapo after they caught you –

MAREK. I have already told everything.

OFFICER. I'm asking *everything* . . . once more.

Pause.

MAREK. I was tortured. I was threatened with execution. Several people were shot in the yard outside my cell. Then one day they sent me to Germany.

OFFICER. Why not a concentration camp in Poland?

MAREK. How should I know? What's the difference between death in Belsen and death in Auschwitz?

OFFICER. But you are alive, after all –

MAREK. In two weeks I would have been dead.

Pause.

OFFICER. You weren't in *such* bad condition –

MAREK. I'm sorry about that!

OFFICER. Communists had a higher survival rate in the camps than most other groups –

MAREK. I told you I am a Communist. And so? It is a question of psychology, of mutual solidarity.

OFFICER. Once more. How *did* Stanton die?

MAREK. In an Allied bombing raid.

OFFICER. But you didn't.

MAREK. The pig was so ideologically treacherous as to fall on the wrong man!

OFFICER. Not *that* bloody silly story again. *Please!*

MAREK. As you wish.

Pause.

OFFICER. We can discharge you to the West or to the East. Which do you want?

MAREK. I already said: to Poland.

OFFICER. Very patriotic!

MAREK. I am not patriotic in any sense you would understand.
OFFICER (*calling out*). Corporal –

A CORPORAL *enters.*

OFFICER. I'll see him again tomorrow –

The CORPORAL *holds the door open.* MAREK *gets up.*

MAREK. You have not the right to hold me –
OFFICER. I've no intention –

They look at each other a moment, then MAREK *goes out followed by the* CORPORAL. *A* CIVILIAN *enters.*

CIVILIAN. Well?
OFFICER. As far as I'm concerned the poor sod's off his rocker.

Pause.

CIVILIAN. And Stanton.
OFFICER. There we go again, Sir. Stanton was dropped in the wrong place by some idiot of *ours* – and subsequently had his neck broken when getting in the way of a bombed pig!
CIVILIAN. How surrealistic!

The CIVILIAN *goes out. The* OFFICER *takes a sheet of paper and begins to write.*

Scene Twenty-four. *Interior. Olivia's living-room: evening.*

She is dictating again.

OLIVIA. . . . Although a dedicated Party activist, he never ceased to be openly critical of the Party's subservience to Moscow, its implementation of Stalinism in his own country, and the destruction of the ideals of dedicated fellow-communists. (*Pause.*) In the early fifties he was expelled from the Party, arrested, his books condemned – and the man himself, to use

Orwell's term: an unperson. (*Pause.*) Released in nineteen fifty-nine, he promptly circulated an essay declaring that his country, far from being socialist, was a degraded workers' state controlled by a bureaucracy with its feet in Poland and its head in the Kremlin. Quoting Lenin, he reminded that '. . . revolution cannot be exported on bayonets . . . and that this was in effect what had happened in his country. (*Pause.*) At the same time, his novel FACES IN THE DARK had a startling success both in East and West. (*Pause.*) Indefatigable in his public and scathing attacks on capitalism in general and American imperialism in particular, we might assume that this gifted and complex man . . . had the comrades oscillating between fury and cautious expediency. (*Pause.*) Meeting him, one is immediately struck by an almost physical emanation of passion and despair. He defends his country and expounds its tragic history with fanatical intelligence. At the same time, he gives the private impression of being a tormented hulk of a man, prone to both physical violence and mental, or perhaps rather emotional, self-destruction.

Camera pans to the door, which is slightly ajar. MAREK, *dressed to go out, stands listening. As* OLIVIA *stops to light a cigarette, he quietly withdraws.*

Scene Twenty-five. *Interior. Taxi: evening.*

MAREK *lolls in a corner of the cab, drinking from a half bottle of whisky. He looks out.*

Scene Twenty-six. *Exterior. King's Road: evening.*

(*After all, what do we all expect* this *shot to convey?*)

Scene Twenty-seven. *Interior. Taxi.*

Scene Twenty-six from MAREK's *point of view for about a hundred yards. Close-up* MAREK *drinking.*

Scene Twenty-eight. *Exterior. Taxi. Chelsea side street: evening.*

MAREK *pays off the taxi, and walks quite steadily up some steps to the door of a big house.*

Scene Twenty-nine. *Interior. Dining-room. Chelsea house: evening.*

A long dining-table with candelabra. The elaborate remains of a meal set for ten people. MAREK *sits hunched before a coffee cup. A* GIRL, *expensively and fashionably dressed sits opposite him sipping wine.*

GIRL. I can't pronounce your second name.
MAREK. Try the first one. Marek. That's easy, isn't it?

    Pause.

GIRL. Marek –
MAREK. Why didn't you go into the other room with the rest of them?
GIRL. You didn't say a word throughout dinner. You didn't eat. Were you trying to attract attention to yourself?
MAREK. I've had more than my fair share of attention, one way and another.
GIRL. I haven't read your books.
MAREK. It doesn't matter.
GIRL. What does? (*Pause.*) To you, I mean.
MAREK. Do you work?
GIRL. I'm a journalist. And my father's rich.
MAREK. What do you write?
GIRL. For a women's page. Clothes and all the rest of it. (*Pause.*) You needn't sneer –
MAREK. I'm not sneering.
GIRL. Then what is it your face is doing?
MAREK. I have a stomach ulcer. It just bit me.

GIRL. Well, you've certainly been giving it plenty to drink.

MAREK. Those people disgusted me –

GIRL. That's a pity. We were all invited to meet *you* –

MAREK. I should think they were relieved to get away from me.

GIRL. Self-pitying as well?

MAREK. If you like.

Pause.

GIRL. I stayed.

MAREK. To irritate me?

GIRL. Mrs Carlton told me most women find you attractive. Since I don't, I thought you might welcome a change.

MAREK. Who is Mrs Carlton?

GIRL. Your hostess. I doubt if a single well-known foreign writer can slip through London without her grabbing at him.

MAREK. Or her. I mean, at women writers too?

GIRL. Oh yes. And painters. And sculptors. Designers. Actors. Etcetera.

Pause.

MAREK. I remembered the address only. Not her name.

GIRL. Are you going back to Poland?

MAREK. I don't know.

GIRL. Are you writing something now?

MAREK. I don't know. I plan.

GIRL. Mrs Carlton told me you once pulled a diplomat's ears in Amsterdam.

MAREK. He insulted me.

GIRL. How?

MAREK. He had this enormous chandelier. I was swinging on it. It broke loose from the ceiling and – *crash!* All there were most shocked, and he in particular. He told me I was a drunken barbarian. He was correct – none the less I objected.

GIRL. As one does, on these occasions!

MAREK. Which occasions?

GIRL. When one's indisputably in the wrong – and extravagant with it.

MAREK. The chandelier was no antique, I assure you. Also, I paid for it from my Dutch royalties.

GIRL. And nobody hurt?

MAREK. A waiter slightly cut in the cheek. I wept, and kissed him. He didn't like this.

Pause.

GIRL. Do you often swing from chandeliers?

MAREK. If I am bored, and if there is a chandelier present. I swallow a lot of drink very quickly, then I make a tremendous acrobatic leap –

GIRL. What pity Mrs Carlton hasn't got one.

MAREK. Ah well. I prefer this candlelight.

GIRL. Where are you staying in London?

MAREK. With a woman called Olivia Stanton.

GIRL. The poet?

MAREK. We are friends for many years.

GIRL. You look to me a bit out of condition now for swinging on chandeliers.

MAREK. That is true. In any case, it is stupid behaviour. On the other hand it is a beautiful sensation . . . swinging . . . backwards and forwards –

GIRL. Yes. And it all adds to your reputation. Wild Polish writer and all that. What else do you do in that line –

MAREK. If drunk enough, I declaim.

GIRL. Are you drunk enough now?

MAREK *climbs on to one of the tables, picks up a candelabrum and stands holding it, silent.*

GIRL. Cat got your tongue?

Pause.

MAREK. I will declaim an article for a glossy magazine.

GIRL. Vogue?

MAREK. What?

GIRL. Nova?

MAREK. Although a dedicated poet, she never did stop to criticize the cult of liberating the women. This not because she disagrees with such liberation, but she is old enough and experienced enough to find cynicism in herself for such things. When at grips with the Sisters she has them oscillating between fury and an inadequacy to outwit her intelligence. (*Pause.*) Meeting her, one is struck by the radiating of passion and despair. She writes of self-murder in her verses, yet lives with a kind of compassionate urgency –

Pause. The GIRL stands, flashing with anger.

GIRL. You maudlin, self-indulgent, adolescent *creep!*

MAREK. Indeed yes. Except I do not know the word creep, though it has the sound . . . how do you say it? . . . the onomatopoeia . . . of being insulting.

GIRL. You're dead right!

MAREK carefully gets down from the table and walks round to her, still holding the candelabrum.

MAREK. What were you doing in . . . let us say . . . nineteen forty-seven?

GIRL. Pushing my way out of my mother's womb. And why nineteen forty-seven?

MAREK. Not special. I chose the year at random.

GIRL. All right. So I'm twenty-five. So what?

MAREK. I find the abuse from young women touching.

He sets the candelabrum on the table and lights a cigarette.

GIRL. And I find the patronizing from older men both arrogant and pathetic!

He touches her cheek gently. She slaps his hand away.

GIRL. I've heard all about your so-called charm as well, you know. And I'm not swooning.

Pause.

MAREK. Touch *my* cheek –

She is trembling with anger and moves to one side.

GIRL. Get out of my way –

He does so, and she goes to the door. She stops and turns to him.

GIRL. You're pretty bloody loathsome.
MAREK. Such insight!
GIRL. Such cheap sarcasm!

Pause.

MAREK. I thought you were leaving –
GIRL. I am.

And she goes out. MAREK *sits down and pours himself a glass of wine. He goes to the window, drinking. It is a large, penthouse window, and from his point of view: the Chelsea night skyline and the river.*

Scene Thirty. *Interior. Girl's bedroom: early morning.*

MAREK *is in bed with the* GIRL *from the last scene. The bedroom is luxurious in a rather austere fashion. She is asleep. He lies staring at the ceiling. On the floor beside the bed, a telephone. He reaches down and dials a number.*

MAREK. Olivia?

We hear an indistinct murmuring from the phone. The GIRL *wakes up. He covers the phone and turns to her.*

MAREK. The address here?
GIRL. Foolsville.

He again speaks into the phone.

MAREK. She says foolsville. The joke escapes me.
GIRL. Thirty-two Marlin Road, Haverstock Hill.
MAREK. Thirty-two Marlin Road, Haverstock Hill.

Again a murmuring from the phone.

MAREK (*to the* GIRL). It is your house alone?
GIRL. It is my house alone.
MAREK (*into the phone*). Yes. (*Pause.*) You will find me? (*Pause.*)
One last time? (*Pause.*) Yes. All right. (*Pause.*) Thank you.

He puts the phone down. The GIRL, *wrapping the sheet around her, reaches for cigarettes and lights one.*

MAREK. You said you did not smoke.
GIRL. Yup. I said that.

Pause.

MAREK. I phone Olivia Stanton for her to come for me.
GIRL. You can imagine my surprise!
MAREK. Catherine –
GIRL. My god! You remember my name?

Pause.

MAREK. I shall not go to Poland.

Pause.

GIRL. Look – I'm absolutely exhausted. Are you going to insist
on talking?

Pause.

MAREK. Why do you want to seem hard?
GIRL. I don't want to *seem*. I bloody well *am*.
MAREK. Which is why you let me come back here?
GIRL. I was pissed up to the eyebrows.

Pause.

MAREK. You were . . . passionate. During the night –

GIRL. Nothing to do with you. I always am.

MAREK. It doesn't matter the man?

GIRL. Of course, it matters!

Pause.

MAREK. I don't understand.

GIRL. Aren't Polish birds more or less the same these days?

MAREK. Catherine –

GIRL. You'd better get dressed and wait for Olivia Stanton downstairs. Does she make a *habit* of ferrying you back from your women?

MAREK. What a bitch!

GIRL. I'm a highly educated, intelligent, attractive woman. The fact that I'm inconsistent – like bawling you out then letting you into my bed – is just one facet of my rich complexity.

She stubs out her cigarette and rolls over on to her stomach. MAREK *gets out of bed and starts dressing. After a moment, and very softly.*

GIRL. Marek –

MAREK. Yes?

GIRL. I want to see you again. (*Pause.*) I want you to tell me about your life –

Pause.

MAREK. The phone number?

GIRL. There's a notebook and pad. Copy it from the phone.

He does so. As he approaches the bed, she pushes her face deep down into the pillow.

MAREK (*quietly*). Are you sure, Catherine?

Pause.

GIRL. I often say things I don't mean. But self-humiliation's only bearable when I'm being honest.

Pause.

MAREK. You are not self-humiliating now!

GIRL. Yes I am. Because quite a big part of me wants to say to you bugger off and don't come back.

He sits on the bed and strokes her hair. She shakes his hand off.

GIRL. But just at this minute – *blow*, will you?

He finishes dressing and goes out, shutting the bedroom door quietly.

Scene Thirty-one. *Interior. Olivia's car : early morning.*

OLIVIA's *face is set and hard.* MAREK *looks desolate.*

OLIVIA. At least for once I didn't have to confront the girl in question!

Pause.

MAREK. Tonight, you and I will go out together –

Pause.

OLIVIA. Everything's finished for you – isn't it?

Pause.

MAREK. I don't know what you mean.

OLIVIA. Lying to yourself is worse than lying to other people. At least *they* can make up their own minds what to do if they find out. (*Pause.*) Accept you . . . reject you . . . they can choose. (*Pause.*) But you can't – can you Marek?

Pause.

MAREK. I lie to myself?

OLIVIA. Of course, you do. You know you do.

MAREK. Writer X? The man, the work and the legend?

Pause.

OLIVIA. I do believe you've been eavesdropping on me –

Pause.

MAREK. I heard something you were saying . . . into your tape-recorder.

OLIVIA. About *you* – you think?

MAREK. Yes.

OLIVIA. And if it were?

MAREK. It could not be published.

OLIVIA. Why not?

MAREK. It has no relation to now –

OLIVIA. But I haven't got as far as 'now' . . . yet.

MAREK. You don't know how it *is* now – for me.

OLIVIA. No? (*Pause.*) Do you spew it out during the night for these dollies? Would they have the faintest idea what you were talking about? War . . . camps . . . partisans . . . politics . . . dating back to before they were *born?*

> *Pause.*

MAREK. How I *hate* Western countries!

OLIVIA. Yes. And how you hate the others too!

MAREK. Stop the car. Let me out –

> *But she is already parking the car – they are in front of her own house. She gets out.*

Scene Thirty-two. *Exterior. Olivia's house: early morning.*

OLIVIA *goes to her door, looking in her handbag for her house keys. On the top step, she turns to look down at the car.* MAREK *gets out and stumbles up the steps towards her. She opens the door and stands back for him.*

OLIVIA. Are you coming in?

MAREK. I don't know.

OLIVIA. You ought to go to bed.

> *As in Scene Four he starts going through his pockets, confused and incoherent.*

MAREK. My passport . . . wallet . . . photographs –

He stands helplessly as she puts her hand into the inside pocket of his jacket.

OLIVIA. There! Passport . . . wallet . . . and –

She opens the wallet and takes out some photos.

OLIVIA. And photos –

She hands them to him. He flings them on the doorstep and rushes into the house. OLIVIA *bends down to pick them up. She puts them into her handbag and goes into the house.*

Scene Thirty-three. *Repeat Scene Twenty-one.*

Except that: MAREK *and* STANTON *are played by two* ACTORS. *The dialogue is in Polish, with English sub-titles as in Scene Twenty-one.*

Scene Thirty-four. *Interior. TV studio.*

A line-up sort of interview. At a table: INTERVIEWER, MAREK *and* OLIVIA. INTERVIEWER *to camera.*

INTERVIEWER. We have in the studio Marek Sienkiewicz, from whose novel FACES IN THE DARK that film was adapted . . . and Olivia Stanton, whose much-praised volume of poems WANING LIGHT was translated into Polish by Mr Sienkiewicz in the mid-sixties. (*Pause.*) Mr Sienkiewicz, would it be true to say that whilst your novel was extremely successful, this extraordinary film attracted little interest.

MAREK is drunk and noticeably glazed. He sips at a glass of whisky and sucks noisily at a cigarette.

MAREK. It was experimental film, made by a student. Very short. Made from only two chapters of the book.

INTERVIEWER. But would it be true to say that the . . . lack of interest . . . despite the obvious talent of the director . . . was more a question of official disapproval than anything else?

MAREK. Who knows?

Pause.

INTERVIEWER. Yet . . . the director went on to make several distinguished full-length features in subsequent years. And he, like yourself, appears to be obsessed with the war, the problems of the liberation . . . indeed with what one might call a 'lost generation' of your contemporaries – ?

MAREK. A 'lost generation'? What? Like some American writers after the First World War who got pushed into such category?

INTERVIEWER. I didn't intend any specious comparisons –

MAREK. Who more obsessed with the *Second* World War than you English and Americans? And look what bloody awful films came out of *that!*

INTERVIEWER. I couldn't agree more, but I meant something rather different –

MAREK. This is boring.

INTERVIEWER. I –

OLIVIA. I think what Marek means is that –

MAREK. He doesn't know *what* he means! (*He stands, drinking – slams down the glass.*) He is trendy shit who knows *nothing* –

MAREK *lurches away. The studio lights dim. The* INTERVIEWER *is left staring at* OLIVIA *in angry consternation.*

INTERVIEWER. Oh, *Jesus!*

OLIVIA. I did warn you –

INTERVIEWER. Thank god it wasn't live. That's all I can say.

OLIVIA. I'd better get after him –

As she gets up, the PRODUCER *comes storming on to the studio floor.*

PRODUCER. Well, Olivia! You can tell your Mr Sink-what's-his-name thanks very much!

OLIVIA. None of it was my idea –

PRODUCER. Granted. And neither will the boot go up your backside or his. It'll go up *mine!* (*He picks up* MAREK's *glass and gulps the remaining whisky.*)

OLIVIA (*to* INTERVIEWER). Tom – did you really expect to edge him into politics?

INTERVIEWER. I honestly didn't mean –

OLIVIA. You honestly didn't do your homework, did you?

PRODUCER. Christ! Who cares about the bastard any more? Who's even *heard* of him any more?

OLIVIA. Then why have him on the programme?

PRODUCER. We were relying on *you* to –

OLIVIA. To nurse him through? That's even more insulting to him than he was to deliberately cock it up.

PRODUCER. One might have thought you'd have a bit of influence over an ex-lover!

There is a long silence. Then OLIVIA, *quietly.*

OLIVIA. I never had much influence over you – did I?

And she leaves the studio.

INTERVIEWER. Whoops!

PRODUCER. And bloody whoops to *you*, man!

Scene Thirty-five. *Interior. Olivia's sitting-room: evening.*

OLIVIA *is pacing up and down, smoking.* MAREK *lies on the couch – a whisky bottle on the floor beside him, a full glass in his hand. After a moment.*

MAREK. It is incest.

OLIVIA. *What* is incest?

MAREK. Because you know them – they think they can get me into the studio and make fool of me.

OLIVIA. On the whole, it doesn't really work like that. And if it

did – I wouldn't be a party to it. (*Pause.*) It was *you* who blew
it – If you agree to do a programme, you *do* it –
MAREK. Not *I!*

> *Pause.*

OLIVIA. Years ago, you –
MAREK. I'm not years ago. I'm now.

> *Pause.*

OLIVIA. That's the trouble, isn't it?

> *Pause.*

MAREK. Olivia –
OLIVIA. Yes?
MAREK. Read me the last verse of the title poem –

> *Pause.*

OLIVIA. The Final Grace?
MAREK. Yes, please –

> *She hesitates, then goes to fetch the book. Opening it, she
> hesitates again, then begins to read:*

OLIVIA. And then, when ice shrouds the exposed
And stricken roots –
MAREK (*cutting in*). It is an adolescent girl's poem!

> *Long pause.*

OLIVIA. That's what I think too –
MAREK. Dodo must have encouraged you because he loved you.
Or else he was an idiot.
OLIVIA. The bloody thing was published, at any rate –
MAREK. Later poems better. Later ones very good.

> *Pause.*

OLIVIA. *I* didn't think very much of the pig scene in the film. *Or* that section in the book –

MAREK. Yes. It was a mistake.

Pause.

OLIVIA (*drily*). But true?

He begins to laugh convulsively, rolling from side to side.

MAREK. Yes! Yes yes yes yes –

He takes a drink and starts coughing. As the coughing fit subsides.

OLIVIA. I'll read you something else.

She goes to her desk, puts the book of poems down and takes up a sheaf of typewritten notes. MAREK *swings his feet off the couch to the floor, clutches his glass, watches her. She sits at the desk and switches the desk lamp on.*

OLIVIA. Ours is hardly a period when the romantic view of the artist or writer can survive as anything but a subject of bored amusement. 'X', on the other hand – a bloodthirsty scavenger from the ruins of Warsaw – graduated so to speak from the heroic sewers to the no less grim business of virtual civil war. The Left and the Right engaged in a process of mutual assassination. (*Pause.*) Before the Communist regime was firmly established, 'X' proved himself as skilful with a submachine-gun as he was later to prove himself in Marxist dialectics.

She pauses a moment and looks at him. He stares at the floor, his body rigid.

OLIVIA. At a time when Western youth was idolizing rebels without causes, 'X' emerged fully fledged as man of action and man of letters combined – his charisma all the more compelling for the fact that he was no servile hack to the regime. (*Pause.*) On the contrary, before his political eclipse, he seemed to have carried the national and traditional virtues of stubborn courage and patriotism into a new dimension. (*Pause.*) We are used to the idea now that only the poseur, the phoney, the self-deluded, can pass off a romantic bohemianism. Poverty, exhibitionism, drinking . . . and what used to be quaintly known as 'womanizing' . . . when flaunted as sanctions to the creative temperament . . . have long been as dead as Modigliani. (*Pause.*) But dated myths, like dated fashions, tend to reassert themselves in new forms at precisely those times when the informed sceptic hopes they have been debunked once and for all. And who have until recently been more acquiescent in these largely male-devised charades than women? (*Pause.*) It used to be said that 'X' had only to walk into a room for the women's heads to turn and yearn. (*Pause.*) That anguished face . . . those sensitive hands which had fingered pen and trigger alike . . . those ghosts of Belsen behind the eyes . . . and much else. (*Pause.*) And yet?

Again she pauses to look at MAREK. *He raises his head.*

MAREK. And yet?
OLIVIA. 'And yet' isn't part of the article –

Pause.

MAREK. You are going to let them print all that? And more?
OLIVIA. I don't think so.

Pause.

MAREK. *Is* it some article?
OLIVIA. There was supposed to be one. This isn't it. This is . . . sort of . . . mine.

Pause.

MAREK. I go out now –

Pause.

OLIVIA. Tom wasn't *wrong* to talk about a generation. At least some of you. (*Pause.*) Certainly *you* –

MAREK. What did you know about any of it? *I* told you everything –

OLIVIA. And meantime . . . the years go by.

MAREK. Don't tell me. Don't say I will not be older. I hear this
too many times.

Pause.

OLIVIA. Forty, you said –

MAREK. What?

OLIVIA. You couldn't imagine living much past forty you said –

Pause.

MAREK. *And yet?*

Pause.

OLIVIA. I think you probably *have* been very much loved by
women –

MAREK. I loved, also –

Pause.

OLIVIA. Do you remember your line about a bureaucracy with its
feet in Poland and its head in the Kremlin?

MAREK. It seems you remembered it!

Pause.

OLIVIA. Well. Didn't you eventually come to live with your
prick in women and your head in the *war?*

MAREK. Olivia – what do you want to say to me? Get it over with.

OLIVIA. You're wrecked, Marek. Aren't you?

MAREK. So?

OLIVIA. And the young women aren't the same, are they?

Pause.

MAREK. So?

OLIVIA (*shouting*). I just wish you'd bloody well let some of it
out!

He goes towards her unsteadily and puts his arms round her.
She pulls away sharply.

OLIVIA. And I don't mean *that!*

He swerves away, back to the bottle – another drink, a cigarette.

MAREK. Women now – hah!
OLIVIA. And self-pity now –hah!

Pause.

MAREK. You are wrong. I have no self-pity.
OLIVIA. I'll tell you this much. If you can't live off your past any
more in Warsaw – you certainly can't in London!

Pause.

MAREK. You are right –
OLIVIA. Don't phone me from *anywhere* in the morning –

And she leaves the room. He goes to the desk, picks up her
typewritten pages – tears them to pieces. Close-up his face.

Scene Thirty-six. *Exterior. Country road : day.*

A British Army open truck is driving along the road. Inside – ten
or fifteen men. Some of them emaciated, all of them dressed in odd
bits and pieces of clothing. They sit listlessly, their heads nodding.
MAREK *is one of them – dressed as in Scene Twenty-three. A*
YOUNG MAN, *in better condition than most of the others, begins to*
sing softly.

YOUNG MAN.
Es geht alles vorüber,
Es geht alles vorbei.
Nach jeden Dezember –
Kommt wieder ein Mai.

MAREK *stands in the lurching truck and grabs the young man*
by the lapels of his ragged jacket.

MAREK. Deutsch?

The YOUNG MAN *is frightened. He murmurs.*

YOUNG MAN. Polski˙–

> MAREK *swings a very hard punch at the boy, who collapses. Everyone in the truck looks on – no one moves or says anything.* MAREK *resumes his place. The truck comes to a frontier post – the driver shows papers to the guards. They wave the truck on. The frontier-post barrier comes down behind it.*

Scene Thirty-seven. *Interior. Olivia's house: evening.*

We see MAREK *come out of the sitting-room and go down the stairs, through the front hall to the door.*

Scene Thirty-eight. *Interior. Olivia's bedroom: evening.*

She is lying clothed on the bed, the room illuminated from the street only. She hears the front door slam. She gets up and goes to the window: from her point of view.

Scene Thirty-nine. *Exterior. Street: evening.*

MAREK *walking up the street. He staggers against a garden wall, then stumbles on.*

Scene Forty. *Interior. Olivia's bedroom: evening.*

She lies on the bed. Close-up her face.

Scene Forty-one. *Interior. Hotel foyer: night.*

It is late, and there are few lights on. OLIVIA *is helping a drunken* MAREK *through the entrance lounge and towards a wide, curving staircase. A* MAN *is sitting with a last drink at one of the tables. He goes to* OLIVIA, *who is having trouble holding* MAREK *up and takes his arm.*

MAN. Lumbered with our Polish friend again, Olivia?

OLIVIA. Looks like it, doesn't it –

MAN. Here, let me help –

He takes on the job of manœuvring MAREK *up the stairs.*

MAN. What did you think of the party?

OLIVIA. *He* had a fight. Not much. The other man was drunk as well.

MAN. Really? I didn't see it. Still, in *that* crush! You know what?

OLIVIA. What?

MAN. Our charming hostess had the caterers put the gateaux in the bath for some bizarre reason. And that French writer, what's-his-name –

OLIVIA. Charbeaud –

MAN. That's right. Charbeaud. Well, he goes into the bathroom pissed out of his wits – can't find the light. So well, he waves it about more or less –

OLIVIA. All over the gateaux!

MAN. Exactly. He told me afterwards. God, I hope you didn't –

OLIVIA. I didn't eat anything at all –

They are at the landing leading to MAREK'S *room. The man props him against the wall.*

MAN. About the only thing I enjoyed, really – when the catering chaps started bringing in the bloody cakes! Thank god the conference'll be over tomorrow –

OLIVIA. Yes. Before we're all run out of town!

MAN. Do you think he can manage from here – ?

OLIVIA. Yes, it's all right. (*Pointing.*) That's his room –

MAN. See you tomorrow then –

OLIVIA. Thanks. Goodnight –

MAN. 'Night –

He goes back down the staircase. OLIVIA *takes* MAREK'S *arm and leads him to his door. She has the key in her hand. Opens the door and helps him in.*

Scene Forty-two. *Interior. Olivia's bedroom: evening.*

As in Scene Forty. She stares at the ceiling.

Scene Forty-three. *Interior. Hotel room: night.*

OLIVIA *and* MAREK *lie side by side in bed.*

OLIVIA. So tomorrow, you'll be gone –
MAREK. I shall be back.

> *Pause.*

OLIVIA. Why did you hit that young man at the party?
MAREK. I don't know where he heard it, but he was singing a song the Nazi troops used to sing when they were pulling out sometimes. When they knew it was all over –
OLIVIA (*softly chants*).
Es geht alles vorüber,
Es geht alles vorbei –
MAREK. No . . . please –
OLIVIA. What does it mean?

> *Pause.*

MAREK. After each winter . . . there will come another spring.
OLIVIA. Another victory –

> *Pause.*

MAREK. Yes. (*Pause.*) I could bear neither the words nor the language.
OLIVIA. But . . . that young writer is English –
MAREK. I know. I have unpleasant reflexes. I don't defend it.

> *She turns to him, smiling.*

OLIVIA. And is it some of your other reflexes which have been . . . working on me?
MAREK. No. (*Pause.*) But. I go away.

OLIVIA. As usual!

MAREK. I can never see any future. I fear everything. Nowadays many people are exiles in their own country. (*Suddenly and fiercely*.) It all goes to hell!

> *He puts his arms round her – she doesn't move. Looking across his shoulder.*

OLIVIA. It does here, too –

Scene Forty-four. *Interior. Olivia's bedroom : evening.*

As in Scene Forty. OLIVIA *gets up and goes downstairs.*

Scene Forty-five. *Interior. Olivia's sitting-room : evening.*

She enters and goes to her desk. Takes up the microphone and sits holding it. She sees the torn sheets of paper in and around the waste-paper basket. She picks out one or two of the pieces, reads the fragments, throws them back into the basket. With the microphone again.

OLIVIA. What do we make of men who intellectually and un-patronizingly accept our revulsion ... our rebellion ... whether we are spitting extremists, or cool non-servitors – (*Pause.*) yet are themselves trapped? (*Pause.*) Who are as split and divided as many of *us?* (*Pause.*) And who, in the end, can no more throw off their conditioned attitudes to women than most women can throw off their own conditioning? (*Pause.*) For myself, I can only admit with bitter rancour that to fall in love is to abdicate my sense of justice ... to voluntarily give up so much hard-won ground –

Scene Forty-six. *Interior. Girl's bedroom : evening.*

The girl CATHERINE, *whom* MAREK *first encountered in Scene Twenty-nine.* CATHERINE *lies on the bed, wearing trousers and a short embroidered caftan.* MAREK *sits on the floor beside the bed, one arm flung across her legs and a glass in his other hand.* CATHERINE's *eyes are closed.*

MAREK. . . . . I survived the camp because I hadn't been there long enough to die or be exterminated before the British arrived. (*Pause.*) I survived the early years after the war by a mixture of luck and experience. Because I was still fighting, you see . . . and later, there were good reasons why the most honest Communists still deluded themselves about what was going on. (*Pause.*) And anyhow I managed to write as well . . . *somehow* –

He drinks, pauses.

CATHERINE. Will you give me a cigarette?

He lights a cigarette and puts it between her lips.

MAREK. Afterwards –

She suddenly leaps off the bed.

CATHERINE. I'd like to go out –
MAREK. But you said –
CATHERINE. In fact I'm *going* out. Are you coming?

Pause.

MAREK. Where?
CATHERINE. Oh, anywhere –

She is smiling, and puffing exaggeratedly at her cigarette. MAREK *leaps to his feet and smashes her across the face with the flat of his hand. She staggers, but recovers at once. She stands looking at him with her arms straight and rigid beside her – her face expressionless.*

MAREK (*slowly*). You . . . asked me . . . to come back –
CATHERINE. I'd forgotten.
MAREK. Forgotten?
CATHERINE. What to expect, anyway –

She slowly rubs her cheek with the back of one hand. MAREK
*seems paralysed. She goes to the telephone and lightly takes up
the receiver. She speaks tauntingly over the mouthpiece in a
baby-voice.*

CATHERINE. Find me, find me, find me –

*And slams it down. He still neither moves nor speaks, staring at
her.*

CATHERINE. You know what 'putting down' means?

Pause.

MAREK. Yes –
CATHERINE. Nobody ever put you down?

Pause.

MAREK. I am sorry I hit you –
CATHERINE. That's the least of it.
MAREK. And what is . . . the most?
CATHERINE. Didn't you know there's a war on –

Pause.

MAREK. In my life . . . there has never not been –

This gets CATHERINE *really laughing. She stands laughing
with her hand over her mouth.*

CATHERINE. I don't mean bloody *Vietnam!* I don't mean just
bang-bangs! And kill-kills!

He stands to face her.

CATHERINE. We've had *them* all *my* life –

Pause.

MAREK. Do you know Olivia Stanton?
CATHERINE. I've met her –

Pause.

MAREK. I think she has . . . 'put me down' once already this evening –

CATHERINE. She rises in my estimation!

CATHERINE goes to her wardrobe and takes out a heavy suède short coat. Puts it on. For a moment she goes limp, exhausted-looking.

CATHERINE (*quietly*). I *could* love you. (*Pause.*) But I won't.

MAREK. Because?

She is now jaunty, but suspiciously so.

CATHERINE. Your historical recitations are boring for one thing –

Pause.

MAREK. I bore myself!

CATHERINE. No, you don't. Your *distinguished* past still fascinates you. (*Pause.*) Zybulski died – long live Marek!

MAREK (*shaken*). *Zybulski?*

CATHERINE. But I guess he was the real thing, man –

MAREK. *Catherine!*

CATHERINE. And I doubt if you are!

He slumps down on the bed, his arms folded across his knees, his head down.

MAREK. You know what you are talking about?

CATHERINE. Yup –

MAREK. There is nothing to compare between us!

CATHERINE. Who's comparing?

MAREK. Why mention him?

CATHERINE. Oh, we try to keep up, you know. Us kids. We go to the movies . . . and read, and all that.

He gets up again and goes to her.

MAREK. Do you mean to be so vicious?

Pause.

CATHERINE. No. I'm sorry. I just wish you could have found some other way of hitting me – if you had to.

He lifts his right hand, forefinger extended, moving it from side to side.

MAREK. You go this way . . . that way . . . I am lost.

Pause.

CATHERINE. Well. I *did* provoke you. It won't burn me up if I confuse you as well.

Pause.

MAREK. Do you think I invent all I say?

CATHERINE. No. But I'm not going to get stuck *on* you or *with* you.

MAREK. Did I ask that?

CATHERINE. Oh yes you *did!* In your fashion – but I don't count the honour unique. After all, whose hang-ups could be as panoramic as yours? There isn't room for anybody else!

She goes out. MAREK *begins to dial a number.*

Scene Forty-seven. *Interior. Olivia's sitting-room: evening.*

As in Scene Forty-five; but now OLIVIA *is typing. The phone on the desk rings. She reaches out to it then pulls back. She sits looking at the phone as it rings. When it stops, she carries on typing.*

Scene Forty-eight. *Interior. Girl's bedroom: evening.*

As in Scene Forty-six. MAREK *has the phone on the floor beside the bed, with an open address-book next to it. Holding the book open with one hand, he dials another number. Whilst the number is still ringing, he puts the phone down. He dials a three-digit number. We hear the* OPERATOR's *voice.*

OPERATOR'S VOICE. International?

MAREK *puts the phone down again. He leaves.*

Scene Forty-nine. *Exterior. Pub. Chelsea: evening.*

The saloon bar door opens, and the PUBLICAN *pushes* MAREK *out into the street, holding him firmly by the arm.* MAREK *is swaying, his head lolling. The* PUBLICAN *props him against the wall farther along.*

PUBLICAN. Just don't come back in there again – you understand?

> MAREK *nods his head. The* PUBLICAN *goes back into the pub.* MAREK *staggers a few yards to a telephone kiosk and goes in.*

Scene Fifty. *Interior. Telephone kiosk : evening.*

MAREK, *fumbling, manages to dial a number. He holds a 2p piece jammed against the slot with his thumb.*

Scene Fifty-one. *Interior. Olivia's sitting-room: evening.*

OLIVIA *is in an easy chair with a pile of manuscript on her knees. She is going through it making corrections with a Biro. Beside her on the floor, a tray with the remnants of a meal, a bottle of whisky and a glass. The phone rings. As in Scene Forty-seven she sits looking at the phone until it stops.*

Scene Fifty-two. *Exterior. Street. Chelsea : evening.*

MAREK *comes out of the telephone kiosk and waves a taxi. It stops, and he gets in. The taxi pulls away.*

Scene Fifty-three. *Interior. Cold room. Wholesale meat storage: night.*

A vast room, with rows of beef carcasses hanging – looming shapes in the darkness. MAREK *is staggering between the carcasses. He falls*

*against one of them and lurches away with a cry as he sets it swinging.
We see him moving in and out of the carcasses in a semi-frenzy. At one
point he flings his arms around one of the carcasses, his face pressed
against it. Close-up his face.*

Scene Fifty-four. *Repeat Scene Two.*

Scene Fifty-five. *Interior Cold room. Wholesale meat storage:
night.*

MAREK *springs back from the frozen meat in horror. Close-up as he
put his hands over his face. He stands swaying. A few more steps
and he jolts another carcass. He begins to moan.*

Scene Fifty-six. *Repeat Scene Two.*

Scene Fifty-seven. *Interior. Cold room. Wholesale meat storage:
night.*

MAREK *is running between two rows of carcasses. Again he falls
against one of them and begins to pummel it. He sinks to the floor
panting, and as he looks up we see the dim shapes of the frozen meat
from his point of view. He gets up and begins to scream. The screams
echo. Suddenly he stops. Complete silence. He staggers away into the
darkness.*

Scene Fifty-eight. *Interior. Olivia's house. Marek's bedroom:
morning.*

MAREK *is lying in bed.* OLIVIA *stands near the door. A doctor has
just given* MAREK *an injection. He stands at the bedside for a
moment holding the empty hypodermic.* MAREK *is conscious, his eyes
open. He tries to speak but cannot. He closes his eyes. The* DOCTOR
puts the hypo away in his case and closes it.

DOCTOR. For Christ's sake, Olivia – what are you into *now?*
OLIVIA. He's staying with me –

DOCTOR. You say you found him lying in the front hall –

OLIVIA. Yes. He has a key. But I heard nothing.

DOCTOR. Well, he's in a state of shock. Otherwise – seems to be unhurt, at any rate. Obviously been drinking. He should sleep for quite a while after that shot. I'll call back this evening. (*Pause.*) Have you *any* idea what he'd been doing?

OLIVIA. None at all.

DOCTOR. He managed to walk upstairs?

OLIVIA. With a bit of help –

Pause.

DOCTOR. All right. I'll be back about six. (*Pause.*) I'll let myself out, Olivia. (*Pause.*) All you need do is look in on him from time to time –

OLIVIA. Thank you. Thanks very much for coming so quickly –

DOCTOR. I'm sure he'll be all right. (*Pause.*) I'm glad it wasn't one of . . . *your* . . . freakouts –

Pause.

OLIVIA. No. There hasn't been one for a long time, has there?

He half smiles, embarrassedly, takes his case and goes out. OLIVIA *goes to the bed.*

OLIVIA (*softly*). Marek –

He opens his eyes, speaks with difficulty.

MAREK. Polish writer defects to West. Polish writer declares still a Communist! (*Pause.*) Truth and nonsense. Nonsense and truth –

Pause.

OLIVIA. Sleep, Marek –

MAREK. I can't . . . keep . . . awake.

His eyes close. She waits a moment then goes out.

Scene Fifty-nine. *Interior. Olivia's sitting-room: morning.*

It is empty. The door opens and she comes in. As she does so, the phone rings. She picks it up.

OLIVIA. Hello –

Scene Sixty. *Interior. Girl's bedroom: morning.*

CATHERINE *lies in bed with the phone on her stomach.*

CATHERINE. Is that Olivia Stanton?
OLIVIA'S VOICE. It is –

> *Pause.*

CATHERINE. This is Catherine Raynor. We've met once or twice –

> *Pause.*

OLIVIA'S VOICE. Yes . . . I remember.

> *Pause.*

CATHERINE. Is Marek at your place?

Scene Sixty-one. *Interior. Olivia's sitting-room: morning.*

OLIVIA *is holding the phone, distracted.*

CATHERINE'S VOICE. Hello – ?
OLIVIA. I'm sorry. (*Pause.*) No . . . he isn't.
CATHERINE'S VOICE. Do you know when he'll be back?

> *Pause.*

OLIVIA. Why don't you wait for him to phone you?

> *She puts the phone down. She sits at the desk and lights a cigarette. Stares out of the window, smoking.*

Huggy Bear

HUGGY BEAR was first presented by Yorkshire Television on 11 April 1976, with the following cast:

HOOPER	Bill Wallis
MRS HOOPER	Aimee Delamain
JANINE LASSOO	Sharon Mughan
JAWS McILROY	Paddy Joyce
MRS SCRIVEN	Molly Weir
BARBARA	Madeleine Cannon
MRS HOYDEN	Joyce Heron
MR HOYDEN	Maurice Denham

Director : David Cunliffe
Executive Producer: Peter Willes

1. Interior. Maternity Hospital ward. *Rows of cots containing new-born infants. Feeding time. The cacophony of howls and wails is ear-splitting. Nurses enter with bottles and begin to feed the babies. We close-up the small, clutching, sucking, greedy creatures. Gradual subsidence of yells, and a sudden loud banging as of a walking stick on a door. Cut to:*

2. Interior. Hooper's flat. Bedroom. HOOPER *in bed. A large, heavy, rather moon-faced man of about forty. He is in foetal position, thumb in mouth, sucking and dreaming. The banging noise wakens him. Naked from the bed, though pulling round him a tatty old fur rug and still sucking - HOOPER goes to the door. He opens it. A tiny, skinny old lady sits in a wheelchair. Grey hair pulled tight in a smart bun, blue eyes with a deadly glitter, black dress and pearls. She sits with walking stick poised in the air, as HOOPER bursts upon her.*

MOTHER. Where are the servants, Aldous?

HOOPER. Oh, Mother!

He bangs the door shut and leans against it, panting. A very fast montage of HOOPER dressing follows. His unmodish clothes are scattered all over the room - under the bed one shoe, vest in an old german tin helmet, other shoe on sideboard, shirt pinned to dart board. Collecting and pulling on his clothes, HOOPER has unfortunate encounters with almost every object in the room - including the near-destruction of a toy train set which occupies about a quarter of the space. At last, hopping and shambling, a final tussle with the door and he goes out. Cut to:

3. Interior. Hooper's flat. Bathroom. HOOPER's *ablutions - two fingers under the tap, the water stroked with loving care round* *his eyes. He momentarily contemplates his image in the mirror. A round sad face (life is a battle-field on a trivial scale and no victories), tie under left ear, short hair standing on end.*

HOOPER. The servants, Mother, are - (*pause*). What bloody servants? We haven't got any servants. We have this every day, Mother. Quiet suburb of Cambridge, yes once a genteel sort of house. Room for my swing in the garden. Shattered greenhouse from sonic booms or something. One sick lime tree which must remember to climb this evening. Cuckoo up there, the cheeky feathered get. (*Pause.*) But oh dear me no! *Pas d'esclaves.*

His glance fall on his toothbrush in its rack. He grabs it and rams it into his mouth. The handle breaks off and is petulantly thrown into the sink. He lurches out - but do we hear a fart, as he strains at the doorknob? Cut to:

4. **Interior. Hooper's flat. Living room.** *More like a trendy junk shop in the King's Road, Chelsea. Posters, ancient weapons and bits of armour, a dressmaker's dummy dressed in a nineteenth century hussar's uniform, piles of books on the floor and elsewhere in manic confusion. A rocking horse, an old winding gramophone with a horn. On this last, a saucer of jammy butter revolves gravely on a recording of songs from the people's democratic republics. Yet by open windows leading onto the small garden (lime tree and cuckoo), a table is exquisitely laid for breakfast as if in a hotel. Egg in its cup, silver coffee pot, toast in rack, vase of flowers.*

MOTHER is wheeled into position (supervisory) by the table, her walking stick placed across her knees.

As HOOPER makes his entrance, we note that he does not so much move around as hurtle about in miscalculated trajectories. Thus many bumps, cracked shins, suppressed curses, overturned and sometimes broken objects — or else crushed beneath the huge flat feet encased in what appear to be small black rowing boats. He crashes over to the table, flings himself onto his frail and protesting chair. Aims a spoon at his egg — squashes it flat.

HOOPER. Ah well. The shell, you know. *Grit.* Hens must eat a certain amount, they say. So why not I?

He pokes about with his spoon in the ruined egg, meanwhile his left little finger is exploring left nostril. A piece of toast is engulfed in his massive hand - crumbs and bits of yolk besmirch his chin.

MOTHER. You must speak to the gardener this morning, Aldous.

HOOPER. Ah yes?

MOTHER. The drive, dear boy. The drive needs weeding.

With HOOPER and from his point of view, we contemplate the modest garden, the privet hedge, the street beyond with passing milk-float and a scampering child in school uniform whirling a satchel.

HOOPER. Yes Mother. And the stables. Oh God, the stables!

He pours himself coffee, sloshing half of it in the saucer. Greedy gulps - mouth wiped on sleeve. One elbow, by now, is squashed into the marmalade dish - no matter, for HOOPER scrapes it with a knife and pops the mess between his working jaws.

MOTHER. You'll cut your mouth, Aldous -

HOOPER. Don't be hypocritical, Mother. It's manners you care about.

MOTHER. You don't take after me, Aldous. Nor your poor dear father. (*Pause.*) Babsie phoned -

HOOPER. Who?

MOTHER. Your fiancée.

HOOPER. Good old Barbara.

MOTHER. Such a tactful girl -

One of HOOPER's ever-wandering paws has grabbed the corner of the table cloth and is cleaning his left ear.

HOOPER. Tact in Barbara, you know - (*pause*). Tact in old Barbara -

MOTHER. She ignores your habit of continually breaking wind. Credit where credit -

HOOPER. Is due. Yes. (*Pause.*) But not an erotic person, Mother. (*Pause.*) Fails to titillate, don't you see? She's not. . . not sensual. No.

MOTHER. Don't speak of sex, Aldous.

HOOPER. Was I?

HOOPER *meditatively sucks a forefinger.*

MOTHER. Babsie is wholesome. (*Pause.*) That Lassoo girl also telephoned. From your surgery.

HOOPER. *Lassoo*, now! She -

MOTHER. She has a common voice. And *will* refer to you as 'Olly'.

HOOPER. She was a find, was young Lassoo.

MOTHER. 'Tell him,' she said. 'Tell him that Jaws McIlroy is here.' (*Pause.*) Can I have got that right? *Jaws?*

HOOPER. Right on target, Mater. He bites through telephone directories in pubs for free beer. (*Pause.*) Well the thin ones, you know. The yellow pages.

MOTHER. You do seem to have some extraordinary patients, Aldous -

HOOPER. Yes. I get them. I don't know where they come from. Last week I had an elephant keeper with an impacted wisdom tooth. And just the other day -

MOTHER. When you told me ⸌ 'dentistry'. When I heard the word, the mere word - I felt quite faint. I distinctly remember.

HOOPER. The mouth is a world of its own, Mother -

MOTHER. One only has to think of you. Spending hours each day poring over. . . over -

HOOPER. Gobs. Caverns. Craters.

MOTHER. Year after year -

HOOPER. Hard times when hungover. These high-speed drills. Miss the tooth and end up God knows where, but certainly the patient yelling and screaming. (*Pause.*) Lassoo puts vodka in my water-bottle for the shakes. Keeping up appearances. (*Pause.*) Sometimes I have a terrible urge to drill right out on the other side. Through the back of the neck - eh? But the unrealised fantasy permits me to get through the day, Mother. (*Pause.*) A slip is one thing, we all make mistakes. But inside my head - oh, the carnage!

MOTHER. Aldous!

HOOPER. Yea - I fear the wrath of the Lord.

MOTHER. Your father should not have left us in reduced circumstances.

HOOPER. Mother are you really batty? Sorry to put it to you so maladroitly each morning - did you flip in some genuine sort of way? I mean, you're functional after all. Can you be truly marbles? At the loss of father, I would have thought . . . a certain *joie de vivre*. A certain. . . *reculer pour mieux sauter*? No?

MOTHER. I'm a burden to you, Aldous -

HOOPER. Absolutely no, not at all no. (*Pause.*) I *do* get to wondering where the rubbish that clutters your old grey head comes from -

MOTHER. Impertinence is no substitute for wit, you know -

HOOPER. And you do have your feelings -

MOTHER. And parody a trivial form of aggression, Aldous.

HOOPER. You certainly have style - crackers or not. *Beaucoup de* style - eh? That's what counts when the faculties begin to wane.

MOTHER. I think it is time you were off to the surgery.

She raises her stick and jabs it not unkindly into his paunch.

MOTHER. Scamper, then. Off with you -

Cut to:

5. Interior. Staircase. HOOPER *is stomping up the linoleum stairs to his surgery. His shirt, hanging out of his trousers at the back, peeps below the old stained sports jacket. The jacket is much stained - many soups and ice-creams have passed this way, the casual wiping of greasy hands after chomping bones, the pockets are heavy with objects of the Hooper-trouvé variety - memorabilia such as large nails, plastic animals, screwed-up Kleenex. And the crutch of his trousers hangs somewhere between thighs and knees. Feet at right angles to torso bounce the stairs. A briefcase, naturally half open, swings from a bunched fist. And the man sings joyfully - his own words to the tune of 'Rose Marie'.*

HOOPER (*singing*). Oh, Miss-Slassoo, I love yer, Hi'm always dreamin' of yer -

At the surgery door, a hand like a mighty dumpling is raised to thud the news of his coming. He aims and swings wildly, but the door opens before he makes contact and under momentum, he skitters into the waiting room flailing in all directions.

Cut to:

6. Interior. Surgery. Small waiting room. HOOPER *fetches up against the wall opposite the door, at which* JANINE LASSOO *is languidly poised. . . No one is ruffled - this is morning routine.* JAWS McILROY *is stretched flat on a G-Plan sofa, fast asleep and snoring.* HOOPER *bends over him affectionately:*

HOOPER. Hello dere, Jaws -

And turning to fawn somewhat on the desired JANINE, *inevitably the slight stammer which passes, in* HOOPER, *for the communication of lust.*

HOOPER. Jer-her-her-Hanine? Dear gir-hir-hir-hirl. Morning.

JANINE. Fliesopen -

HOOPER. Eh?

He examines that sensitive area of his crumpled pants. Indeed, the zip is at half mast, showing a square inch or two of pluto-patterned knicks. JANINE *watches, eyeballs rolled to heaven, as* HOOPER *fumbles.*

She is one of those small, slender girls endowed with large breasts (for HOOPER - *the ideal). Pale silvery, back-combed hair like fine wire, with hints of mauve shadow. She has a pert little face - 1940s make-up, and wears a smart starchy white overall, white sneakers and a black canvas belt with snake buckle.*

JANINE. Wholebuildingshakesthway - cumupthem stairs -

Still holding his briefcase, HOOPER *steps onto a small set of scales in the corner, sending the needle in rapid oscillation. With a sigh,* JANINE *yanks the briefcase from his hand.* HOOPER *peers downwards, blinking.*

HOOPER. Glasses -

JANINE. In your *pocket* Olly -

From his breast pocket he pulls the heavy black-framed spectacles, repaired with plaster in two places. He fixes them on the tip of his nose. Things are blurred, down there on the scales - his lenses filmed with thumb and finger marks.

JANINE. Themboots - weighaton, shd think.

HOOPER *precariously lifts a massively-shod foot for inspection. As he starts to over-balance,* JANINE *leans against him.* HOOPER *gets off the scales and sinks to his knees, eyes to the needle.*

HOOPER. Nought pounds! Don't weigh a thing! (*Pause.*) I don't exist. I'm *not here,* Jer-her-her-

JANINE. Oh, Olly!

HOOPER (*standing*). What to do about Jaws? I mean -

JANINE. Yer. He's smashed -

HOOPER. How does he manage? So early -

JANINE. Cd not describe his condition on arrival.

HOOPER *bends over* JAWS *and pulls his mouth wider open with two inserted fingers. A blast of foetid air makes him wince.*

HOOPER. Last week's bridge missing. Already. (*Pause.*) Good old Jaws -

He firmly presses JAWS' *jaws together.*

JANINE. Gotcher tapioca ready. Nice an'ot.

HOOPER. Yum!

He goes into the surgery. JANINE *looks down at* JAWS. *Suspicion. She feels in his pocket. An empty half bottle, whisky. She feels in the other pocket. A half-empty bottle.* JANINE *takes this and the briefcase and follows* HOOPER.

Cut to:

7. Interior. Surgery. *A light, airy, well-equipped surgery. But the floor-covering is lino, and cracked. There are cracks in the walls too, and a large stain on the ceiling. On one wall hangs a large framed photo of Stalin. Opposite - the Queen and a corgi*

or two. One corner of the room is divided off by a bench.
Behind the bench is a combination of work area and kitchenette.
On a gas stove sits a simmering pan of tapioca.

Sniffing the aroma of a favourite food, HOOPER *is helped*
into his overall. JANINE *serves him the tapioca in a basin.*
HOOPER *gorges it with much eye-rolling and lip-smacking. Soon*
his upper lip and chin are plastered with tapioca. Old HOOPER
mops at these places with the tail of his overall.

JANINE *leans against the dental chair, buffing her nails.*

HOOPER. Any letters?

JANINE. Na.

He wanders to the tall window, which overlooks a cluttered
railway siding. Spoons tapioca absently.

HOOPER. The great Dental Mechanic in the sky, Janine.-

JANINE. Yuh?

HOOPER. Heedeth me not.

JANINE. Huh?

HOOPER. Do we not pray for merciful release from our little
mise en scène?

JANINE. Eh?

HOOPER. I've been thinking of going strictly private. Cash on
the nail, Ja-hah-hah - and one day you and I to Barbados -

JANINE. Thoughtcher'd come round to it.

HOOPER *wipes the bowl clean with his forefinger, sucks the*
finger and wipes it thoughtfully on his overall.

HOOPER. Coconut milk, Jer-her-her. (*Pause.*) Great. . . great
things full of it. In Barbados. The Whatyoumacallit. The
Car-Car-Caribbean. Sea. (*Pause.*) Cross over to marine biology?
Sharks' teeth? Oh Janine! Got it that time, eh? The
ss-sss-sstammer. . . only when I. It is shyness, old J. The
guardian of my - er, lust. For example I do not stammer at
Mother. And others.

JANINE. Not talking about Barbados. Talking about private
practice. Got sick, I did, hearing you go on about people's right
to free treatment. Miner c'n earn nearly what you. Nowadays.

HOOPER. There *was* money in it you know. Round about when
- when you were rising puberty, I should think. Golden days.

Crocks of lucre. What mattered curvature of the spine, when mouths were cornucopias or something like?

JANINE. And Babsie phoned.

HOOPER. Who?

JANINE. Don't come that.

HOOPER. Babsie frightens Hooper. Yes she does. Babsie has a wide range of deodorants. And some of them are intimate. (*Pause.*) The deodorised flesh, Ja-ha-han. Anine. Is not my meat. If God had intended, would he not for example - a tiny faucet in each sweat gland? Spraying blossomy breezes? (*Pause.*) Babsie waxes her legs, too. Total depilation, that is old B. Calves shine like polished eggs -

JANINE. Shall I drag McIlroy in?

HOOPER. Let the poor sod sleep. Let him dream. Being Irish is not amusing, J. And never was. (*He flops into the dental chair.*) Ice cream?

JANINE fetches a mound of ice cream on a saucer from the fridge. She sits on the bench, swinging her legs and buffing at the nails. Her rather vacant blue eyes do not miss a thing about HOOPER. As he crams in the ice cream:

JANINE. Yer a big baby, Olly -

HOOPER. And hungry for dugs. Yes.

JANINE. Watchyerlanguage!

HOOPER (*musing*). Dugs? It offends?

JANINE. Like pickingyernose. And some of your other little habits. Can'timaginewhystay. Really can't.

None the less, JANINE arches her back - her hard breasts swell under the crackling starch. JANINE does believe that every one is entitled to his ration. At a price.

HOOPER. God would be, I often reflect - a pair of great scrubbed arms reaching down from the sky. (*Pause.*) Gently pushing the pram of one's life. Dandling a mobile of enormous lollipops over the head.

A small, thin, battered-looking old lady pushes a brown saurian head round the surgery door. It is MRS SCRIVEN, with her habitual brown paper parcel under her arm, dangling its string.

JANINE. Not yet, Mrs Scriven!

MRS SCRIVEN. He's not working -

HOOPER *looms round, his wide glance upon her, fear and compassion battling.*

HOOPER. This is our morning conference, Mrs Scriven. To proceed otherwise would be frivolous.

MRS SCRIVEN. He's eating ice cream!

HOOPER. *Testing* ice cream, Mrs Scriven. Miss Lassoo and I - we conduct these experiments.

MRS SCRIVEN. Oh yer! I seen some on yer experiments - (*she wheezes away into an asthmatic cackle*).

JANINE. Gerraway, y'oldstringer-bones!

MRS SCRIVEN. Scriven sat on me teeth.

HOOPER (*rising, dignified*). A classic situation, Mrs Scriven. The material of music halls, and offensive jokers.

MRS SCRIVEN. A spanner in 'is back overall pocket - (*more wheezing cackles, the bag is a 'character', she thinks*).

HOOPER. How are the gums, then?

She scuttles over to him baring her gums. HOOPER *places one hand on her head, the other under her jaw and firmly effects closure.*

HOOPER. I'm so bored with you, Mrs Scriven -

MRS SCRIVEN. Eh?

HOOPER. Careless little old lady. Isn't she, Jer-her-her?

MRS SCRIVEN. Got me rights -

HOOPER. Indeed you have. The great anguished cry of the oppressed. What would revolution mean to you, Mrs Scriven? An endless supply of free false teeth?

MRS SCRIVEN. Oh, I'm thirsty -

HOOPER. Give her a glass of water.

JANINE *goes to the tap with a glass.*

MRS SCRIVEN. Not from the tap, dearie. From Mr Hooper's bottle - (*cackles.*)

HOOPER *and* JANINE *exchange eyeball-rolling looks.*

JANINE *pours a mean measure of his precious vodka —
swigged at once by Mrs S. with much lip-smacking and gum-
chomping.*

MRS SCRIVEN. Not like gin, though -

HOOPER. The best Stolichnaya, Mrs S. From Russia's windy
steppes. Bites like a bee up a Cossack's nose -

MRS SCRIVEN *grabs the 'water' bottle from* JANINE,
*and collapses like a bundle of rags in the dental chair - her
mouth wide open.*

MRS SCRIVEN. Hum on, hen -

As HOOPER *bends over her with slightly averted face:*

JANINE. Don't forget Babsie called -

Cut to:

8. Interior. Fish and chip shop. *In a corner, three or four plastic
tables.* HOOPER *sits, a vast handkerchief tucked bib-like into his
collar. In front of him is a mound of three cod and chips, dripping
with ketchup.* HOOPER *is burrowing into it with fork and fingers,
pausing only for great gulps of milk. From a ketchup-smeared
face he peers at the foxy dreamer,* JAWS McILROY. *He has an
Irish accent, but no bog phrases or stagey turns of speech. He is
gazing at the half inch of scotch remaining.*

JAWS. Is it not the case, Mr Hooper? We would make a team, I
would be your man. I would iron your trousers, Sir - and
freeze you a daily supply of iced lollies. The wreck confronting you these last months on pretext of dental urgencies . . .
the ruin of McIlroy is but the naughty husk of the potential
man, Sir. (*Pause.*) My teeth, ah I will not go into it. You have
studied them Mr Hooper. And found them wanting. The real
business of my purpose with you, I will point out that if I
did not exactly fight my way from Calais to the Rhine in the
last Great Conflict - I was at any rate always on hand to Major
Trumpkins, Sir. Bumpkins Trumpkins, Mr Hooper - an old-
world gentleman, Harrow and Ascot. Nothing less than fine
wine and pâté could start the day. (*Pause.*) That wound in
his arse, the cause of much foul snickering. He was not
directing his tank the wrong way. He had his back to the Hun
out of a mighty contempt. (*Pause.*) And in Vienna, Sir, the
spoils of war were ours. It was there I refined the art of caring

for a gentleman. Bumpkins died astride a fulsome whore,
Mr Hooper. An American general took me to West Point,
where after some years I took to drink - not pining for
Ireland, Sir, but gunsmoke, caviare, Pouilly Fuissée and
Bumpkins' roisterous way of life. That brings us up to
nineteen sixty-eight. Disgrace, Mr Hooper, and -

HOOPER *interrupts, whilst picking for shreds of codflesh in
his own impeccable teeth, mangling the words round a questing
finger:*

HOOPER. Now hang on a minute, Jaws. Hang on -

JAWS. I do ramble, I know. It is loneliness and the rejection by
my fellow men has brought me down -

HOOPER. Can we skip the last seven years?

JAWS. Yes indeed Sir. It's but a tale of drink and degredation.
I ended up in Moosejaw -

HOOPER. You are possibly an anachronism, McIlroy -

JAWS. In fact. I would not have been out of place with Lord
Raglan in the Crimea. I have a theory about aristocracy,
Mr Hooper.

HOOPER. No time, no time. I'd like to have your precise drift,
though. You'd like to be my man, is it?

JAWS. In a nutshell.

HOOPER. I'm getting married next week -

JAWS. A complication. I can spot them.

*The waitress brings a mountain of lemon meringue pie, which
HOOPER attacks at once.*

HOOPER. In other circs, though. My mother tries to care for
me, but it's a lost cause. A jumped up working woman, Jaws
- *avec delusions de grandeur.* She too served at table, and
what's more scuttled round at every whim of Lady Thing.
My grandfather was a coachman, and Dad himself a reluctant
chauffeur. Whatever else you can say about a Rolls Royce,
he warned me, it does not drop the steaming golden balls which
are so encouraging to roses. (*Pause.*) He drove the Rolls Royce
into the Loire one night. He and Lord Thing - you will
appreciate this, *re* Bumpkins - were looking for a whorehouse.
Drowned in style, as one should live Lord Thing used to say.

(*Pause.*) And Mamma flipped, dear old Jaws. I only dug her out of the madhouse six years ago. Our modest flat is her mansion. Our garden her acres. And the single tree, where presently a cuckoo is tossing forth the eggs of better birds - this tree is her Dunsinane. (*Pause.*) So if I were not hooked, Jaws. To Barbara. You've seen her - the anxious girl who carries a box of Kleenex for Men. Well otherwise you and I might have done a deal.

JAWS. I wouldn't have thought marriage your scheme, Mr Hooper.

HOOPER. You are right. It is Barbara's. (*He is now nervously scrubbing at ketchup and meringue on his face, with a grubby handkerchief. JAWS proffers a square or two of crinkled paper from the serviette stand, but these are ignored.*) What's more, she'll be here any minute. Won't eat with me in this place. Not the humble, the lowly fish and chips. But condescends to join me for the disastrous coffee they have here -

JAWS. More lemon pie, Mr Hooper?

HOOPER. I can see you have caught on to my ways. The weakness - dreadful revealing this to a layman - is for sugar and milky things. (*JAWS shouts for the waitress for more pie.*) You recall Barbara, you can bring her to mind? Has the fog of booze not crippled you yet, Jaws?

JAWS. No Sir. The one that looks like a pressed leaf? A sort of dry young lady with nimble manners?

HOOPER. I think you have her measure, old shamrock!

JAWS. But in these free-and-easy days, begod?

HOOPER. You mean - eat one's Barbara and not have it?

JAWS. Would she be above the progress we've made in sexual habits, Mr Hooper? I gather things are pretty loose. Enough to get conservative ladies and gentlemen hopping mad, Sir -

HOOPER. Barbara is not above all that. She is behind it. (*Pause.*) I know her not carnally, McIlroy. And I have not proposed, I have been manoeuvred. It reminds me of my youth, when merely to get inside a blouse required an engagement. I was nearly caught that way. In the air-raid shelter behind the Church Hall. My first nipple. Rosy in the moonlight, it was.

And as I gave it a jocular tweak, that one too announced our wedding. (*Pause.*) Barbara is of the same ilk. I wonder if they need dentists in Ghana -

A breathless wail - 'Aldous' - from the door ushers in the woman herself. BARBARA is festooned in parcels, a plastic bag from a less than trendy shop in Chelsea, her handbag slipping off her shoulder, one soberly unfashionable shoe has quit her foot - she hops about near the till at the shop entrance. BARBARA is a thinnish, rather gawky woman in her early thirties. Her appearance is a rebuttal of trends and fashions, her selling-point is invisible, being efficiency. Adoring HOOPER for months has twisted her cool, though. In or near his presence, she is a little dislocated, as if some of his own failure to integrate has rubbed off. She is not at all unattractive, but maybe a little too roman of feature, verging on the camel. Her fine-boned face is now taut with concentration as she assembles herself and her extensions - including a tightly-rolled red umbrella with a vicious point. She has straight hair cut in a rectangle round her face, and is short-sighted, squinting at the world as if it were about to vanish, or at least withdraw support, at any moment.

BARBARA is for culture and high manners, for what an earlier time would have called refinement. She is neither foolish nor ignorant, but somehow caught in a time-warp which renders her modestly old-fashioned values eccentric. She would have loved Shelley and been terrified of Byron. She finds HOOPER's regressive anarchy sweet, holding in reserve the notion that it too - like everything else - must surely be susceptible of training. Now she descends upon the flinching dentist, a warm creature with a tolerance of steel.

BARBARA. Oh, Aldous -

She organises herself on a chair opposite HOOPER and beside JAWS. Her unconscious has already rejected JAWS as having any sort of credibility in her universe.

HOOPER. Oh, Barbara -

BARBARA. A fright. Such a fright. I nearly ran over a teeny kitten. Between the wheels, though. I gave it a cuddle and put it on a wall -

JAWS is gazing at her in disbelief. He coughs.

HOOPER. This is McIlroy -

BARBARA. It's what? You can't imagine how flustered I am. Bobbins went off early for lunch, and -

HOOPER. Mr McIlroy, Barbara -

She jerks erect against the chairback, looking JAWS up and down. Her first impression remains uncorrected. JAWS awards her a shy smile but is regarded sternly.

BARBARA. How do you do, Mr McIlroy.

JAWS. I'll just be off, then -

BARBARA. The point is, I think Bobbins is having a thing with one of the Under Secretaries. Last time it was an M.P. - a sort of division bell affair. Well I looked at one or two rings, Aldous. And -

HOOPER (*croaking*). Rings?

JAWS. There's a Saturn Rings in the three-thirty at Newmarket, Mr Hooper. The coincidence might be providential -

Pause.

BARBARA. You refer to a horse, Mr McIlroy?

JAWS. It is more than a horse, Ma'am. It is speed incarnate, you might say. It is a poem. It -

BARBARA. Betting, Mr McIlroy, is not so much immoral as irrational. Are you addicted?

JAWS. I'll just be off, then -

BARBARA. Aldous?

HOOPER. We. . .er. . .we deploy a few bob now and then Babsie.

BARBARA. You needn't look shifty, Aldous. Disapproval is not my - scene? I know everyone thinks me a prig, but I assure you I am not in the least conventional.

HOOPER. In that case: three quid each way, Jaws?

JAWS. 'Tis done, Mr Hooper. (*He gets a little more Irish in strange company.*)

BARBARA. On the other hand -

JAWS. I'll skedaddle at once -

BARBARA rises, pushing her chair back. The way out is indicated and JAWS has no alternative. He sidles past her.

JAWS. Three quid it is then. And you'll think on the other business, Mr Hooper?

HOOPER. Er - what?

JAWS. Like you know - me and the Major?

HOOPER. The Major?

JAWS. Bumpkins, Sir?

Pause.

HOOPER. I'll think it over.

JAWS. Then good day, and to you Miss Er. (*He inclines towards her.*) It is not amusing to be Irish, Miss. Not by any stretch of a leprechaun's tit -

And JAWS *sprints away, yodelling some republican ballad for* BARBARA's *benefit. He turns at the till to administer a wink at* HOOPER.

BARBARA. You do know some odd people, Aldous -

HOOPER. A patient. A tattered shamrock washed up on Time's great shore -

BARBARA. And who is 'Bumpkins'?

HOOPER. A soldier long dead, Babsie. Might have been the Conservative Candidate for High Wyckham, in another world -

BARBARA. Leprechaun's tit, indeed!

HOOPER. Jaws has a vivid tongue, sweetie -

BARBARA. And will you stop this Babsie business? You know I cringe -

HOOPER. I will.

BARBARA. Oh, Aldous -

HOOPER. Oh, Barbara -

BARBARA. What are we to do with you?

HOOPER. I imagine you have a few reforms in mind -

She grasps his hand, squeezing fondly, and looks into his eyes - over which he coyly lowers his lids. To protect her.

Cut to:

9. Interior. Surgery. JANINE *at lunch: an apple and a cup of coffee. Outside, the sun shines. The Queen and Stalin on their respective walls look amiable.* JANINE *drains her cup, puts the apple core in the waste bin, and with a compact begins to repair her lipstick.*

HOOPER *crashes in. She ignores him and works away at her mouth. He collapses in the dental chair, gazing wistfully at the white and brisk* LASSOO. *She speaks to him with difficulty, through fingers and stump of lipstick.*

JANINE. Yot ya hum hack ho early hor?

Pause.

HOOPER. You know what I've hum hack ho early hor!

JANINE sucks her lips in and out, snaps the compact shut, touches an eyebrow.

JANINE. BeenwiBabsavewe?

HOOPER. Ler-hun-hun-hunch -

JANINE stretches, smiling her 'up babsie' smile. She is not wearing shoes, and wriggles her little toes inside her tights. Hands on hips - out shoots her tongue. At the same time one small paw smooths her sprayed hair.

JANINE. CnIbeabridesmaid?

She slinks over to the chair and perches on one arm. The lunchtime game is on.

HOOPER. In the depths of my sou-ho-hole, Janine -

JANINE. Yerwha?

HOOPER (*singing*). Oh Miss-Slassoo, I love yer, Hi'm always dreamin' of yer -

JANINE. Got to get you a new tie, haven't we? It's all what looks like ketchup -

HOOPER. And lemon meringue pie -

JANINE. What you got? In the depths of your soul, Olly?

HOOPER. I tremble with lust, little old Lassoo -

JANINE. For Ja-ha-ha-hanine?

HOOPER. Unorthodox visions. (*Pause.*) The overall? A little higher, coz?

JANINE *hitches the skirt of her overall two more inches up her thigh.*

HOOPER. The buttons, J -

She unfastens the top two buttons of her overall.

JANINE. How'sat?

HOOPER. Lovely. You took off the, er - the?

JANINE. Yer. Itookoffmebra - don't I always?

HOOPER. This is bliss -

JANINE *takes a chocolate from her pocket and prettily unwraps it.*

JANINE. Tonguey?

Out slips HOOPER's main sensory organ, glistening. She ritually places the chocolate, and HOOPER levers it back into his mouth. Face ecstatic at the munching. He places his forefingers on her overall where the nipples are, and relaxes with his eyes closed, chewing.

HOOPER. Nothing like digital sex, Lassoo -

JANINE. Iwillsay. Yer not hard to please, Olly -

He gulps, holding his fingers in position. A warm shudder through the vast HOOPER frame.

JANINE. 'Nother choc?

HOOPER. Can I manage twice?

JANINE. You did last Wednesday -

Another choc is unwrapped and engorged. His forefingers and thumbs essay a tiny squeeze.

HOOPER. Haaaaaaaaaaaaaah!

Reaching down to the dental tray on its flexible arm beside the chair, JANINE takes a square of gauze and swabs gently at HOOPER's beaded brow.

JANINE. Wentabit toofar, didn'we though? No *squeezies,*

Janine said before -

HOOPER. A man has to cut a dash, Janine. In the Hooposophy -

JANINE. The wha'?

HOOPER. Hooper's philosophy, J. I believe in the greatest good for the most of Hooper. A rogue, dammit!

JANINE slips off the chair and smiles down at HOOPER. She wags a reproving finger.

JANINE. Squeezies is almost rape, Olly -

HOOPER. I have violated you!

JANINE. Needn't look so chirpy about it.

HOOPER. But you forgot something -

JANINE. I did?

Pause.

HOOPER. Scratchies, you cheeky bundle!

JANINE. Scratchies? Diddums!

She lightly touches his cheeks with her silver-polished nails. Up and down, up and down. HOOPER arches his back and purrs.

JANINE. Olly -

HOOPER. Yass?

JANINE. Can I have a little car?

HOOPER. Well, now -

JANINE. We been doing this for two years, Olly -

Pause.

HOOPER. Two years of stark, staring joy, Jah-ha-ha-etcetera.

JANINE. Funny way of putting it.

HOOPER. How many chocasms make a car, Lassoo?

JANINE. Didn't think you were mean, Olly. Saving all yer loot for Babs?

HOOPER. Barbara is well-endowed, if only in that respect.

JANINE. I'm yer *mistress*, Olly. (*Pause.*) Every day at ten to two. This has been a long-lasting relationship of great intimacy, Mr Hooper.

This, for JANINE, *wildly articulate and stylish outburst jerks* HOOPER *upright in the chair.*

HOOPER. A moped?

JANINE *holds up an imaginary telephone, her eyes glinting.*

JANINE. No, Miss Hoyden. Yes, Miss Hoyden. He's still in bed, yes I suppose. You know Mr Hooper. I think his mother is still at this moment in time, combing the egg from his hair, Miss Hoyden. (*Slams down imaginary phone.*) Every fucking morning, Miss Hoyden!

HOOPER (*in wonder*). Janine - you have an inner life!

JANINE *grabs the dental drill and switches it on. She pulls him towards her by the tie and holds the whining instrument an inch from his nose.*

JANINE. I oughter carve you up. Straight, I did -

HOOPER. Jer-her-her. Put down that expensive Czechoslovakian drill. It is not paid for. This is Cambridge, not Balham High Street.

JANINE *switches off the drill and hangs it up. Affecting remorse, she hangs her head.*

JANINE. I turn you on though, Olly -

HOOPER. Twas the Great Dental Mechanic in the sky sent you to this humble surgery. Divine imagination. Cosmic compassion. (*Pause.*) Out there beyond the stars, Janine -

JANINE. Yes and I've earned a prezzy -

HOOPER. A car is not a prezzy, Janine. It is a major shift in the balance of power.

The surgery door bursts open, and in stalks BARBARA's mother, MRS HOYDEN. She is a large-boned, florid woman in her sixties with gimlet eyes and a scathing manner. As she quickly takes in the surgery and MISS LASSOO, it is clear that Hoopersville is not at all to her taste. She is immediately followed in by JAWS. She puts a firm hand on his chest and propels him backwards into the waiting room, closing the door in his face.

MRS HOYDEN. Aldous!

HOOPER. Er - *qui?*

MRS HOYDEN. Barbara is in tears. She is demoralised.

HOOPER. *Quel dommage!*

MRS HOYDEN. *Aldous!*

HOOPER. *Je crois que -*

MRS HOYDEN. What have you done to my daughter?

HOOPER. Who?

MRS HOYDEN. You are a middle-aged man, Aldous -

HOOPER. Oh, I say -

MRS HOYDEN. And I shall not play absurd games with you.

HOOPER. My age is a sore point, Mrs H.

MRS HOYDEN. Who is this person?

HOOPER. Why, Madam, 'tis Miss Lassoo. Now what gives with Babsie?

MRS HOYDEN. And who is that impertinent little creature outside?

HOOPER. That's Jaws. My man. Trained in Vienna - *Kinde, Kirche, Küche.* Is the betrothed in a state? My goodness, that's a dodgy set of molars Mrs H. And look here, I know that forty-three's over the hump, but -

MRS HOYDEN. Kindly empty your pockets, Aldous -

JANINE *takes up what she imagines to be an elegant pose in the dental chair, fascinated.* MRS HOYDEN *seems the archetypal Waterloo for any man. A little further nail-buffing is called for.*
   Shy HOOPER *digs out his treasure. A melting iced lolly, a condom, a miniature alarm clock, much screwed-up paper, and a flimsy brassière. He holds this up as if he has never seen one before.* MRS HOYDEN *snatches it off him.*

MRS HOYDEN. *Barbara's -*

HOOPER. *Mais non, mais non -*

MRS HOYDEN. But I recognise it!

JANINE. Oooooooh - Olly!

MRS HOYDEN. Did you or did you not remove this from my daughter's person? In her car this lunchtime? Without her consent? They should bring back the cat, in my opinion.

HOOPER. Hang on, hang on -

He delves in one of his trouser pockets and brings out another bra.

HOOPER. Now whose is this one?

MRS HOYDEN. Miss. Whatever-your-name-is - please leave us.

With a sexy leer at HOOPER, JANINE *sways out of the surgery.*

MRS HOYDEN. What kind of a person are you, Aldous?

HOOPER. Oh, I dunno. I get scared at zebra crossings. Prefer countries where a policeman whistles you across. (*Pause.*) A Russophile. Yes, I know a thing or two about the Slavonic soul. Pushkin by heart, and as far for Lermontov - don't you think the offence is flimsy, Mrs H? All I said to old Barbara was: can I have it for my collection? It's those little embroidered flowers between the, er - cups, is it? She doesn't allow me *inside* her clothes you know. By heaven, Mrs Hoyden, there is none of that! It was a gift. A concession.

MRS HOYDEN. Your collection, indeed!

HOOPER (*picks up the other bra*). Well take this one for example. Pretty rare, design-wise. I -

MRS HOYDEN. What do you *do* with them, Aldous?

Pause.

HOOPER. Stroke them. It's the nearest I ever get. There's a long history to all this, Mrs H. I don't know why Babs blabbed. Could have spared me. Bottle-fed, and my mother a stickler for regularity. Since the biffy days in the cradle, this gap in my experience. Hungry-pooh for the real thing. Clockwork baby, mother said. The expression has a sinister ring - no? Man as machine. If mind is no more than an epiphenomenon of matter? I was shy of telling you before - no ordinary dentist. Do you think I am in this racket for money? Out of idealism? No. I am haunted. I fancy the soul is there behind the teeth, somewhere. Don't you agree we all feel we are somewhere behind our teeth? A little above, perhaps. At any rate in that area. Why are you so miffed? Why Barbara so outraged? Some men will not stop at the bra, Mrs H.

Fortunately I am timid. Insecure. I am - pardon me - a sucker for the sexual morality of harsher times.

MRS HOYDEN. In other words, you are a pervert, Aldous -

HOOPER. Shy when rebuffed, you know.

MRS HOYDEN. The other bra?

HOOPER. One of Lassoo's cast-offs I imagine. Not the spoils of war, by no means. Wouldn't you like me to take a squint at your teeth? There's usually a lurking cavity or two. Or what about a quick polish?

MRS HOYDEN. Aldous, you will have dinner with us tonight. I think Nigel will want to know more about all this.

HOOPER. Ni-hi-hi? (*He sighs, peering distractedly out of the window.*)

MRS HOYDEN. Eight o'clock sharp.

She snaps BARBARA's bra into her handbag with a flourish, and exits - spilling the listening JAWS into the room as she goes out. There is a tremendous bang from the outer waiting room door.

HOOPER. My mother-in-law to be.

JAWS. I'll not comment, Mr Hooper. Jokes about them are on a part with those about the Irish. County is she? The Major was wry about such people. You de-bra'd the young lady, Sir? There's nothing like high jinks in a car.

HOOPER. What puzzles me, Jaws, is why Barbara made a song and dance? Why the histrionics? Old Ni-hi-hi, you know - he's a magistrate. Bi-focals and a hearing aid.

JANINE enters, proffering a choc.

JANINE. Tonguey -

Absently, HOOPER flicks out his tongue and flicks in the choc.

JANINE. Cuperteanabun? There's no patients -

HOOPER. Please J. I am shaken. I am shoo-hoo-hook-up. Right up. Babs telling all? Revealing our little secrets? Our wee and pathetic intimacies? The mind doth bo-ho-hoggle.

JANINE busies herself with kettle and mugs. From a cupboard she takes a bag of large and wicked-looking currant buns.

HOOPER. What to do, Jaws dear boozing friend?

JAWS. Talking of, Sir -

HOOPER. The water bottle, Janine -

She hands JAWS *the bottle and he swigs meditatively.*

JAWS. Not Smirnoff. No. Aromatic. Ah, the blood of the Romanoffs, Mr Hooper -

HOOPER. Stolichnaya. Present from a dentist in Novosibirsk. We parted on the Oder, Jaws. The bridge at Brest-Litovsk, is it? His poems snug in my underpants -

JAWS. D'ye not think, Mr Hooper - (*A mournful pause.*) There we go again. The 'ye' will creep in at times of stress. Our accent is as much maligned as our alleged mental confusion. I was about to say - a council of war, Sir?

HOOPER. In the Soviet Union, Jaws, even dentists tend to knock off the odd poem. And there I was at Brest-Litovsk I think, and as Yevgeny said through tears of frustration: the cause of the Jews in Russia is a noble one. But don't you Westerners realise? *All* Russians want to leave Russia. We would like to abandon the place lock, stock and sputnik. Give it back to the Mongol hordes, Gospodin Hooper. (*Pause.*) By God I sweated at the Customs, Jaws. His verses damp against the crutch. The ink running, I fancied.

JAWS. The point I wish to make. The woman is outraged. Ye - *you* - have the advantage, Mr Hooper. (*Pause.*) What if - what if I came with you tonight? My presence would compound any offence to human sensibility.

HOOPER. Er . . . aar . . . er - this is my man, Mr Hoyden. A poor wretch, but an honest one. Accompanies me everywhere, the faithful hound.

JANINE *thrusts a mug of tea and a bun under his nose. The same for* JAWS.

JANINE. You'll always be top teeth man for me, Olly. Your cosmetic work unrivalled and what's more untaxed. I have the money in a suitcase.

HOOPER *munches, showering crumbs. Blight has settled on his crown.* JAWS *finds the tea distasteful and energetically swings vodka to his cracked lips.*

JAWS. Platitudes never in order, Mr Hooper. But no one has to marry. There are plenty of bras over the hill, Sir.

HOOPER. Could we do a bunk? Mother would be desolate.
How much in the suitcase, Lassoo girl?

JANINE. More'n three thousand.

HOOPER. My trains? My scale model of the Trans-Siberian
Railway?

JAWS. In a crate, Sir. Labelled for any place you should name,
across five continents.

HOOPER. The cunning fellow tempts me. But what is three
thou in these days of inflation? 'Twill not buy a bauble for
Lassoo's pretty neck. (*Pause.*) Where *are* the patients by the
way?

JANINE. You're always asking that, Olly. We made a packet
when you stuck to bridge work. But since you had them
sawing away with nylon thread, and scrubbing the plaque -
well prevention is a mug's game I think.

HOOPER. Drilling at the nation's chompers is a mug's game J.
Sugar is lethal to the old fangs, everybody knows it but who
cares?

JANINE. And your teeth? Ice-cream and chocs? Currant buns
and vodka?

HOOPER. Exactly. My cake hole is a graveyard. A rotting
tomb . . . a dereliction -

JAWS. Digressions, Mr Hooper. Tonight -

HOOPER. Run me a bath, J. - lots of bubbles. Bubbles for
Barbara - and Mater and Pater. Then we'll shut up shop and
all go to the pictures. I think, yes - there's a mammary sort
of film showing in Cambridge. *Allons y mes enfants.* Let us
hunt the nipple -

10. Interior. The Hoydens' living room. *A large chintzy room*
with open French windows looking out onto a garden.
Restrained comfort verging on the shabby is the key note - with
one or two hints that there is wealth behind all this: a good
baby grand, one or two excellent eighteenth century oil
sketches, Dresden porcelain. BARBARA *sits at the piano, in a*
maxi-dress, playing the Joplin/'Sting' theme, MR HOYDEN *is*
thrown up against the mantelpiece like a grappling-iron - tall

stooping, thin white hair, gaunt sorrowful face, hearing-aid. He is peering into a glass of sherry.

MR HOYDEN. I say, Barbara -

BARBARA. Yes Father?

MR HOYDEN. Gets on the nerves that piece. Don't you think?

BARBARA. I'm sorry.

She closes the piano and sits apathetically, hands on her lap.

MR HOYDEN. Never were a strong girl -

BARBARA. I beg your pardon?

MR HOYDEN. I meant - in the head.

BARBARA. *Father!*

MR HOYDEN. Don't get tearful old thing. What about me? I've had you and your mother for well over thirty years. It must be. (*Pause.*) An occasional verbal stab in the back - have to do it. I wasn't referring to the music. You tinkle quite prettily. No. (*Pause.*) No it just occurred to me. I feel as if I've been standing here for a thousand years. In this room. With this glass of sherry. You draped on the piano stool. Mother kicking hell out of that poor dumb girl in the kitchen. French windows open. (*Pause.*) A thousand years. (*Pause.*) When I was a young man, used to go up to town to a show now and then. You know what? When the bloody curtain went up, it was invariably a replica of this scene. Or something like. (*Pause.*) Haven't seen a show since Suez. Read about that angry chap's play in the *Telegraph* at the time. (*Pause.*) I suppose he's settled down now. They all do. I expect even anger and so on . . . are old hat by now? Sheer despair is in, I should think. Seen the *Financial Times* Index? We are slowly inching our way up from poverty to penury -

BARBARA. Daddy -

MR HOYDEN. How nicely you say that!

BARBARA. Did Mother discuss Aldous with you?

MR HOYDEN. I think a spot more of this. (*He helps himself to more sherry.*) You know Babbers, I sometimes have the feeling - and now is one of the times - that I am not alive. No. Merely wandering about in some blighter's parody of how he *imagines* my despicable existence. (*Pause.*) When you say

'Daddy' for example. The tone of voice. It actually is true
that only women of what they used to call 'breeding' can
hit that unsublime note. That combination of the filial and
the irritable. (*Pause.*) Young Hooper, did you say? The tit-
fetishist?

BARBARA. *Please* - (*a finger to eye corner*).

MR HOYDEN. Oh, don't snivel poppet. Rabbit, or whatever I
used to call you. I merely expressed with commendable
brevity what your mother took an hour to hint at. Round
and round she went . You know your mother. At least you
might do. Damned if I do. (*Pause.*) Language is not a means
of communication to your mother. It is an indefatigable
skirmish with menacing silence. (*Pause.*) I like Hooper. He's
engaging, the podgy fellow. Some people go to seed - others
have known the condition from the cradle. Mustn't knock a
chap because of his tailor. Not any more. Not in - my God! -
nineteen seventy-five. And being a dentist. Must be nerve-
wracking.

BARBARA. I'm not complaining about Aldous. I love Aldous.
I wish I'd never said a word to Mother. (*Pause.*) It's just -

MR HOYDEN. Sock it to me right between the peepers, Babsie -

BARBARA. Well I'm still a virgin, for one thing. And -

MR HOYDEN. Christ! Are you? My God! How extraordinary!
Incredible. Frightening. (*He sips his sherry.*) I reel with
incomprehension.

BARBARA (*not without spririt*). I'm not retarded, Father. I wish
you wouldn't *perform* so. I'm sure I could be an athlete of
carnality, given the right man. But Aldous -

MR HOYDEN. Premarital jitters? That *would* be quaint, in these
enlightened - (*pause*). That phrase! Enlightened times. I
keep using it when I'm on the bench too. Some pimply thug
only has to rip out a few telephones and I find myself in
court using expressions like that. Why do I have to prove how
enlightened I am? *He's* the enlightened one. *He* knows that
vandalism quite clearly establishes him as how does it go?
Socially disadvantaged? Everybody tells him so. What am I?
A beak. One of the oppressors. A spoil-sport in bi-focals and
a deaf-aid. As if I didn't know. I have a terrible urge to rip
out telephones myself. And as for wrecking railway carriages -

pass me the axe at once, please. (*Pause.*) Am I wandering off the point? Poppet? Cuddles?

BARBARA. I think Aldous needs a weaker woman than I, Father. After all. It takes a person of character, you know? To sit in a car opposite King's College chapel in broad daylight, and remove her bra. This is the point I am trying to make. Both Aldous *and* Mother have misunderstood. *That's* why I got rather hysterical-pooh. It's all he *ever* wants -

MR HOYDEN. The bra -

BARBARA. Right.

MR HOYDEN. Your mother *has* got the wrong end of the stick - hasn't she?

BARBARA. Mummy has been clutching that since I was a little girl.

MR HOYDEN. Poor old Mummy. Such a thick old bag -

MRS HOYDEN *has made her entrance on the last line.*

MRS HOYDEN. I heard that, Nigel -

MR HOYDEN. Not for the first time - eh?

MRS HOYDEN. I know how you both talk about me behind my back.

MR HOYDEN. Alicia, you look charming in that - flour sack, is it? And what have you been doing all day? Hounding that poor bloody dentist? Are we giving him his favourite pudding?

MRS HOYDEN. I really don't see how this marriage can take place.

MR HOYDEN. That ought to cheer him up. I wasn't looking forward to this evening at all. Let's tell him, eh? And watch him, er, exude relief.

MRS HOYDEN. On the other hand, the humiliation -

MR HOYDEN. Who's? Barbara's? But she'd be ditching *him* - no?

BARBARA. I'm not ditching anyone.

MR HOYDEN. He's the only one you've got. Of course the fellow's hardly presentable, but I find that touching. The very idea of being presentable belongs to another age, I should imagine. What a ghastly business it used to be! Girls coming out and hordes of hot young officers braying at them.

I refused to compete. Your mother was the disaster of her season. I proposed on the comfortable assumption she wouldn't dare take me seriously. (*Pause.*) Set and game to Mum-mums. What *do* you want to do with your life B?

BARBARA. I want Aldous.

MR HOYDEN. Splendid! That settles it then. A spot more sherry?

MRS HOYDEN *goes to the sherry bottle and sniffs.*

MRS HOYDEN. This is not sherry, Nigel.

MR HOYDEN. It's the right colour.

MRS HOYDEN. It is not sherry -

Pause.

MR HOYDEN. Ukrainian vodka, matter of fact. Little wrinkle young Hooper told me about. I'm as high as a kite. I gather you love him Barbara. And why not? Someone has to endure the misfortune of loving Hooper. Or is it more a question of the challenge? The gamble? I've noticed you are such a tidy person, darling Bab. Is that it? You wish to put Hooper straight? To correct the faults in his design? He does tend to hang a bit askew, on life's great wall. Alicia you should try this stuff. It produces a delightful whanging sensation at the top of the head.

BARBARA. One can't choose the person one falls in love with.

Pause.

MR HOYDEN. Eh? (*Pause.*) The girl is monumentally serious, I have to admit.

BARBARA. I don't think you and Mother know me at all. Not the slightest bit. I should never have told her, this afternoon. I can see now. What we have to do is ritualise the bra kink. We must incorporate it into our love-play. Yes. I mustn't get upset any more. Nor about his fondness for plastic animals in the bath, either. He has a sweet little platypus. I want him. I'm going to have him. (*Pause.*) I shall bring the bastard to heel, you mark my words.

MR HOYDEN. What *have* we spawned, Alicia? Babsie you frighten me -

BARBARA. I've set my sights on that dentist. I was wrong about him being too weak. He's just exactly right. (*Pause.*)

How I shall pummel him into shape! He's only a baby. A man would have been most unsuitable. I hate men. I love babies. I think, to begin with - a large playpen in the sitting-room. And what about a large, inflatable rubber dog? (*Pause.*) We must take him at face-value, don't you see?

HOOPER *has appeared at the French windows, drumming his fingers on the glass.*

HOOPER. Hello dere -

He staggers into the room, halts, executes a little dance entailing the shaking of his right foot.

HOOPER. Steppin' out . . . steppin' out. For tonight it's the time to step out - din-dins ready? Hello dere, Mr Hoyden. Hello dere, his good lady. (*Pause.*) I left my man in the car. He is not fit to eat with the servants. (*Sniffing the 'sherry' bottle.*) The Ukrainian hooch - yes? Begod, these actually *are* French windows! And a rosebush did prick my arse on the way in. That is how I like it. That is the setting for my Babsie. But alas - no, let it wait. Barbara, Kiss me!

MR HOYDEN. Hello dere, Olly -

HOOPER *bends over* BARBARA, *eyes closed, extending a cheek - which she pecks. Now he lumbers towards* MRS HOYDEN, *but she sidesteps and he is left flailing.* JAWS *appears at the windows, dressed as a butler.*

MR HOYDEN. Olly -

HOOPER (*swinging round*). Yass?

MR HOYDEN. Who dat man?

HOOPER. That is Jaws McIlroy. I've taken him on. Reviving the old ways, Mr Hoyden. Jaws will handle me. At my elbow is his rightful place. We are fresh and clean-smelling from the bubble bath. You should see Jer-her-her-Hanine. Foam on the tip of her sharp little nose, and -

MRS HOYDEN. A *manservant?*

HOOPER. Step forward and say your piece, Jaws. He will serve at table, Mrs H. I want you to have the benefit. A new era. An epoch. Well. Let history speak for itself.

He gives himself a generous glassful from MR HOYDEN's *bottle, and waits beaming on all sides.* JAWS *comes forward.*

JAWS. Well now. Considering the way things have been going since the war, Oi mean - I mean *I* mean - the servant problem and the decline of the class war into a mere jostling for advantage. (*Pause.*) D'ye think a dram of that sherry? I contracted a terrible affliction in Moosejaw, the throat seizes up and the eyes shrivel. Unless - is it from Kiev, Mr Hoyden Sir? I was nearly in Kiev with Major Trumpkins, where he was to be honoured by the Bolsheviks -

MR HOYDEN. Bumpkins Trumpkins?

JAWS. The same, Mr Hoyden -

MR HOYDEN. Old Bumpers!

JAWS. You knew him?

MR HOYDEN. I was hunting Martin Borman -

JAWS. Who wasn't?

MR HOYDEN. Bumpy Trumpy! A sodomite, as I recall -

JAWS. That is - pardon me - a perversion of the truth, Sir.

HOOPER. Oh, Jaws!

MR HOYDEN. What are you doing with young Hooper? (*Raising his glass.*) Incorrigible batman -

JAWS. That's it, Mr Hoyden. I have renounced Moosejaw and all its works. And passing this gentleman's chomper factory one day. Well. A bridge brought us together. As bridges should. (*Pause.*) Now we shall bring him to trial.

HOOPER. What's that Jaws? Treachery?

JAWS *goes to the French windows and whistles.* JANINE *steps in - heavily made up, dark wig, mightily pregnant. Her cheerful eyes flash behind turquoise fly-away spectacles.*

JAWS. May I introduce Miss Breeze? Doddie Breeze, bearing within a small Hooper. Mr Hooper - yes. Treachery. How can I raise you up without doing you down? Tell them Dodie -

JANINE (*in a West country burr*). Last winter, it was. Day and night I had this powerful pain in my tooth. (*Demonstrating - finger pulling at upper lip.*) Wisdom, I think. I sees the plate on his door. Aldous Hooper, L.D.S. He was kind, I will say. But when he got me in his dental chair -

All are ostentatiously bating their breath. 'Dodie' is a one for histrionics, and savours her own performance.

MRS HOYDEN. Come come, girl -

JANINE. Ooooooo! You 'igh an' mighty!

BARBARA. (*A squeak.*) Aldous?

JANINE. He pumped me up -

MR HOYDEN. Good Lord, Olly -

HOOPER. What she mea-hee-heens is. I elevated the chair as is customary with small persons. By means of the foot pedal.

JANINE. That's right. And then -

Lowers her glance, moves the toe of her left shoe from side to side.

JANINE. Impacted, he says. For sure. But let's take a photo of your pretty little jaw. (*Pause.*) Well after he'd done that -

BARBARA. Miss Breeze - *blow* -

JANINE. Shuttup, you!

MR HOYDEN. Sounds impeccably professional so far. And what did this splendid Hooper here actually *do*? You assert the bulge is his?

JANINE. He showed me how he plays bears - (*singing*) 'F'you go down in the woods today, you'll sure have a - (*speaking*) Know what I mean.

MR HOYDEN (*leans forward, pats her tum*). You certainly do sure have a -

JANINE. Played bears all round the surgery, we did -

MR HOYDEN. Care to demonstrate, Olly? Harmless enough. So far -

JANINE *holds up her little clenched fists, and begins to lumber about.*

JANINE (*singing*). 'F'you go down in the woods today, you'll sure have a big surprise -

MR HOYDEN (*waving his glass, crooning*). For every bear that ever there was, te tum te tum te -

JANINE. And then he had me.

MR HOYDEN. In the dental chair?

MRS HOYDEN (*gleefully*). He raped you!

JANINE. Oh no. (*Primly.*) I gave myself.

MR HOYDEN. Quick off the mark, young Breeze -

JANINE. I wished him to know me carnally, Mr Hoyden. That is all there is to it.

MR HOYDEN. Charming turn of phrase the little poppet has - (*reflectively*). Carnally - that was Trumpkins' favourite sport too. But he preferred -

HOOPER. A fondness for bears -

JAWS. I thought, your Honour - a paternity order?

HOOPER. I once knew two bears in Edinburgh zoo that could hummmmmmmmmm -

MR HOYDEN. Now McIlroy. To turn on one's benefactor. Mr Hooper, here - did you say Moosejaw a while back?

HOOPER. Extremely musical bears -

JAWS. That was where Dodie wrote me, it could be ten years ago Brigadier. My little girl, drummed out of the convent.

MR HOYDEN. I was in Moosejaw, looking for Martin Borman -

JAWS. He was seen in Buenos Aires, Colonel. The winter of '59.

HOOPER. You went up to these bears - and you just sort of . . . hummed. Then they'd hum back.

JAWS. Dodie was a virgin, Captain. And until ten years later was still unacquainted with dentistry.

BARBARA *marches over to* JANINE *and gives her a terrific thwack on the navel area.*

JANINE. Oops!

BARBARA. It's a cushion. I know what you're up to McIlroy - (*she grabs* JANINE's *hand*). Come with me - (*yanks her out through the French windows*).

MRS HOYDEN. I think you know what to do, Nigel -

MR HOYDEN. Do I?

MRS HOYDEN (*points at* JAWS). This riff-raff -

JAWS. Mr Hooper, you didn't forewarn me of insult -

MR HOYDEN. Have you any serious interest in what's going on at all, Olly?

HOOPER. I don't know how I got mixed up with B. you know. Abercrombie's Ice Cream Parlour on a Saturday night. She came in breathless from her amateur dramatics. (*Pause.*) One evening across a crowded ice cream parlour. I was fleeing from my mother, Nigel. The things she gets up to in her wheelchair. Zooming about. Well dear me. I *had* staggered into the show a little boozy. Woke up in the middle. Saw this entrancing creature. Pocahontas I thought, confused as always. But no. Could have been Electra. Almost anything, really. (*Pause.*) It was her teeth. Well, a draughty hall with a mere sprinkling of Civil Servants. She seemed shy, round at Abercrombie's -

MRS HOYDEN. There's no such place -

HOOPER. Exactly. I am a dreamer, Mrs Hoyden. I -

MRS HOYDEN. A liar!

Prolonged shrieks from beyond the French windows - everyone turns in that direction. BARBARA drags in JANINE, dishevelled. Triumphantly waves a cushion, a wig, the deplorable specs.

HOOPER. Why, it's Jer-her-her my goodness me! Jaws, it wasn't your Dodie at all.

BARBARA flings the cushion at him. JANINE takes out a compact, a Kleenex, and works on her face.

JAWS. I've seen her before, though -

BARBARA. Pathetic!

JANINE. Watchyertongue -

HOOPER (*bending to examine*). My my, a cushion it is. Babbers, you have an eagle eye -

BARBARA. Explanations, Aldous?

MR HOYDEN. Chin up, Olly. *Think* of something -

JANINE. 'Sall quite simple Nigel, reelly. Birds like your daughter. What a bitch! Mr Hooper must be protected. I think. He is not good marriage material. He is not understood. Lives in his own little world. Thinks I am dim, your Honour, but underneath I am quite educated and articulate. If she's determined, he'll shuffle along. That's his trouble. One of them. We cooked up a scheme, d'you see? In the bubble bath this afternoon.

After all, I reckon if Mr McIlroy had a daughter - it would be
Dodie. And he connived, Mr Hoyden. Sat there in the
bathroom polishing a shillelagh, dreaming of Vienna, tanks
and whores. And Mr Hooper had glum thoughts on matrimony.
Babbers, he said, must be out of her tiny mind. Save me! Save
me! He took the rubber platypus between his teeth and sank
under the foam. I got in beside him, intending to comfort.
Coaxed him out. Towelled and powdered. I can only tell you
that he just about cried his little heart out. Jaws sang Republican songs and I capered about. That is how we cooked up
Dodie, in a mood of inspiration. Thinking to outrage you at
sherry time. And get Hoop off the hook. I tell you straight,
Babsie - we feared what you had in mind, we were a party to
his anxieties. (*Pause.*) Shall they not speak with tongues
also? - those who only hang about with the plastic cup
muttering: Rinse your mouth out -

Pause.

MR HOYDEN. I never much cared for the Babo, I confess. And
you want him yourself, Miss - er?

JANINE. Lassoo. An incredible monniker, I know -

MR HOYDEN. You hanker for Hooper? Is it vocational?

BARBARA. He's *mine*!

JANINE. I have the training -

MR HOYDEN. We can set him up in business, if he's fed up with
teeth -

BARBARA. I saw a dear little house, yesterday -

MRS HOYDEN. And once removed from certain *influences* -

MR HOYDEN. Comb out a few of the idiosyncracies -

BARBARA. A kind of rehabilitation. Quite painless.

MR HOYDEN. Can't live one's life in rompers, y'know -

HOOPER. But -

   BARBARA *slinks over and links her hands behind* HOOPER's
   neck.

BARBARA. You'd like to be a grown-up Aldous, wouldn't you?
   (*Patting his cheek.*) Wouldn't he? Blow his nose instead of
   picking? Learn how to use a knife and fork? Break windies in

the loo, instead of making a thing out of it? No sweetie?
Make a little Aldous with Barbara instead? A real one -

*Disbelieving HOOPER removes her paws, places them by her
side. His head swivels pleadingly at an incomprehending
universe. A deep breath, and:*

HOOPER. Aaaaaaaaaaaaaaaaaah -

*And he hurtles off through the French windows, his cry of
protest dying away across the garden.*

Cut to:

11. Interior. Hooper's flat. Living room. *Evening. The curtains
are drawn. The TV is on, soundless. In front of it sits* MRS
HOOPER *in a rocking chair. By the fire,* JAWS *is sonorously
reading aloud* Finnegan's Wake.*in an Irish accent, pausing now
and then to beam around at the cosy little scene. In the middle
of the room, a large play-pen surrounded by the circular track
of a model railway. A little engine quietly purrs round the track,
pulling a few trucks.* HOOPER - *dressed in what appears to be
a vast 'Babygro' - sits cross-legged whilst* JANINE *deftly spoons
pink blancmange into his mouth.* JAWS *lays aside the James
Joyce and sips at a huge tumbler of whisky. He gets up and
saunters over to a pile of luggage at the other side of the room.*

JAWS. Mr James Joyce now, that great dreamer in words! Might
envy us en route to Barbados I should think. (*He raises the
lid of a suitcase crammed with bundles of banknotes.*) The
Major's family sprang, I think, from the loins of a pirate in
those parts. (*Pause.*) The Hoydens of this world, Mr Hooper -
could not grasp your drift. Not in a million. Not in epochs or
aeons, Sir. Slaves of the Reality Principle. (*Pause.*) I feel a
destiny in you, Mr Hooper -

JANINE *has scraped the last of the blancmange, transferred
it to* HOOPER's *gullet - and wipes his mouth expertly with a
napkin.*

JANINE. There we are, Olly. (*She rattles the spoon in the empty
dish.*) A' gone.

HOOPER *burps comfortably.* JANINE *smiles, handing him a
rattle which he shakes reflectively.*

HOOPER. It was a near thing, Jaws -

JAWS. I thought you'd give in -

HOOPER. Babsie just a wee nightmare now, Jaws. One must grit the chompers, and opt for integrity.

JAWS. Master Joyce's own words, Sir, in effect. (*Pause.*) *Non serviam.* (*Pause.*) The wily Celt -

HOOPER. I wish I'd known Major Trumpkins -

JAWS. A man of your stamp, Sir. (*Raising his glass*). How many go to greet their Maker on the rolling tide of an orgasm? The Knights Templars of happy prurience, Mr H. A select company -

JANINE. Time for bye-byes -

HOOPER. What about one last glug of scotch?

> JAWS *half fills a tumbler, and passes it to* HOOPER. *He holds it up.*

HOOPER. Looking at Ma, over there. Dreaming I bet, of sprightly times when she had wind and limb. Yes. Peeking at Mums, I would say my wistful wishes have never included the inter-uterine. Never so far back, Jaws. Just the first few biffy months. Before the awful nature of things became, so to speak, as clear as the teat on one's bottle. (*Pause.*) I well remember the first salutary hint of things to come. Astride the pot. Refusing to perform. (*Pause.*) I would peruse a woolly rabbit. Batten down the sphincters. By God, Jaws, I can still feel that cold ring of enamel! Face red. Lungs constricted. Totty paws beating the air. (*Pause.*) Helpless one is, attended by what seems to be an importunate giant. (*Pause.*) The junction of pot and backside, Jaws, triggered off the first word. The first precious unretractable statement. (*Pause.*) Up it came - a gust of air, twanging and strumming the virgin vocal cords. Up - hup hup hup! Out with it! Let it come! The gift of language, the first coherent sound from smacky bubbling lips: *No!*

JAWS. I'll drink to that -

> *They drink and* JANINE *lovingly tweaks* HOOPER's *cheeks.*

HOOPER. The rest, dear old leprechaun - is the corrupt workings of civilisation.

JANINE (*to Jaws*). Isn't he a lovely old bear? (*To Hooper, tweaking again.*) You're a huggy bear, you are. A real huggy bear -

> *Titles over Toytown music.*

Printed in the United Kingdom
by Lightning Source UK Ltd.
122052UK00001B/11/A